God's Time-Records
in
Ancient Sediments

Evidences of Long Time Spans in Earth's History

by Dan Wonderly
(For background of author see back cover)

Crystal Press *Publishers*
Flint, Michigan

COVER PHOTOGRAPH
The cover photograph shows a slab of rock with several types of fossils which were embedded in it before it became lithified. The two large ones are members of Phylum Brachiopoda, genus and species *Mucrospirifer arkonensis* (S. and G.). Most of the other fossils seen in this rock are brachiopods and crinoid rings. (Photograph, courtesy of the Smithsonian Institution, Washington, D.C.)

For an explanation of why fossils which are very diverse in form and size appear in the same stratum, see the last paragraph on page 52.

Published by: CRYSTAL PRESS
1909 Proctor Street
Flint, Michigan 48504
ISBN 0-930402-01-4
Library of Congress Catalog Card Number 77-085681
Printed in the United States of America

TABLE OF CONTENTS

Page

ACKNOWLEDGMENTS

I want to express my sincere thanks to the many friends and colleagues who have helped with the preparation of this work. Without them its composition would have been impossible. Particular credit is due the following for reviewing the chapters related to their fields of specialization, and for making many helpful suggestions which have been incorporated into the text: Dr. George W. Andrews, the U. S. Geological Survey; Dr. Kenneth L. Currie, the Geological Survey of Canada; Dr. Wayne Frair, The King's College; Dr. Jesse D. Humberd, Grace College; Dr. James R. Moore, The Open University of Milton Keynes, England; Dr. John H. Stoll, Grace College; Dr. John W. Stuber, LeTourneau College; Dr. William L. Wonderly, The American Bible Society; and Dr. Donald H. Zenger, Pomona College.

The librarians of Indiana University at Fort Wayne; Grace College, Winona Lake, Indiana; Frostburg State College, Frostburg, Maryland; and the Ruth Enlow Library, Oakland, Maryland, have rendered invaluable service in obtaining materials for me. This I greatly appreciate.

A truly great amount of credit is also due my wife Edna, and my daughter Eunice, for their untiring encouragement, their suggestions, and their secretarial help.

D. E. Wonderly

FOREWORD

In recent years, many sincere Christians, anxious to uphold the Biblical record of creation and to combat the theory of evolution, have sought to dismiss the geological evidence for an old earth. This has commonly been done by claiming that such evidence is based entirely upon radiometric dating schemes which are said to be unreliable. This, however, is not the case, as this work by Daniel E. Wonderly so clearly indicates.

Because few Christians have extensive training in geology, and because most Christian geologists have tended to dismiss proponents of a young earth as misguided, there has been little attempt to catalog non-radiometric evidences for an old earth. Prof. Wonderly's article, "Non-Radiometric Data Relevant to the Question of Age," which appeared in the Journal of the American Scientific Affiliation 27 (1975), 145-152, is a notable exception, and I was pleased to be able to include it in my book Genesis One and the Origin of the Earth (InterVarsity, 1977).

It is an even greater pleasure now to recommend God's Time-Records in Ancient Sediments as an expansion and explanation of this previous article. I have enjoyed reading this book and found it to be sound in its science and Biblical in its theology.

This is not surprising as Prof. Wonderly is an earnest Christian who holds firmly to the inerrancy of Scripture and is a diligent and thorough student of science. He has an excellent academic background for this work, with graduate degrees in both theology and science, including graduate-level work in biology and geology. He has taught for over 15 years in both secular and Christian colleges, and is a member of several scientific societies.

I hope that this manual will receive wide circulation among evangelical and fundamental Christians, with the result that the old-earth creationist position will be more favorably considered. I am concerned on the one hand that theistic evolution tends to minimize the Biblical data on origins, while on the other hand young-earth creationism too easily ignores the scientific data. It is only through a serious handling of both sources of information that a sound Christian view of origins will be reached and severe damage to our young people will be avoided.

Dr. Robert C. Newman
Biblical School of Theology
Hatfield, Pennsylvania

v

LIST OF FIGURES

LIST OF TABLES

PREFACE

THE PURPOSES AND METHODS OF THIS WORK

We are directing this book to the Christian reading public. Numerous groups of Christians in North America now recognize sizeable problems having to do with the relation of science to the Biblical account of creation. However, I believe that it is possible to properly understand God's meaningful world, and at the same time participate in the fellowship which He wants his own people to have with one another. The sharing of observations and ideas concerning God's record in nature can be a source of much joy and fellowship, as well as an enhancement of our love for God. We hope that at least the early chapters of this work will be found to be inspirational reading, while the other chapters may be used as a manual of important information concerning the earth and the studies which Christians have made with respect to creation. (Therefore we will sometimes refer to the entire work as a manual.)

One of our primary purposes is to encourage Christians to become aware of and benefit from the sedimentary time records found in nature. In chapters 3 and 5 through 9 we have made a deliberate attempt to translate some of the scientific reports of these time records into language which laymen, ministers, and theologians can understand. It is also hoped that the materials herein presented will lead thinking readers not to be satisfied until they have directly investigated some of the abundant source materials which deal with natural events related to time.

There are now widespread misunderstandings among conservative Christians concerning the evidences for the age of the earth. Many conservative Bible-believing Christian leaders in the early part of our present century were willing to accept the natural evidences which indicate that the earth was created long before man was put upon it. This view was stated briefly in the early pages of the Scofield Reference Bible, together with appropriate warnings against acceptance of a dogmatic evolutionary position. Yet we have now seen many theologically conservative leaders turning against the principles set forth by these Christian founders. Almost all the observations of geology relative to time are rejected as unbiblical, and it is supposed that the major sedimentary layers of the earth were somehow formed by events which have occurred during the relatively brief time man has been on the earth. Unfortunately, this belief concerning the nature of earth's geologic "treasures" fails to make use of the many marvelous discoveries which God has allowed man to make within the past 100 years concerning the nature of sedimentary rock layers--such as limestone deposits. This strange position taken by some Christian groups surely amounts to a backwards retreat in the work of God's kingdom. It has recently brought turmoil and disagreement into many churches and schools, and has greatly narrowed the field of ministry of those Christian workers who now feel that they must separate themselves from people who take geologic research seriously. Both the present author and those who have helped him in the writing of this book (see the "Acknowledgments" page) sincerely hope that our efforts will help to alleviate this confusion and loss.

1

It is true that Christians have often become perplexed when trying to deal with scientific observations which are related to the Bible. Frequently those who are well trained in the Scriptures and theology encounter difficulty in understanding the language and methods of science. Likewise, those Christians who have developed skills in research science are often unable to relate their work to the Biblical message. Biology and geology are disciplines which can be very useful in unraveling some of the problems faced by those who wish to properly relate modern science to the creation account found in the Book of Genesis. There seems to be no possible way of satisfactorily relating these without acquainting oneself with at least some of the elementary facts and principles of biology and geology.

In this manual we will make use of these two disciplines, but will not attempt to follow or employ all the usually accepted theories or lines of reasoning used in biology and the earth sciences. We will proceed mainly by discussing certain local sequences of sedimentary strata with respect to the lengths of time required for their deposit and subsequent modification. (We use the term "local sequence" here to refer to strata which are found at one particular geographic location, and can be observed in a single bore hole or test well made through the sequence.)

A method which uses mainly local sequences of strata will not supply us with a precise and composite estimate of the total age of the earth, nor even of the total length of time since the deposition of fossiliferous strata began. Arriving at a precise theory as to the total age is unnecessary for our purposes here, as this is not intended to be a technical book. Our main interest here is in taking a simple look at specific, local sedimentary records in the earth, in order to prevent us from falling into the error of ignoring their meaning, or of adopting illogical or unrealistic methods of explaining them. The characteristics of these sedimentary records are almost never presented in young-earth creationist publications and are unknown to most evangelical Christians. Actually, these natural time records are relatively easy to understand, and do not require more knowledge of mathematics than one normally uses in everyday life.

For examining the sedimentary records we will use only the more simple principles and forms of data. Thus we will not attempt to make use of radiation dating methods, because of their complexity which is not easily mastered by busy laymen or by theologians who are unable to find large segments of time for scientific studies. When persons who have only a minimum knowledge of radiometric dating attempt to relate the results of this technique to theological knowledge, misunderstanding and confusion are the usual result. Such confusion has already become a stumbling block in some Christian circles.

Our setting aside of radiometric studies undoubtedly calls for somewhat of an apology to the numerous Christian geologists and biologists of our country, but it is hoped that they will understand our purpose in doing so. We decided on this procedure so as to enable us to concentrate on the more obvious and simple methods of understanding the record in nature. It is hoped that this method will result in showing us at least several examples of God's record which can be accepted and understood within a Biblical framework by using little more than common everyday forms of thought and understanding. Geologists and biologists may consider the results of such a procedure to be minimal, because the greatest ages can not be demonstrated by it. Nevertheless, it is our conviction that it is sometimes better to obtain minimal results which are positive and thoroughly acceptable than a set of maximal results which seem to rely too heavily on theory, or on techniques which our readers find difficult to understand. And of course it is true that radiometric dating often leaves us in the realm of uncertainty, due to the fact that it frequently has to depend upon one or more presuppositions which defy our efforts at verification.

The reader will find it advantageous to make use of the footnotes (found at the end of each chapter), especially because a number of definitions and explanations are found therein. Most of the other definitions needed can be found by consulting the index for pages defining the terms. For those wanting more information, most of the sources are readily available in any university library, and several are available in moderate to large sized public libraries.

It is hoped that no reader will misinterpret our extensive use of materials based on research done by petroleum geologists. We are not in any way trying to promote any particular segment of American industry. It is only that a high percentage of the information which will reveal nature's time record comes from deep drillings; and the petroleum industry is the main source of such drilling records.

The Biblical quotations in this book are from the New American Standard Bible.

CHAPTER 1

NATURE AND SCIENCE

Christians are naturally interested in the world around them. The Bible encourages us to see God in the beauties and complexities of nature. In Psalm 92:4-5 we find the writer rejoicing in God's creation with the prayer, "Thou, O Lord, hast made me glad by what Thou hast done; I will sing for joy at the works of Thy hands. How great are Thy works, O Lord! Thy thoughts are very deep." Numerous other Psalms express the same appreciation of nature, as Psalm 104 which is devoted almost entirely to this subject. Both the physical (nonliving) and biological realms of the earth are important to the Christian, because God is the author of them both. In this manual we are presenting a body of information from nature which we hope will further illuminate the fact of divine creation. This body of information is recorded in great detail in recent scientific publications, but is not commonly known to the Christian public. However, it is hoped that a greater sense of need for the study of this data concerning God's works will be developed among Christians.

Our interest in God's natural world should extend to the point of causing us to ask what God has done, and the order in which He did it. The Bible itself gives us some basic answers to these questions, but God has left to us the privilege of ferreting out many of the details of his works with the scientific tools (methods) which are at our disposal. As we discover these details we not only gain an increased appreciation for God, but also enhance our ability to help the non-Christian world to come to a knowledge of our God and Saviour. In this space age there is renewed interest among non-Christians concerning the origin of the earth and the order of events upon this planet. For example, popular news and science magazines, as well as professional journals, are constantly publishing articles on the history of the earth and of its satellite the moon. This interest among people around us will improve our opportunity to guide them into God's way, if we properly inform ourselves concerning God's creation.

In this book we will be dealing primarily with the order of some of the events in the earth's history, and with some indications of the length of time required for those events. For us as Christians, the main facts concerning origins are settled. "He spoke, and it was done; He commanded, and it stood fast" (Psalm 33:9). We therefore accept the information on origins which the Bible presents, and then proceed to examine the natural record of the physical and biological processes which have taken place in the past. As we do this, we must seek to be truly honest, never casting aside or ignoring any of the evidences we find. We must recognize that the body of data we find in nature is primarily a record of the works of our God, and that the evidences He has left us are meaningful and for our use. To consider them as unworthy or unintelligible, as some Christians have done, is a grave error. We find a great many types of evidences

4

in nature which give us useful information concerning the amount of time which has passed since the creation of life upon this earth. Much of this time-indicating information comes from a recognition of the many types of sediment layers on the earth, and from the kinds of microscopic-sized particles of which sedimentary rocks are composed. Thus our knowledge of age is not actually dependent upon radiometric dating or upon any form of "circular reasoning" related to fossils, as has sometimes been asserted. Likewise, the evidences for age which we recognize are not dependent upon a "system" of uniformitarianism. Rather, each case of sedimentary evidence described in the following chapters is able to stand upon its own merits.

In the pages which follow, we will be using the terms "nature" and "science" frequently. The word "nature" refers to all of the natural world, as distinguished from things which have been built or produced by man. Nature includes not only the biological realm, but also non-biological things, such as rocks, oceans, volcanoes, and all the minerals of which the earth is composed. The word "science" refers to "the body of knowledge obtained by methods based upon observation."[1] Thus, the body of knowledge which we call "science" is obtained by the gathering of facts and drawing conclusions based on those facts. Strictly speaking, science is separate from philosophy, but it does find some of the more basic philosophic principles to be essential to its work.

Order in Nature

Any careful consideration of nature soon reveals that ours is a world of order, and that the tools of science will be useful in examining that order. The philosophers, Bible students, and theologians of ancient times took note of some aspects of the order in nature, for example, the similarities of certain kinds of animals and plants, the bilaterally symmetric structure of the legs and other parts of animal bodies, and the radial symmetry of many plants, jellyfishes, and other lower animals. Now, in recent times, science has demonstrated that there is far more order in nature than was formerly observed. Examples of this are: (a) the highly organized crystalline structure of many minerals, (b) the arrangement of the cells of the human body which allows nerve cells to control muscle cells and gland cells, (c) the functional arrangement of molecules within a cell, (d) the cooperative ecological relationship between many plants, animals, and microorganisms, and (e) the systematic relationships of the elements which make possible their arrangement into the familiar "periodic chart" which hangs on the wall of every chemistry laboratory.

Another phase of this discovery of more order in the earth has been carried out by geologists and other earth scientists, as they have studied the strata (layers) of the earth. It has turned out that there is a very meaningful order in these layers--an order which was established by events on the earth and in the earth's crust in the past. The general public usually does not realize how very useful this knowledge of the order in the rock layers has been. An understanding of the events of the past has enabled man to discover large numbers of mineral deposits which the old "hit-and-miss," random explorations would never have revealed. For example, many ancient gold seekers, not understanding these past events, wasted their time and efforts looking for gold in sedimentary layers which were far from any outcrop of gold-bearing igneous rock. Likewise, a host of other prospectors in the past have been frustrated because they had no understanding of the natural orderliness of the earth's strata. But in this present generation, prospecting for minerals and petroleum, being based on a fairly adequate understanding of events of the past, is highly successful.

Thus the various branches of science have greatly amplified man's early knowledge of the orderliness found in nature. As a result, the human population has been benefiting immensely from this revealing of "earth's secrets."

The Methods of Science

At this point it is logical that we briefly examine the nature of the scientific methods man uses for investigating the created world. People often misunderstand the work of the scientist. Some think of his work as a creating (or inventing) of new ideas, instead of a discovering of facts and principles. Others think of scientific research as a sort of game in which the scientists select what evidences they want and throw out the unwanted.

Actually scientific research is an investigative process in which all observations are used as a basis for the most unbiased conclusion. (We must of course remember that when we say "all observations" we will exclude those measurements or readings which have been distorted by error or by some irrelevant factor. For example, if the temperatures at various points in a lake are being measured periodically for the purpose of determining the amount of natural seasonal temperature fluctuations, one should discard a thermometer reading which was inadvertently taken near to a release point for waste from a sewage plant.) There is nothing mysterious, secret, or tricky about scientific research. In reality the work of the earth scientist consists of a reading of the record of God's works. It is true that such a scientist may not always be aware of the Creator who formed the meaningful record which he investigates, but this lack of awareness does not invalidate the results obtained.

Another way to define the work of a scientist is to say that it is a collecting of data and an investigation of the meaning of that data. The word "data" refers to observed facts or bits of information. These are the raw material from which scientific principles are derived.[2]

It has sometimes been said that even the collecting of data by a scientist is influenced by the personal bias and prejudice of the scientist. In the strictest sense there is probably truth in this statement, for we have limitations as to the perfection of our work. However, it is very incorrect to say that a significant amount of bias is always present. Consider how absurd it would have been for the scientists of the polio vaccine research teams of the 1940's and 1950's to have made significantly prejudiced selections of data, and thus delay their work. Or again, what petroleum geologist would make biased selections of data as he takes well core samples to investigate the underground strata, with a view to discovering oil? Such a defect in his work would frustrate both himself and his employer; and, if his work is published, subject him to the criticism of other geologists working on the same types of strata. We might also add that it is fortunate for those of us who are interested in learning the facts of God's record in nature, that much of the data which we use comes from petroleum geology research. This gives us a safeguard not enjoyed by those who use data which was collected for some less practical purpose--such as that of supporting a controversial theory. This is very evident when we read the descriptions of various local stratigraphic columns [3] in petroleum journals. In these we readily notice that there is much less of the theoretical, and more genuine analysis of the underground environments of petroleum formation. This research characteristic is largely responsible for the phenomenal success of petroleum geology during the past few decades.

How then does a scientist collect and use data? To illustrate the process, let us assume that a geologist in an oil producing part of our continent is assigned the task of determining the relation of a particular rock formation or set of strata to the limestone which lies beneath it. After fixing in his mind a clear statement of the problem he is to solve, he sets about the task of collecting data. The first step in this collection process will usually be an investigation of the scientific journals which record previous observations on these same rock layers. After learning as much as possible in this way, the geologist will go and examine the well cores and drilling records from wells which have penetrated these and adjacent rock layers.[4] He will also compare the samples from the wells with layers of the same or similar rock which are exposed (outcrop) in the vicinity, all the while taking notes on his observations. These observations include not only simple visual examination, but also chemical analyses and microscopic examination of many samples taken from the strata the investigator is studying.

While our geologist is collecting data, certain hypotheses as to the meaning of them and as to the solution of his problem will naturally come to mind. These hypotheses are ideas or possible explanations based on the previous experience and knowledge of the investigator.[5] The successful investigator, however, knows that he must not allow any of his hypotheses to dominate his thinking or obscure the meaning of the data he is collecting. He recognizes that a hypothesis is an idea yet awaiting verification, and does not adopt any one hypothesis until a large amount of data has been collected. The next step for the scientist is the process of carefully analyzing, comparing, and interpreting the data. This may result in one of his earlier hypotheses being confirmed, or it may show all the hypotheses to be wrong and give a different answer. Thus the scientist is able to formulate a sound conclusion to the problem he set out to solve.

It is of course true that many such research projects do not result in an immediate solution of the problem. However, this is not to be considered a failure. The investigator publishes the facts and principles which he has learned in one or more of the technical journals which serve his field of study. These journals are widely circulated among scientists, and are available in large libraries, so that other investigators are able to take up where other men have left off. In brief, this is the way that modern scientific research operates.

It should be further explained here that the processes of scientific investigation are largely inductive; that is, scientific investigation is based primarily on the principle of collecting small items of information (facts), systematically tabulating and analyzing these facts, and then drawing a conclusion based on the same. This is the method which was championed by Francis Bacon during the Renaissance, and is now the main procedure used in thousands of research science laboratories. Visit practically any biological or medical research laboratory, and you will find the scientists and technicians painstakingly collecting and tabulating many individual units of information from which they hope to--and often do--arrive at a useful conclusion. Likewise in a geological research project, the investigator may go out to study many individual strata, collect many samples, and record the results of careful microscopic investigations of those samples in the laboratory. Finally, after a great deal of work with these small items of information, he can arrive at a valid conclusion concerning the nature of the rock formation being studied. This conclusion may or may not be what was expected when the research was begun, but that is a commendable characteristic of the scientific method of research, and illustrates the fact that it is a logical and valid process of obtaining information about the world around us. However, when considering this inductive process of scientific investigation, we must remember that there are also disciplines in which deductive reasoning is necessarily prominent and right. A case in point is that of Bible study, where we are approaching a body of divinely revealed truth, from which we are to draw the finer principles by a deductive process. For example, we start with the larger principle that God created the entire universe, and by deductive reasoning arrive at the conclusion that He is the creator of each of the separate heavenly bodies which we observe, even though most of those bodies are not specifically mentioned in the Bible.

Facts, Theories, and Hypotheses

It is true that scientific investigation is a precise and accurate procedure, but this does not mean that everything written by scientists is to be taken as truth or fact. The collecting and reporting of data by scientists can be trusted, for they learned long ago that honesty in this matter is absolutely necessary; but there are certain areas of investigation which do not lend themselves to a rapid solution or analysis. During the process of investigation of such an area, it is natural that the scientists involved will express their opinions as to the final outcome of the research.

If the research is drawn out over a period of time, a rather stable "theory" may be formulated by the scientists. This theory is usually a synthesis of the opinions which the researchers have expressed. It is of course always necessary that we do not confuse such a theory with fact. The scientists themselves usually realize this more fully than the general public does. This is illustrated in the treatment of certain evolutionary theories. A brief conversation with a scientist who has done extensive research on the past history of sharks will reveal that he readily recognizes the uncertainty of the theory of origin of sharks, whereas the general public usually thinks it is an established fact. Many similar examples could be cited.

Unfortunately, the explanations of certain types of scientific research projects which we find in newspapers and popular magazines often give an impression of more certainty than the scientists would express. In order to get the true picture, one should go to the professional journals in the field of research involved. In such journals we do not find the dogmatic statements concerning unsolved problems which are so prevalent in popular magazines and textbooks. This is because the scientists who have written the journal articles are very much aware that both their expression of opinions and their reporting of the data will be carefully scrutinized by fellow-scientists working in the same field. (The efficiency of communication is of course far better now than it formerly was.)

We should stop here to explain that there are a few emotional factors by which some scientists and science teachers are sometimes led to make more dogmatic statements concerning the certainty of their findings than is warranted. This is particularly true in the field of evolution. Such dogmatic statements are usually made orally, after which they make their way into popular writings (often magnified) by various means.

In closing this chapter we must take note of another, somewhat related, form of confusion into which people sometimes fall. This is the error of using a series of hypotheses, rather than a series of facts (data), to explain a certain phenomenon or condition in nature.

Suppose there were an isolated island in the Pacific Ocean which had recently had all the observable forms of life which were upon it destroyed by an earthquake, tidal wave, and near-by erupting volcano. A group of travelers come upon the island, not knowing anything of the real reason for its present condition. One member of the party formulates a hypothesis that this devastation was produced by a hydrogen bomb. He knows some things about the effects of such bombs; for example, that they produce a great amount of heat, and that they release sufficient energy to crack open the surface of the earth. On the basis of this knowledge he begins to explain the process of destruction to his companions. Together they notice the cracks in the earth, and the effects of heat (but fail to look for evidence of the very intense heat and radiation which hydrogen bombs produce). The hydrogen bomb hypothesis strikes them as being very plausible, except that there is evidence of the action of water. This problem is soon solved by someone's suggestion of another hypothesis; namely, that the explosion of the bomb pushed the water away from the island, allowing it to return later with great force. The members of the party may then go and publicize their discovery of "an island destroyed by a hydrogen bomb." They might even go so far as to give or write lengthy explanations of the effects of heat, force, and water when hydrogen bombs are used.

What is wrong with this sort of observation and explanation? Perhaps several things are wrong, but the primary error was in the outright substituting of hypotheses for collected data. To be sure, the observers were collecting some data, but this data was not a group of factual observations systematically set aside to be analyzed at the end of the investigation. Thus the original hypothesis, supplemented by various lesser hypotheses, has taken the place of the data, and a false explanation has resulted. This erroneous method of investigation (with variations) has misled great numbers of the common (non-scientist) population ever since the dawn of written history, resulting in all sorts of superstitions and false beliefs. Both the non-Christian and Christian populations, including some Bible students, have frequently fallen into this snare. Sometimes the resulting error is a small one having to do with such matters as the supposed influence of the moon on growing crops; at other times it has had large effects upon people's beliefs concerning past events on the earth. Whatever the subject treated, the main reason that the observations have misled the people is that the observers have not systematically collected data as the basis for solving the problem. Instead, they have placed one or more hypotheses into a position of supremacy above the data. Needless to say, this is no proper way to obtain information from God's record in nature.

FOOTNOTES

1. R. B. Fisher, Science, Man, and Society, 1971, p. 4.

2. The expression "the data" is usually used in the plural sense, but sometimes is considered to be a single mass of collected information.

3. The expression "local stratigraphic column" refers to a series of strata which lie one above another, as observed (often by drilling) at a particular geographic location. This is in contrast to a composite column, which is constructed on paper by combining drilling records from various locations. See Chapter 4 for a description of such columns.

4. Oil corporations maintain extensive records of previous drilling operations, together with identified "cores" of some of the rock and sediments which have been removed from the wells. Cores are obtained by special drill bits which lift out sections of the well.

5. Sometimes the word "hypothesis" is defined as "an educated guess." This is correct, but one must realize that useful hypotheses are based on a certain amount of information, and are never <u>wild</u> guesses.

CHAPTER 2

REVELATION AND SCIENCE

There are different ways by which man obtains information. Revelation and science are two of these ways or methods. In God's revelation of himself to man He has informed us of certain truths concerning Himself, man, and the universe. Science, as we have already seen, obtains information about the universe by making observations of things, processes, and events within the universe. There is no necessary conflict or disagreement between revelation and science.

Types of Revelation

The Bible contains many statements declaring the reality and objectivity of revelation. We have a simple statement of God revealing himself in Psalm 103:7, "He (God) made known His ways to Moses, His acts to the sons of Israel." In the books of Exodus, Leviticus, Numbers, and Deuteronomy we find many very explicit statements concerning God's revelation of himself and of his message to Moses (Exodus 3:1-4:17; 19:1-31:18; etc.). In other parts of the Bible we have numerous equally explicit statements that God revealed himself to David, the prophets, Peter, Paul, John, and others; and divinely inspired them to accurately record the message.

In each of the cases we have cited, the revelation was communicated in human language. This is what is sometimes called "special revelation," and is by far the most precise and understandable form of God's communication to man. However, it is true that many things about God and his works are also revealed in nature. The Bible itself refers to the reality of a revelation of God's power, beauty, and orderliness in nature (Isaiah 40:21-26; Psalms 19:2-6; 94:8-10; and Romans 1:19-20). Thus we accept the validity of both of these forms of divine revelation, and rejoice in knowing both the Revealer and his message. Man sometimes has trouble properly interpreting and understanding both the written revelation of God and the revelation in nature, but this does not make these communications from God imperfect or inaccurate in themselves.

Since we are blessed in having such a "double revelation," we should respect and use both forms of it, and recognize both forms as meaningful. In doing this we should recognize the reliability of human language as a medium of communication, and consider the entire Biblical record to be meaningful. We should therefore never consider a part of the Bible to be allegorical or figurative unless there is some definite indication in the text to show that it is of this nature. The first chapter of Genesis is an example of a Scripture portion which has often been wrongly taken as poetry, and thus mistakenly thought to be largely figurative. Actually the chapter has only a very small amount of poetic form, and in this respect contrasts sharply with the poetic descriptions of creation which are found in Job 38:8-11 and Psalm 104:5-9.[1]

We are, in this book, concerned mainly with God's revelation
through nature, and with the ways by which we interpret and understand it. The person who neglects to use information from the study
of nature is missing out on a great deal of the revelation of God.
This is because the Bible gives us very little detail concerning
nature or what we might call "the world of science." Instead, God
has given us the privilege of investigating this for ourselves.
In so doing we discover a great deal about his wisdom and works
which the ancients were not privileged to know.

We should of course accept the numerous broad statements which
the Bible makes concerning the natural world and God's works in
nature, for they are true and reliable. The reason these statements
are true and reliable is that they were given by divine inspiration,
just as the rest of the Bible was (II Timothy 3:16). Furthermore,
experience has shown that whatever the Bible teaches concerning the
earth or other parts of the universe is reasonable and acceptable
in the light of modern science. Many ancient writings contain a
multitude of superstitious ideas concerning the earth and the heavenly bodies which are absurd, but God guided the Biblical authors
in such a way that they did not assert the validity of these ideas.
They did refer occasionally to some of the currently believed non-
factual ideas concerning the earth and universe, especially in poetic
sections such as the Psalms, but there is no effort to declare such
ideas to be truth. It has often been claimed that the Bible contains
scientific errors, but such claims are always based either on a
misreading or a misunderstanding of what the text actually says.
For example, an overliteral reading of certain passages such as
Isaiah 11:12, which speak of "the four corners of the earth," resulted in much misunderstanding in earlier times.

Certain parts of the Biblical account of the creation of man
obviously demand a literal interpretation, but even here one needs
to avoid making extreme interpretations. Thus the fact that Genesis
2:8-23 gives the precise geographic location of the Garden of Eden,
and describes Adam and Eve as real people, forces us to recognize
this account as true history. But we must then guard against such
extremes as that of saying that the Garden of Eden was arranged like
Solomon's gardens. Likewise, to demand that the serpent in the
Garden was turned into a certain species of snake with which the
reader is personally familiar is a harmful extreme. These are some
of the many aspects of the events of creation which are just not
explained in the Bible. When they are not explained we must be
careful not to read into the account more information than is there.

The Usefulness of Science in Investigating Nature

Since the primary method of science is the collecting of data
by making objective observations, it is very useful in investigating
nature. Thus science can provide a great benefit in helping to understand the other type of revelation--the revelation in nature--to
which we referred above.

However, some Christians are fearful of using science as an aid

14

to understanding God's natural revelation. They are conscious of the
fact that scientists occasionally make errors in the collecting or
recording of data, and because of this are afraid to trust science
for helping us "read the book of nature." This fear is unjustified,
because the making of an error does not indicate that accurate measurement is impossible. For example, we may buy what has been measured
for nine feet of lumber, only to find out later that we obtained
only eight. The error of the clerk who made the measurement may
annoy us, but it never causes us to say that a nine-foot piece of
lumber can not be measured out. You will likely go back to the
lumber yard and insist that your own observation be added to that
of the clerk in cutting off a piece of the correct length. Or, if
you felt that two persons could not make sure of the measurement,
you could call in a third.

Of course one might say that no matter how many times the measurement was checked, there would be some slight chance that all
observers would read the figure 8 on the measuring tape as a 9, and
thus obtain the wrong length. Theoretically this may be true, but
when we examine cases in the Bible where God expected human beings
to make observations and measurements, we find that He knew that
measurements could be made with satisfactory accuracy. In other
words, human observation can be reliable and can be trusted, at
least when it has to do with the more common things of nature and
life. A few of the many examples of this found in the Bible are as
follows:

1. God commanded Moses and the Israelites, "You shall work
six days, but on the seventh day you shall rest" (Exodus 34:21).
Thus God showed his belief and knowledge that human beings have the
ability to observe days and keep a record of the number of days.

2. God commanded Moses concerning the building of the ark of
the covenant, and some of the other pieces of furniture of the tab-
ernacle, that they should be built out of acacia wood (Exodus 25:10,
23, etc.). An offering of various building materials was received
from the people, "and every man, who had in his posession acacia
wood for any work of the service, brought it" (Exodus 35:24). Thus
God was recognizing the ability of man to classify types of wood,
and to select one particular kind out of the group.

3. God commanded Moses to have any person who had commited
theft or robbery return the stolen property, and to "add to it one-
fifth more" (Leviticus 6:1-5). Thus God assumes the ability of man
to measure fractional amounts of substances.

4. God commanded Moses that if anyone was found offering
sacrifice to heathen idols, to the sun, or to the moon, during the
period when Moses was in command, the person who had done so was
to be put to death. God further commanded that the conviction of
guilt for such an offense was to be based on the testimony of two
or three witnesses (Deuteronomy 17:2-6). Thus God was recognizing
the ability of the common people to accurately observe the event

of an offering being made to an idol, to the sun, or to the moon.

5. Jesus recognized the ability of the common people to distinguish between bread and stones, and between a fish and a snake (Matthew 7:9-10).

6. Jesus recognized that people are readily able to distinguish between old cloth and new cloth, and between old wineskins and new wineskins (Matthew 9:16-17).

Even in this incomplete list we have quite a range of types of observing ability which God has openly recognized to be valid and accurate. So, any argument that man does not have the ability to observe with satisfactory accuracy, or that scientific observation of the natural world is of little value, can be dismissed. Those who are inclined to wonder if scientific observation is really effective need only to consider the fact that scientific investigation has delivered us from most of the fearful superstitions which haunted our ancestors, and has discovered the cause of most diseases of man, domestic animals, and domestic plants.

The reason for the reliability of man's observation is found in the fact that man was created "in the image of God" (Genesis 1:27; John 10:34-36). It is of course very true that man lost a priceless portion of that image of God when he rebelled against his Creator in the Garden of Eden. But we must still recognize that the powers of reason, observation, and analysis which man had received as a part of God's image were not lost. As we have seen, Christ himself recognized them as still present in man. God has given us the gift of rationality, so that "the laws of thought are also the laws of things." Or to put it another way, "In God's veracity we have the guarantee that our faculties (in their normal exercise) do not deceive us."[2]

Francis Schaeffer explains that the scientists of Reformation times believed in the reliability of man's observations, and that this belief was rooted in their Christian faith. He says, "The early scientists also shared the outlook of Christianity in believing that there is a reasonable God, who has created a reasonable universe, and thus man, by use of his reason, could find out the universe's form."[3] This ability of man is a reality because he possesses some of the image of God with which he was created, thus allowing his reason to be in agreement with the patterns of God's creation. To summarize, there are similarities between the mind of God and the mind of man, and because of this, man can observe and understand the kinds of things God has placed on the earth.

We must further realize, as Christ did, that the powers of reliable observation in man are not dependent upon his being a Christian. Rationality and the power of analysis are a part of God's universal gift to the human race. This can be illustrated by the case of the counting of the rings of two maple trees of the same species which have been cut down. A layman may approach the stumps, count the rings, and decide that one tree is 40 years old and the

other 60 years old.   This will probably be a fairly accurate count,
but when a trained forester--Christian or non-Christian--approaches
the stumps and makes the count, he knows how to recognize and include the very thin rings which were formed during extremely dry
seasons. As a result, the trained forester may get more accurate
counts of perhaps 42 and 65 years, and we must recognize his superior
ability in this type of research. Similarly, a non-Christian,
trained geologist can recognize, describe, and understand a given
series of sedimentary strata far more accurately than a Christian,
non-trained layman can.[4]

The Stability of Natural Laws

Another of the reasons why we can be confident that science is
useful and reliable in the study of nature is that the natural laws
which science investigates have a stability which is ordered by God.
For example, we know that oxygen is required for the chemical conversion of carbohydrates to produce energy in animals and in the
higher plants. Because of the principle of the stability of natural
law, we have no ground for suggesting that this may not have been
true in the past, or may cease to be true at any time.

There are at least two kinds of teaching in the Bible which
enable the Christian to know that nature is dependable and knowable.
The first of these is the fact of God's unchangeableness (often
referred to as his immutability). We read in Malachi 3:6, "I, the
Lord, do not change,"; and in Hebrews 13:8, "Jesus Christ is the
same yesterday and today, yes and forever." Also, Psalm 102:27
expresses the same idea. God is not in any sense erratic or fickle
as the heathen gods of tradition were. Both the living and nonliving realms of the earth are controlled by a large number of
natural laws which God established in the beginning. He created
these laws as working principles which function in harmony with
each other. The wisdom of God was such that He made this a perfect
system at the beginning, with the laws functioning correctly in
relation to each other. He surely has had no reason to be changing
these laws since that time; and furthermore, his absolute power and
authority in the universe are sufficient to keep all natural laws
intact. We know the latter specifically from Hebrews 1:3, which
says that Christ "upholds all things by the word of His power."
(Compare Colossians 1:17.)

To illustrate how important it has been, and is, that all the
natural laws be kept intact, let us consider again the law of the
oxygen requirement mentioned above. The oxygen which enters a
marine animal, such as a clam, enters by a process of diffusion.
The diffusion process, in turn, operates by the natural laws which
govern the movement of molecules through the water and through the
cell membranes, into the cells of the clam. So if any of the laws
which govern diffusion were to change appreciably, the clam's supply of oxygen would be either cut off or disturbed, and thus kill
the clam (and other animals) in the sea. A similar balance exists
for all animals. And of course the supply of oxygen is only one
of hundreds of natural functions which are dependent upon the stable

laws of nature. We can also be sure that, at the time God first created different forms of life, the natural laws were the same-- if for no other reason, because the first chapters of Genesis describe the animal and plant life as being similar to what we know today. If the natural laws had been different, the animal bodies would have had to be different. For example, if the rate of dif- fusion of oxygen through the film of water in the air sacs of the lungs had been appreciably different from what it is now, the lungs (and consequently the rib cage) of air-breathing mammals and birds would have had to be radically different in size. This would then, in turn, call for a much larger or smaller heart and circulatory system, as the case might be. Furthermore, the differing diffusion rate and the differing circulatory system would greatly alter the size and efficiency of the muscles, and even of the bones of the animal.

The other kind of teaching in the Bible which assures us that nature is dependable and knowable consists of the numerous places where specific statements are made concerning nature. When Christ was here on earth he made statements that showed his confidence in the reliability of nature. In Luke 6:43-44 we find him saying, "There is no good tree which produces bad fruit; nor on the other hand, a bad tree which produces good fruit. For each tree is known by its own fruit. For men do not gather figs from thorns, nor do they pick grapes from a briar bush." Thus Jesus recognized that thorn trees and briar bushes are governed by natural laws of hered- ity, and that these laws are dependable. Somewhat later, when talking to the multitudes, He said, "When you see a cloud rising in the west, immediately you say 'A shower is coming', and so it turns out. And when you see a south wind blowing, you say, 'It will be a hot day', and it turns out that way. You hypocrites! You know how to analyze the appearance of the earth and the sky, but why do you not analyze this present time?" (Luke 12:54-56) In this quotation, Jesus is of course not saying that the people could al- ways predict the weather accurately, but He is certainly recognizing the definite fact that rain comes from clouds and that it is warmer toward the equator than toward the north pole.

From these and other similar statements in both the Old and New Testaments we must conclude that natural laws are stable, be- cause God established them that way. Also, scientific research has unveiled many natural laws which are now known to be definitely true, and need not be doubted. We referred above to the law of the use of oxygen by animals for obtaining energy from food. This has been observed to be true so many times that we have no trouble recognizing its validity. There are a large number of other natural laws of which we are just as certain. William Harvey spent 20 years exper- imenting with animals and examining human beings to determine the relation of blood flow to the heart. In 1628 he published his momentous results, informing the world that the blood is pumped out of the heart through arteries and returns to the heart through veins, to be pumped out again. This was a great discovery, and is a firmly established fact which is redemonstrated dozens of times each day as heart surgeries are performed. Thus science has discovered this principle which God had known from the beginning.

Since William Harvey's time science has overwhelmingly demonstrated many other facts concerning the natural world. A few of these are: that tree rings represent annual growth, that many species of organisms produce reproductive cells which unite (instead of just "seed" growing in a womb), that mosquitoes carry malaria, that many kinds of bacteria exist, that iron is more dense than aluminum, that the sun is farther from the earth than the moon, that there are rocks on the moon, etc. Certainly these are all cases where God has allowed men to finally discover some of what He knew all along to be true.

This principle then gives us confidence that at least many of the discoveries of science are true and reliable, because they are merely a revealing of what was long ago included in God's knowledge of what He had established. Thus the argument which we sometimes hear, that all observations made by man are uncertain and theoretical, is erroneous.

Uncertainty and Change in Science

It is sometimes said that because scientific theories change, and because some of the material of science becomes outdated, that all discoveries of science are tentative and uncertain. This is a misunderstanding, based on a lack of familiarity with science. We frequently hear very misleading statements, such as, "Every science textbook is out-of-date within five years of the date of publication." It is true that the style of presenting the material, additional discoveries of the finer details of living cells, and changes in opinion as to what should be taught in a given course, encourage the frequent revision of textbooks. But the basic facts of the books are not changing. For example, we have recently heard that there is some uncertainty and some new evidence concerning the exact shape of the earth, but the basic fact that the earth is essentially a globe is demonstrated many times daily by air vehicles traveling to distant destinations, and finally arriving at their starting point by flying around the earth. Science may discover numerous high or low points on the globe, but will not some day decide that the earth is thin like a pancake!

As those of us who are in science, work at our profession, we constantly encounter both chemical and biological data which have been published and known ever since the early days of science--the densities of various elements, certain characteristics of various living cells, types of reproduction in organisms, etc. Science is always learning more details concerning the things we study, but as R. W. Maatman says, "New knowledge rarely proves older ideas to be wrong."[5] Maatman then goes on to explain and illustrate this principle:

What does happen is that older ideas may be seen in a new context. Consider the example of quantum mechanics and Newton's laws. Some persons have erred in claiming

that modern quantum mechanics and the uncertainty principle have shown Newton's laws of motion, formulated in
the seventeenth century, to be incorrect. Newton's laws
are incorrect for the smallest particles, particles which
were unknown in the seventeenth century, but those laws
are correct (within experimental error) for the larger
objects for which the laws were formulated.[6]

A further misunderstanding concerning certainty in science often
arises from rumors that there is great disagreement between scientists
on a given subject. Sometimes such disagreements are sensationally
publicized in the popular news media. But when we examine each case
we almost invariably find that the disagreements do not affect the
well established principles of the particular science involved, but
only have to do with the finer details of new, related discoveries.
For example, the Deep Sea Drilling Project, currently being conducted
by the National Science Foundation, is bringing to light many new
facts concerning the sediments on the ocean floors. But this research
is not destroying our knowledge of the nature of the numerous sediments which have already been studied during the past 100 years.[7]

Truth and Scientific Observation

Can science discover truth? In order to answer this question
we can go back to the fact that science devotes its attention to observing God's revelation in nature, which was discussed near the
beginning of this chapter. Since God has incorporated a limited
revelation of himself into nature, and since the Bible encourages
us to accept human powers of observation as reliable, it follows
that certain truths can be derived from nature through scientific
observation. We are not speaking here of spiritual truths, but of
the truth which concerns the natural world. Thus the discoveries of
the need for oxygen and of the flow of blood through the heart are
truths concerning nature, discovered by science. These facts are
true, not because science discovered them, but because they were
known in the mind of God long before man discovered them.

We most certainly regard the Word of God, as spoken by Christ,
the apostles, and the prophets, and as recorded in the Bible, as
absolute truth. However, there is the question, "Are God's words
more true than his acts?" It is well known that corn plants produce
sugar, and that this sugar can be extracted for the making of syrup
and other food products. The reason that corn plants produce sugar
is that God made them with this ability. Now, since God is the creator
of this ability in corn plants, is not the fact that they produce
sugar just as true as the things God sets forth in language? That is,
are not the things which God does just as true as the things He says?
Thus, can we not say that it is just as true that corn plants produce
sugar, as that the Israelites once lived in Egypt, or that the disciples caught fish in the sea of Galilee? One of these facts was
discovered by science; the other two are stated in the Bible, but
all three surely must be equally true.[8]

We do want to make clear here that we are not saying that truth concerning nature is on an equal level with the <u>spiritual</u> truths found in the Bible. There are indeed truths concerning our relation to God, the work of Christ for man, etc., which are "spiritually discerned," or "spiritually appraised" (I Corinthians 2:14), and are in some sense higher than are the facts of nature and of history. However, the higher status of the spiritual truths is due to their quality or classification, rather than to their source.

Perhaps we can now summarize this brief treatment concerning truth by saying that God is the source of all truth, regardless of where it is found, or how it comes to man. A statement from Warren Wiersbe may help in this summary: "We do not look upon truth as something men have invented. We take truth, regardless of where we find it, whether truth is found under a microscope, through a telescope, or wherever God has put truth in this universe of ours."[9] To this we would add the warning, when you are looking through that microscope or telescope, be sure to remember the distinction between genuine observation and opinions you might formulate as a result of superficial observation. We do not declare something to be fact or truth without a long series of repeated observations by numerous capable observers--such as the many surgeons observing the flow of blood through the heart, which we mentioned above.

The Dangers of Compartmentalization

It would be inappropriate to close a chapter on "revelation and science" without a warning against the danger of forming a dichotomy out ot the two. Many scientists who have embraced Christianity have made the mistake of never trying to reconcile their profession with the divine revelation of the Bible. Hence they have often harbored within themselves two contradictory lines of thought, saving themselves from mental torture only by keeping the possibly conflicting ideas separated into two "compartments" of their mind. We are of course not saying that objective observations of science are in conflict with the teachings of the Bible; they are not. But some of the theories which are usually regarded as a part of science are not in harmony with the Bible. In this case there needs to be a true reconciling, rather than a rejection of the idea of reconciliation by regarding science and Christianity as two completely unrelated disciplines. They do have definite dissimilarities, but they are not unrelated, for they both deal with realities.

Francis Schaeffer aptly explains that the modern science of the 19th and 20th centuries has largely given up the principle of antithesis which Francis Bacon and the other scientists of the Reformation held. Thus the recent philosophy of science does not admit the need of reconciling revelation and natural science. Schaeffer comments on the better position of the <u>early</u> founders of modern science as follows:

> They all believed in the rational. This word has no relationship to the word 'rationalism'. They acted upon the basis that man's aspiration for the validity of reason was well founded. They thought in terms of antithesis.

If a certain thing was true, the opposite was not true....
There is no historic basis for the later Heidegger's
position that the pre-Socratic Greeks, prior to Aristotle,
thought differently. As a matter of fact it is the only
way man can think. The sobering fact is that the only way
one can reject thinking in terms of an antithesis and the
rational is on the basis of the rational and the antithesis.
When a man says that thinking in terms of an antithesis
is wrong, what he is really doing is using the concept of
antithesis to deny antithesis.[10]

Evangelical Christians of the present day have not gone so far
as to give up the principle of antithesis, but many are evading the
necessity of reconciling the revelation found in the Bible with the
objective discoveries of science. Such a reconciliation is possible
because both God and the universe are rational.

The habit of mental compartmentalization of the ideas of science
and of the Bible is not only found among scientists, but is also
prevalent among other classes of people. Thus all of us need to
make an effort to keep ourselves free from this error. God can not
accept two opposite teachings concerning the natural world as both
being true; neither should we make an attempt to accept them both.
Christians in particular should realize this responsibility, and
seek to emphasize the wonderful agreement between God's inspired
revelation and the observations of science. Thus we will be properly
relating both special revelation and God's revelation in nature.

FOOTNOTES

1. See Edward J. Young, Studies in Genesis One, 1964, p. 82-86.

2. A. H. Strong, Systematic Theology, 1949, p. 288.

3. Francis A. Schaeffer, Escape From Reason, 1968, p.31. compare
Francis A. Schaeffer, The God Who Is There, 1968, p. 92-93.

4. If the geologist goes on to include some explanation or
theory which seems to contradict the Bible, we must then carefully
recheck the Biblical statement to see if we have understood it correctly. If it turns out that there is still a contradiction, we
should then question the geologist to learn the basis of the explanation he has made.

5. R. W. Maatman, The Bible, Natural Science, and Evolution,
1970, p. 59.

6. Ibid., p. 59-60.

7. One must be aware that disagreements concerning theories
are much greater than are disagreements over observed phenomena or
conditions. An example of this is seen in the great amount of disagreement among biologists over evolutionary theory; but this is because

22

the genetic material (chromosomes and genes) of the fossils is never preserved, so there is usually no way of settling the arguments of past relationships of organisms. In other words, the disagreement is in an area where scientific evidence is lacking, but with human nature what it is, speculations still abound.

8. If an attempt is made to reject this principle on the ground that the production of sugar in corn is known only because of the work of man, rather than being written in the Bible, we should recall the fact that even our knowledge of the Israelites and of the disciples depends on human ability to correctly read human language.

9. Warren Wiersbe, "Truth: A Responsibility," Brethren Missionary Herald, v. 34, Dec. 23, 1972, p. 36.

10. Schaeffer, Escape From Reason, p. 35

CHAPTER 3

CORAL REEFS AS A RECORD OF THE PAST

Just before the destruction of Eniwetok and Bikini atolls in the Pacific atomic tests, the U. S. Geological Survey opened up an important window into the past for evangelical Christians. This "window" was to give us an insight into the long and extensive process of the making of certain biologically produced rock formations. Here was to be found a natural record of at least many hundreds of thousands of years of the growth and building activity of coral animals and other lime-secreting organisms. In this record Christians would have an opportunity to see step-by-step some of the results of the creative acts of God which are described in the first chapters of Genesis. Soon after the Second World War the U. S. Government decided that extensive drillings should be made into the atolls (circular type coral reefs) of the Pacific before the bomb tests were carried out. These investigations were made during the period of 1946 through 1952, and the reports were published as a part of the U. S. Geological Survey Professional Paper series.

Coral reefs are built by the slow growth of coral animals and other organisms which live with them. Since the limy materials deposited by coral animals gradually build up over the skeletal matter left by the previous generation, a hardened, mineral record of the past is built as time progresses. This gives us a natural, accurate record of animal and plant growth on the reef over a long period of time. In some ways this is comparable to the record we have in the successive generations of peat moss which accumulate, one upon the other, to form a peat bog. There are, however, several basic differences between the formation of a peat bog and the formation of a coral reef. One of these is that the reef-forming organisms must have sea water, which is laden with minerals, as their source of building material. Another is that, after the limy skeletons of the coral animals and other organisms have been formed, the continued action of the surrounding sea water fossilizes a great many skeletons, thus forming very long-lasting structures which make up the framework of the reef.

When we speak of the "skeletons" of these organisms, we are not referring to bones. Coral animals and the other organisms which form a reef do not have bones, as the vertebrate animals do. Any hard structure which supports the living cells of a marine animal or plant, and thus gives stability to the organism, is properly called a skeleton. Since sea water contains an abundance of mineral matter (approximately 3.4%, by weight), marine organisms have no problem in obtaining the material for their skeletons. The main mineral used for this purpose is calcium carbonate ($CaCO_3$). Surprisingly, numerous kinds of algae build supporting skeletons of calcium carbonate within their plant bodies. So the corals, snails, oysters, and other hard-bodied marine animals are not the only organisms which contribute skeletal materials to a reef.

24

Fig. 1. Air view of Bikini atoll, in the Marshall Islands. The U. S. Geological Survey made deep test drillings in this coral atoll island soon after the Second World War. Note the white beach of coral sand around the island, and the clumps of trees near the left end and center. (Courtesy of U. S. Naval Photographic Center, Naval District, Washington, D. C.: Photograph no. 80-6-373118, Feb. 28, 1944, altitude 1,000 ft.)

Drilling Records from Living Coral Reefs

The drillings made by the U. S. Geological Survey on the Bikini and Eniwetok atolls in the Marshall Islands revealed that these reefs are extremely thick, and that they are built on top of old, deeply submerged, volcanic cones, called "seamounts." (See Figures 2 and 3 for the location and form of these reefs.) One drill hole on the Bikini atoll penetrated 2,556 feet of reef material, and one at Eniwetok penetrated 4,610 feet before reaching the volcanic base.[1] So it is evident that a great amount of reef growth is represented in these atolls.

We should here explain that some of the volcanic cones which form seamounts are elongate or otherwise imperfectly shaped, but they do have a general circular shape, as viewed from the air. Many of these conical mountains were relatively flat topped before the coral deposits began to form on them. Such a truncated volcanic mountain is called a "guyot" or "flat-topped seamount," and is known to provide a good foundation for the growth of a reef. In the case of the Eniwetok atoll in the Marshall Islands, the drillings made by the U. S. Geological Survey revealed that the guyot on which it was built had the typical broad platform at the top.[2] The guyots are composed largely of basalt, which is the most common form of volcanic rock. Basalt is of course radically different from the fossil-bearing limestone of which the reefs themselves are composed. The research at Eniwetok atoll showed that the guyot on which it was built stands two miles above the surrounding ocean floor, with the atoll rising nearly another mile above it.[3] Several other atolls in the Marshalls were shown to have similar bases. It must of course be remembered that the corals and other reef-forming organisms could not begin their growth until the volcanic platform had cooled to a mild temperature, and until a favorable water depth over the platform had been established.

Growth Rates of Corals

If we want to know the length of time required for forming a reef such as the Eniwetok atoll, a knowledge of the growth rates of corals and the other marine organisms which grow on the reef will be of great value. There are several important retarding effects which influence upward growth of the reef. Some of these are the dissolving action of water, the mechanical destruction accomplished by wave action, and the mechanical and chemical destruction produced by the numerous boring organisms which live in the reef rock. But, if we know the growth rates of the main organisms and then allow additional time for the various retarding effects, it is possible to make a meaningful estimate of the length of time required for the construction of the layers of reef material found during the drilling of a test hole into an atoll or other reef.

A study of growth rates may seem at first sight to be a technical matter with which we need not bother in this book. However, numerous Bible students have often gone astray in thinking that growth rates have no fundamental controls or constancy, and have thus thought that the creatures which form reefs can not be used as a gauge for time.

26

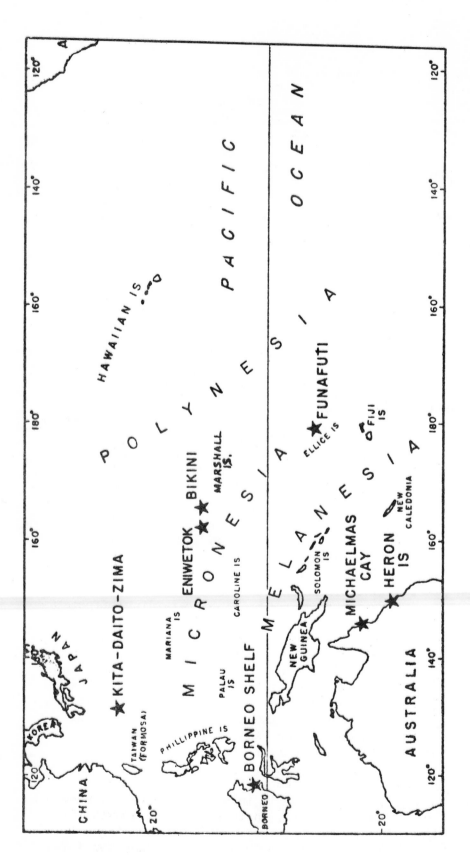

Fig. 2. Sites of some deep test wells drilled on reefs and coral islands in the Pacific. K. O. Emery, J. I. Tracey, Jr., and H. S. Ladd, "Bikini and nearby atolls, Marshall Islands," U. S. Geological Survey Professional Paper no. 260-A, 1954, Figure 65.

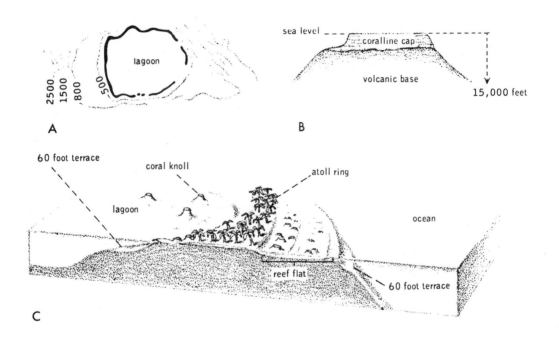

27

Fig. 3. Diagrams of topograph of Eniwetok atoll. A. Config-
uration of atoll and surrounding water depths. B. Cross section through coral cap and volcanic base. C. Section through
part of atoll. R. D. Barnes, Invertebrate Zoology, 1968,
Figure 5-37. (By permission of the W. B. Saunders Co., Philadelphia, Pa.)

A consideration of the growth processes and growth rates of reef-forming organisms will do much to give us a realization that there truly has been order and constancy in the development of reefs and other structures during the past ages.

To many people the term "coral" means only a piece of rock of a particular shape, or an ornament which has been fashioned from a piece of coral skeleton. Actually a coral animal is a small, cylindrical living creature, similar to a sea anemone. An individual coral animal is usually called a "coral polyp." It lives in a small cup of calcium carbonate skeletal material which it forms for its protection. Small arm-like structures called tentacles extend out to, or beyond, the rim of the cup to bring in food. The process by which the skeletal cups are formed is called "secretion," and involves the removal of calcium ions and carbonate ions from the sea water, to form the hard calcium carbonate. The mineral ions are first taken into the cells of the animal, and then secreted to the exterior, where the mineral hardens to form the cup and the base underneath it. Most kinds of coral are colonial in growth habit. That is, the coral polyps grow together in groups, cementing their skeletal cups one to another to form a solid mass. (See Figures 4 and 5 for photographs of living and fossil coral colonies.)

There have been several careful, systematic studies of the growth rates of reef-forming corals in various parts of the world within the past sixty years. One of the most recent of these is the study by J. E. Hoffmeister and his associates off the coast of Florida.[4] Hoffmeister made careful observations on the growth rate of the most dominant reef-building coral in the Florida-Bahama area, Montastrea annularis,[5] by marking many specimens in their under-water habitats, and then observing and measuring them over a period of years. The rate of growth of course varies somewhat, just as the growth rate of larger animals varies within the limits of the governing physical laws, which can not be violated. The fastest growth rate of these corals which Hoffmeister and his associates found was 10.7 millimeters (about two-fifths of an inch) per year in height.[6] This would produce one foot of coral rock in 28.5 years if its growth were not interrupted or slowed down. However, there are numerous influences which directly interfere with the growth processes of the coral animals. Some of these factors as observed by A. G. Mayor during a four-year Carnegie expedition to the Samoan Islands were: (a) silt and mud washing over and smothering coral colonies, (b) high temperatures due to hot sun during low tides, (c) drenching tropical rains which not only smothered and killed many coral colonies by the resulting mud, but diluted the sea water to such a low salt content that the coral polyps could no longer live in it.[7]

At this point we will consider some other examples of the fastest-- and also average--growth rates of reef-building corals, as observed in various waters. There is a fundamental difference in the growth rates of the non-branching ("massive") corals, and those of the kinds that are highly branched. The polyps of some kinds, for example the members of Genus Acropora, arrange themselves on the colony in such a way that the skeleton of the colony will be a highly branched,

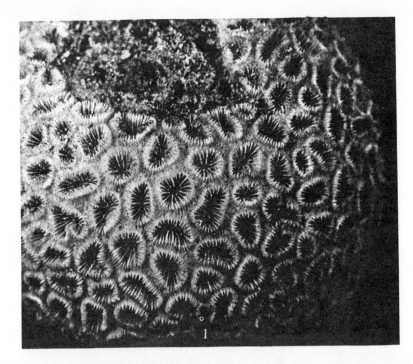

A

B

Fig. 4. Two modern coral colonies from reefs in the Marshall Islands, shown at approximately natural size. Note the numerous
"cups," which show clearly on each colony because the bodies of the
living coral animals have been removed. One coral animal (individual) lived in each cup. The lines radiating out from the center of
each cup are partitioning walls which partially divided the digestive
cavities of the individuals. A. Favia pallida, B. Favites flexuosa.
From J. W. Wells, "Recent corals of the Marshall Islands, Bikini and
nearby atolls," U. S. Geological Survey Professional Paper no. 260-I,
1954, Plate 173, Figure 1, and Plate 175, Figure 1.

Fig. 5. A fossil coral colony from a depth of 937 feet in
one of the test wells drilled in Bikini atoll. This specimen
shows seven of the "cups" in which the coral animals lived.
The number "X 5.5" at the side means that the photographic
process magnified the specimen five and one-half diameters.
Seriatopora ornata. From J. W. Wells, "Fossil corals from
Bikini drill holes, Bikini and nearby atolls," U. S. Geological Survey Professional Paper no. 260-P, 1954, Plate 223,
Figure 4.

antler-like structure, with a great amount of space between branches.
If one measures the rate of growth of the tips of these branches he
will find it to be up to about 100 mm. (about 4 inches) per year in
the Florida-Bahama region,[8] and up to 125 mm. per year in Samoa.[9]
This is the fastest growing genus of the reef-forming corals; however,
it must be remembered that the open nature of the colony (somewhat
like the branches of a tree) prevents this coral from making anything
like 100 mm. of solid buildup of reef per year. Wave action and
other forces wear and break the branches, whereupon they fall to the
base to add their volume to the reef mass.

    Mayor found the average growth in height of healthy colonies
of corals of the massive type, belonging to Genus Porites, to be
17 mm. per year. He also found this kind of coral to be one of the
most effective reef-building types in Samoa. Since coral skeletons
of this massive type are not readily broken up by wave action, Mayor
estimates that "a reef-wall composed of massive Porites might attain
a thickness of 55 feet in 1000 years, while a reef composed of branching Porites might grow upward at least 25 feet in the same period
of time."[10] (This is of course assuming that the ocean level and
other environmental conditions would remain favorable for the entire
period.) It should also be noted that Samoa has a latitude, water
temperature, and other conditions which are more favorable for coral
growth than is found in the Florida-Bahama and Hawaiian areas.[11] It
is important here to realize that the term "average" in these reports
refers to a figure obtained by measuring the growth of numerous
healthy colonies of coral over a period of time (a year or more), and
averaging them. Just measuring the growth rate of a single colony
would not give an accurate picture.

    The growth rates of reef-forming algae also have some effect
on the growth of the reef. These organisms are, as stated in the
early part of this chapter, kinds of algae which secrete a hard,
calcareous skeleton as a part of the plant body. There are several
kinds of red algae and of green algae which have this characteristic,
and contribute large amounts of mineral to reefs. Encrusting types
of red algae often produce a thick crust over colonies of corals
which have died. Different kinds of green algae which grow on the
floors of reef lagoons produce multitudes of small calcareous plates
and needles which make a sizeable contribution to the reef. Scientific reports of reef studies practically always include some observations of the algal mineral deposits being made. Most observers,
including Mayor and Hoffmeister, have recognized the rate of mineral
deposited by algae as similar to, or somewhat less than the rates
observed for coral.[12] One must of course remember that a mass of
encrusting algae growing over a mass of coral stops the growth of
the coral.

Coral Growth Rates vs. Reef Growth Rates

    As a swimmer passes over a submerged reef, he sees numerous
clumps (colonies) of coral growing on the surface of the reef. These
colonies have their own growth rates, as explained in the previous
section, but most of them are destined to be drastically changed

before they make their final contribution to the reef height. Boring and encrusting organisms frequently stop the growth of the colony or of a part of it. Eventually the entire colony may be broken loose by wave action and rolled down the side of the reef to a lower level.

In addition to this sort of delay in reef growth, complete stoppages occur. Each stoppage of the reef's growth leaves its mark in what is called an "unconformity" in the substance of the reef mass. Unconformities are thus caused by major disturbing factors such as a drastic change in sea level,[13] the development of muddy or other unfavorable environmental conditions in the water of the area, and volcanic eruption. In many such cases, the fossil remains which are found on the unconforming surface in the reef mass are abruptly different from those above. At least one such unconformity was observed by Hoffmeister and his associates when they made core drillings into the reefs in the Florida Keys;[14] and many such unconformities were observed in the (far deeper) drillings made in the Marshall Islands by the U. S. Geological Survey.

Thus it is seen that it would be absurd to think that the length of time which was required for the formation of a large reef could be calculated by merely dividing the depth of the reef by the average growth rate of healthy coral colonies. The upward growth of the reef is always much slower than the growth of the colonies. In fact, this phenomenon is self-evident in the observation that most of the numerous coral reef-flats in the Pacific which have been studied during the past 75 or more years are wearing down at about the same rate that they are being built up.[15] Of course we are not saying that no material is permanently added to the entire reef-flat each year, but rather, that the leveling forces spread the deposited skeletal matter out over a wider area, broadening the entire reef as time progresses. This broadening can be compared to what we see when truckloads of gravel are spread upon the top of a large heap of crushed stone. The mass of gravel in the truck bed may be 4 feet in depth, but because it is being spread out on the top of the heap, it will add only a few inches to the total height of the heap.

There have been at least two very careful calculations made, of the total amount of coral skeletal material added per year to a given surface of reef, in areas where normal growth is going on. It is significant that none of the research on growth of corals which we are citing was carried out for the purpose of demonstrating that the reefs are of great age. These research projects were done with a view to showing the rate at which corals can be expected to build up barrier reefs which are of value in protecting harbors.

Mayor made a very careful series of observations to determine the amount of actual mineral (skeletal matter) which was being se-creted and deposited per square yard on one of the typical, normally growing reef-flats. An extended period of observation and measurements made during the Carnegie expeditions of 1917 to 1920, to the Samoan Islands, under Mayor's supervision, revealed that the total thickness added to the reef flat per year was approximately 8 millimeters.[16]

At this point let us compare the upward growth rates we have cited, with the total depth of the thickest known coral reefs--the atolls in the Marshall Islands. During the drillings which were made into these islands, the thickest coral reef deposit found was that of Eniwetok atoll, where one drilling, as stated above, had to go through 4,610 feet of reef deposit before striking the volcanic rock (basalt) base. Another drilling nearby extended through reef deposit for 4,158 feet before reaching the volcanic base.[17] It is of course true that no one is able to determine the exact length of time which was required for growing such an extensive reef, but it is obvious that it was a very long process. If we divide the thickness of the Eniwetok reef by Mayor's 8 mm. of deposit per year, we arrive at 176,000 years of continuous growth required for the laying down of this much thickness. However, this would be a false picture, because of the many factors which retard the build-up of the reef, as discussed above. Thus the total length of time required for forming the 4,610 foot reef deposit of Eniwetok was undoubtedly many times the 176,000 years.[18]

Natural Laws Which Limit the Metabolic Processes of Growth

In considering the length of time required for the growth of a coral reef of this thickness, some who are unfamiliar with the laws of nature may go astray. They may attempt to hypothesize that corals and other marine organisms could have grown many times faster in ancient times than they do now. Here is where we need a brief lesson on the subject of biological growth, and a reminder of what we pointed out in the previous chapter; namely, that God's natural laws--including biological laws--were stable, from the time of creation.

The reef-forming kinds of animals and plants are, and always have been, dependent upon the chemical (metabolic) processes which God established as their "way of life." There are numerous kinds of chemical processes within each living cell, whether it be in a snail clinging to a rock in the surf, a coral polyp quietly collecting its food, or a filament of algae doing its work of photosynthesis. Some of the chemical reactions within the cells are for extracting energy from food, and some for building the necessary organic molecules for cellular growth. Other reactions have to do with the collecting of mineral ions from the sea water and processing them for the production of an external skeleton or shell.

All of these metabolic activities are completely dependent upon the supply of raw materials (mainly oxygen, minerals, and food). The rate of growth of an organism is limited by the availability of these raw materials, and also by the rate at which chemical processes can be carried on in the cells of the animal or plant. The rate of metabolic activity is confined to definite limits for all organisms. For example, a farmer can induce more rapid growth in hogs and broilers by increasing the supply and quality of raw materials for these animals; but there are very definite limits to this increase--as

every farmer knows. The reasons for these limits are several, but
the most obvious of them are: (a) limited capacity of digestion,
(b) limited area of absorption in the intestine, to transfer digested food and minerals to the bloodstream, (c) limited capacity of the
circulatory system for carrying the digested food to all parts of the
body, (d) limited quantities of the enzymes which are so essential
in the construction of the molecules of protein, fat, carbohydrate,
and skeletal materials which make up the body, and (e) limited capacity to receive and distribute oxygen to the cells of the body.
(Any increase of cellular activity, such as in growth processes,
requires an increase of oxygen supply.) All of these limitations
exist because life and growth are based on natural laws of chemical
activity within the cells of the organism. Since these natural laws
of metabolism are a part of life, they were of necessity established
by God simultaneously with the creation of life. Certainly it is
his wisdom that planned the intricate activities which go on within
cells. And we must recognize that God does not change the many
natural laws which He has created, except in very special cases
either for the benefit, or for the judgment, of man. In other words
the laws which control the thousands of chemical reactions within
living cells were so perfectly planned, and so carefully and delicately related to the physical environment, that there has been no
need to make any appreciable changes in those laws.

    Let us take the example of a coral animal (polyp) living and
secreting a skeleton. The amount of skeleton it can secrete per
unit of time is dependent on the rate at which the animal can take
in and assimilate food, oxygen, and minerals. Food is taken in
through the mouth by tentacles from the surrounding water and digested in a central cavity. The amount of digestive enzymes is of
course limited. There is no blood circulatory system to convey
digested food to other parts of the body, for example, to the cells
on the outside of the body which do the secreting of skeletal matter; so the digested food has to be conveyed by the slow process of
diffusion from cell to cell. Oxygen is readily obtainable from the
small amount of that element which is dissolved in the water, but
there are no gills; so the oxygen just has to diffuse into the animal
through its outside epidermis, just as in a frog during hibernation.
The maximum amount of oxygen found in water, at the temperatures in
which tropical reef-forming corals grow (about 27° C.), is approximately 0.001%. (The amount of oxygen which can dissolve in water
is dependent upon the temperature.)[19] Thus the intake of oxygen is
limited both by the limited surface of the animal's body, and by the
physical laws which determine the rate of diffusion. Likewise, the
intake and secretion of the minerals which form the skeleton are
limited. The calcium-secreting cells which form the skeleton can
secrete skeletal matter no faster than they can take in mineral ions
from the water, chemically reprocess these ions, and release them
back to the outside as calcium carbonate. This intake of ions is
dependent upon the physical laws of diffusion and the biological
laws of cellular activity, both of which are fundamental, permanent
laws established by God at creation. Thus we come to recognize
these lowly creatures of the sea as "time keepers of the past."

The Drilled Stratigraphic Column at Eniwetok

We can not, in this volume, give a detailed description of the local stratigraphic column[20] which was elucidated by the Eniwetok drillings, but a brief description of what the drilling cores revealed will help explain why we must regard the atoll as having had a long history. (Drilling cores are sections of the stratigraphic column which have been lifted out intact by means of a special drill.) H. S. Ladd gives a detailed, stage-by-stage description of the materials brought up by the drills on Eniwetok.[21] Of course practically all of it is limestone, with many fossils--especially corals, Foraminifera, and algae--embedded in it. Numerous, and sometimes extensive, sections of the column were composed of hard, fossilized, cemented coral skeletons. Other sections were sometimes composed of limy debris which contained high percentages of the skeletons of other types of calcium-secreting organisms. In some layers the coral fossils showed a great amount of wear (erosion), whereas in other layers much less wear.

As the test drillings were being made at Eniwetok, with the drill passing through successive layers of reef limestone, it was observed that some of the limestone layers showed marked evidence of leaching and weathering. These features can occur only as a result of long-time exposure of the limerock, either in the intertidal zone, or above the level of high tide. Such long periods of exposure represent unconformities which greatly add to the length of time required for building the reef. Three very definite, extensively weathered unconformity levels of this type were found, at depths of 300 feet, 1,000 feet, and 2,780 feet respectively.[22] The fact that these particular unconformity levels represent periods of prolonged emergence is indicated not only by weathering, but also by the type of cementation found in the limestone layers which lie just beneath the unconformity. This limestone shows the typical kind of calcite cementation which occurs when limestone lies for many years just above the salt water level along a seashore.[23] In this environment much of the calcium carbonate of the limestone dissolves and is replaced by a "cement" composed of very small crystals of a more pure form of calcium carbonate called "calcite".

In addition to the evidence from these weathered unconformity levels, the fact that at least parts of the top of the atoll were exposed well above sea level for a long period is further indicated by the presence of large amounts of pollen in several of the layers of sedimentary material. During certain times, either the foundation of the atoll arose somewhat, or else the sea level fell. (We do know that the sea level was much lower than at present during some of the Pleistocene Epoch.) The prolonged exposure of the top of the reef of course resulted in the death of the corals and other lime-secreting organisms which require continuous submergence, except around the outer perimeter where the water was still present. The presence of very high counts of pollen of seed-bearing trees and shrubs in the drilling samples shows that parts of the atoll were exposed for many years--probably many centuries--giving opportunity for the growth of seed-bearing trees to become established.

E. B. Leopold of the U. S. Geological Survey made an extensive study of the pollen of seed-bearing plants, and of the spores of some of the "lower" vascular plants found in the drilling samples taken from the Eniwetok test wells. Appreciable amounts of pollen were found at numerous depth levels of the atoll, but the zone of 2,440 to 2,510 foot depth, and the zones from 820 to 880 feet and 670 to 680 feet, yielded large amounts of pollen from the numerous drilling samples tested. Several of the samples yielded more than 10,000 pollen grains per gram of reef rock or sediment, and one sample from the 830 foot level contained 100,000 pollen grains per gram (28.3 grams = one ounce, avoirdupois weight.)[24] In most of these samples approximately one-half of the pollen was identified as being from various species of mangrove trees. Figure 6 shows photomicrographs of one of the kinds of fossil pollen from drilling samples taken from the 830 foot level in the Eniwetok atoll.

There are modern species of mangrove trees growing on many of the islands of the Pacific at present. They are prolific producers of pollen, but the pollen count in modern sediments taken right near where these trees grow has been found to be no greater than the count in the above described sediments from deep in the Eniwetok atoll. An abundance of pollen such as was found in these ancient sediments of course indicates that there were periods of time when many pollen-producing (seed-bearing) plants grew in the immediate vicinity, and that later the sea level changed, allowing the coral reef to continue its growth. There is no possibility that such high concentrations of pollen could have been blown or washed in from distant points.[25]

Thus a reasonably good reconstruction of the history of the Eniwetok atoll has been made, by taking note of the rock and sediment types, the many kinds of marine fossils, the distinct unconformities, and the kinds of pollen and other remains of terrestrial life. All of these tell us that the reef has had a long and varied history, with numerous major interruptions in its development.

Other facets of this atoll's history have been established through a knowledge of the growth habits of the kinds of organisms which built it, for example, the photosynthetic nature of most of the major reef-forming organisms. Both the reef-forming corals and the various kinds of calcareous green and red algae which help build the reef require light, and therefore can flourish only at shallow depths. This tells us that a great amount of change of sea level, in relation to the atoll, had to occur during the development of such a massive and "high" structure. Very little growth of calcareous algae occurs at depths greater than 300 feet,[26] and corals rarely flourish at more than 100 feet. (Corals are dependent on microscopic forms of algae which grow symbiotically in their outer body walls.) Some of the changes of ocean level were undoubtedly due to the buildup and melting of glaciers at the poles of the earth.

Another factor which most likely helped in maintaining the proper water depth for reef growth was the change in elevation of

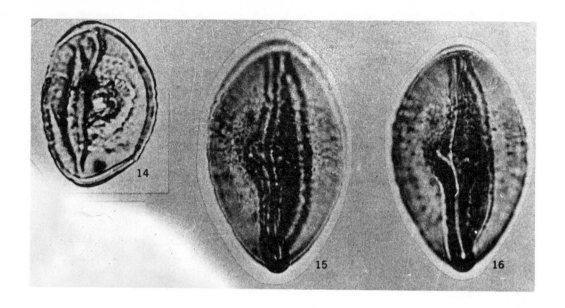

Fig. 6. Three grains of fossilized plant pollen from a
depth of approximately 850 feet in the Eniwetok atoll.
These are microscopic views, shown at a magnification of
approximately 1,000 diameters. This is a species of Genus
Sonneratia. From E. B. Leopold, "Miocene pollen and spore
flora of Eniwetok atoll, Bikini and nearby atolls, Marshall
Islands," U. S. Geological Survey Professional Paper no.
260-II, 1969, Plate 307, Figures 14, 15, and 16.

the seamount on which the atoll rests. Since it is well known that
islands and peaks of land beneath the surface of the ocean often go
through a slow sinking process, it is generally believed that the
extinct volcanic bases upon which the larger atolls were built
underwent a gradual subsidence.[27] In this way the corals, and the
algae which live with them, could have a favorable water level for
growth. Of course it would be unreasonable to suppose that the
rate of subsidence was always equal to the rate of upward growth of
the reef. Thus the reefs underwent periods when they either were
too deeply submerged to allow coral growth, or were projecting up
out of the water and being eroded by wind and waves. Such periods
as these must have been responsible for at least most of the more
radical unconformities.

Some of the alterations of sea level, and of the altitude of
the volcanic bases on which the atolls rest, may have been caused
by catastrophic events such as the Biblical Flood. Therefore, the
Flood could have been responsible for one of the several unconformities in the atoll. However, it would be very difficult to confirm
any hypothesis of such a connection. At any rate, catastrophic
events can not be taken as the cause for the atolls, for these show
every evidence of having been formed by an orderly series of biological growth processes. We also have every reason to believe
that the lower (older) levels of these reefs grew and were fossilized long before the creation of man.

Now to summarize, we have a fairly accurate history of the slow
formation of the atolls, through (a) a knowledge of the volcanic
bases upon which they rest, (b) the natural laws of growth of the
reef-forming organisms, (c) the animal and plant fossils found at
various depths, and (d) the unconformities and erosion representing
the physical changes which occurred in the ocean during the time of
atoll formation. Thus a great deal of specific information is known
about the past without even resorting to the use of radiometric
dating or to the use of highly theoretical assumptions. The Bible
student can be confident that here we have an accurate record of
some of the long period of time which has elapsed since God created
reef-forming animals and plants.

Fossilization of Marine Organisms in Coral Reefs

We have considered the growth processes of coral atolls, but
we must realize that growth of lime-secreting animals and plants is
very often followed by fossilization processes. This leaves a much
more meaningful record for us, of both the immediate past, and of
the distant past, than could growth alone.

To begin with, we should realize that fossilization processes
do not, as is often assumed, belong only to the past. Fossilization
in a reef is a constant process which can be regularly observed to
modify the abandoned skeletons of many of the marine organisms,
transforming them into a more permanent form. For example, when
T. P. Scoffin recently made a series of studies of the reefs around
the islands of Bermuda, he found that only a few years are required

for transforming a visible layer of coral skeletal material into fossil form.[28] When we break a piece of coral rock off the side of a reef, we find living organisms covering the surface of the removed piece. But when the fragment is sawed in two, fossilized skeletons are usually found only an inch or two beneath the outside surface. The fossilized skeletons found in these fragments often exhibit radical differences in texture and composition from what is observed in the unfossilized organisms at the surface.

Fossilization also occurs in the sediments which are found gradually accumulating around the base of the growing masses of coral. Cementation, which is an advanced stage of the fossilizing process, often begins at a depth of 30 centimeters (about 12 inches) in these sediments.[29] This process of cementation fossilizes and binds the shells of many small marine organisms present in the sediment, thus forming a kind of rock which shows a high percentage of very small skeletal units throughout.[30] Whether or not this cementation will progress to the point of forming hard rock depends on the amount of water currents forcing water through the pores of the sediment mass.

Just what is a fossil? Even though we frequently talk about fossils, our conception of their nature seems often to be rather vague. We can gain a better idea of their nature by considering some of the different forms in which fossils are found in reefs and other sedimentary environments. Most of these forms of fossils have been well known for several decades, and some for much longer. We will here concentrate mainly on the kinds of fossils found in reef environments.

1. Essentially unaltered skeletons or skeletal parts. This type of preservation is illustrated in some of the fossil corals found in the drillings in the Marshall Islands.[31] In this case the coral specimens were so perfectly sealed in the reef that the percolating waters did not have opportunity to appreciably alter their chemical make-up or structure.

2. Replaced skeletons. These are represented by marine shells, masses of coral skeleton, and other calcareous bodies which have had the substances of their hard parts replaced bit by bit--often molecule by molecule--by some other mineral. This leaves a skeleton identical in shape and appearance to the original one, but composed of a more permanent type of mineral. The most common minerals which replace the original shell material are silica (silicon dioxide, the main component of hard sandstone), iron pyrite, iron oxide, and calcite.[32]

3. Molds and casts. If a shell or other form of skeleton is buried in sediment and then dissolves away, leaving a cavity in the hardening sediment, the remaining imprint of the outside of the shell against the cavity wall is called an "impression" or "mold" ("external mold," in this case). Frequently such a cavity, with its impression of the shell's surface, is later filled in by fresh sediments. If these sediments harden, we then have a "natural cast." In this case

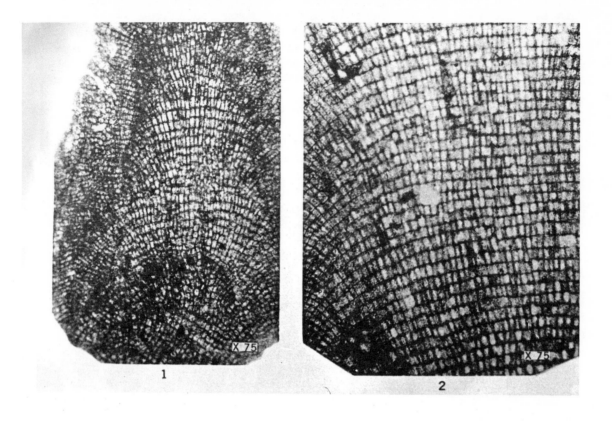

Fig. 7. Fossil calcareous algae from a depth of 2,040 feet
in the Bikini atoll. Each of these two specimens was formed
by an algal plant which possessed many cells. Each of the
minute blocks in the photographs is the fossilized remains
of a cell wall. Note that the pattern of growth in both
specimens was one which radiated upward from the lower part
of the photograph. The magnification, as seen here, is approximately 100 diameters. Lithophyllum oblongum. From J.
H. Johnson, "Fossil calcareous algae from Bikini atoll,
Bikini and nearby atolls," U. S. Geological Survey Professional Paper no. 260-M, 1954, Plate 191, Figures 1 and 2.

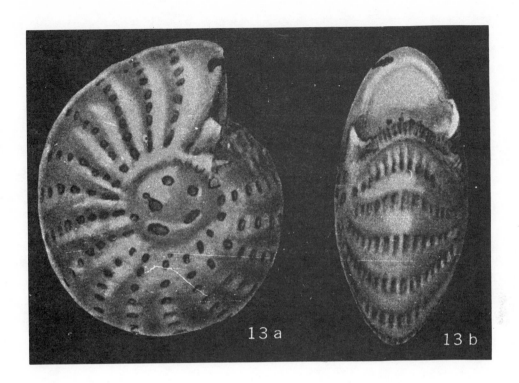

Fig. 8. Fossilized shell of a very small marine animal,
from a depth of 1,800 feet in the Bikini atoll. This is a
member of the very abundant order called the Foraminifera.
The photograph marked 13a is the same shell as 13b, except
that 13b was rotated 90°. The many tiny holes were for
water circulation to bring food and oxygen to the animal,
just as in numerous modern species of the same order. The
shell is seen here at approximately 85 diameters magnification. _Elphidium_ _marshallana_. From R. M. Todd and R. J.
Post, "Smaller Foraminifera from Bikini drill holes," _U_. _S_.
Geological _Survey_ _Professional_ _Paper_ no. 260-N, 1954, _Plate_
198, Figure 13.

Fig. 9. Fossilized shells of small marine animals of the
Order Foraminifera, from a depth of 1,050 feet in the Bikini
atoll. The figure marked 23 is an external view of four
specimens, at approximately 15 diameters magnification. The
one marked 22 is a median section of one of the same species,
shown at approximately 30 diameters magnification. Note the
numerous chambers in the interior of this shell. _Operculin-
oides bikiniensis_. From W. S. Cole, "Larger Foraminifera
and smaller diagnostic Foraminifera from Bikini drill holes,"
U. S. Geological Survey Professional Paper no. 260-0, 1954,
Plate 204, Figures 22 and 23.

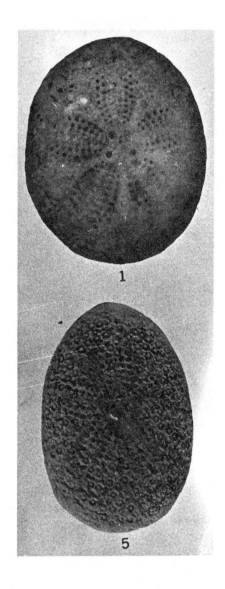

Fig. 10. Fossilized echinoderm specimens from a depth
of 2,900 feet in the Eniwetok atoll. These are close
relatives of the starfishes, sand dollars, and sea urchins. Note the radial symmetry of this animal, with
columns of pores for water circulation radiating out
from the center. Magnification approximately 12 diameters. Echinocyamus petalus. From P. M. Kier, "Fossil
echinoids from the Marshall Islands," U. S. Geological
Survey Professional Paper no. 260-GG, 1964, Plate 302,
Figures 1 and 5.

the paleontologist or fossil hunter can sometimes obtain the entire
fossil cast by breaking open the rock, and prying the cast loose
from its impression. The fossil obtained will have the same form
and shape as the original animal, but will be composed of hardened
sediments which had washed into the cavity. Thus a natural cast
is formed in nature, much as a plaster of Paris cast of a jaw bone
or skull is made for museum displays.

4. Fecal pellets. Lumps of waste material eliminated from the
intestines of various kinds of marine animals, such as crabs and
their relatives, often become fossilized. These mineralized pellets
are frequently of great aid in determining the kinds of life which
were present in or on the sediments in ancient times.

5. Burrows and tubes. The burrows left in the sea shore sands
by marine worms often become filled in with other sediments which
then harden, leaving an identifiable record of the path of the worm.
(The mucus or other slimy material left in the burrow by the worm
is sufficient as a separating material, so that there will be a contrast between the wall of the burrow and the sediment which fills
the cavity.) Also, some types of marine worms secrete hard calcareous tubes which look like small, kinky pipes, in which they live for
protection. These tubes are later transformed into permanent fossil
tubes when the conditions on the sea shore are right. In some
limestone the worm burrows and tubes furnish us with an extensive
and accurate record of the worm population in the marine environment
where the limestone was formed. The present author has seen spectacular arrays of such fossil burrows in the limerocks near to the
shore in the Bermuda Islands.

In summary, we can say that there are several ways in which
the original remains of animals can become preserved or fossilized,
and that such fossils are very abundant in most of the sediments of
the earth. As one looks over the above list of kinds of fossilization, he will be able to note that burial is necessary for the
formation of most fossils. However, since most of the animals and
plants which are fossilized have hard, durable skeletons, the burial
does not have to be a rapid process. The shell or other skeletal
part may lie on the edge of the reef or sea shore for a considerable
time, and then be buried by water currents or waves which cover them
with sediments.

The U. S. Geological Survey has published many volumes describing and picturing fossils in marine sediments. The series of papers
which describes the Bikini and Eniwetok atolls includes the main
types of fossils found in the sedimentary layers of those reefs.
Some of these are corals, calcareous algae, sea urchins and their
relatives (echinoids), and the small shell-producing protozoa belonging to the Order Foraminifera. Figures 7 to 10 show photographs
of some of these fossils which were removed from the test wells on
the islands. The caption beneath each figure gives the depth from
which the fossils were taken, as well as their identification.

FOOTNOTES

1. H. S. Ladd, "Bikini and Nearby Atolls, Marshall Islands, Drilling Operations on Eniwetok Atoll," U. S. Geological Survey Professional Paper 260-Y, 1960, p. 863 ff.

2. H. S. Ladd, "Reef Building," Science, v. 134 (1961), p. 708, 711, and 713. It has been suggested that the truncated nature of guyots is due to erosion by wave action at a time when the top of the volcanic cone was higher above the sea floor, or when the sea level was lower. However, it is now believed that such flat tops could have been produced by multiple explosions around the rim of the volcano, as explained by Haroun Tazieff in "The Afar Triangle," Scientific American, v. 222, Feb. 1970, p. 32-40.

3. Ibid., p. 713.

4. J. E. Hoffmeister, "Growth Rate Estimates of a Pleistocene Coral Reef of Florida," Geological Society of America Bulletin, v. 75 (1964), p. 353-358.

5. Montastrea annularis is the scientific name of this type of coral. Montastrea is the genus to which it belongs, and annularis is the species name.

6. Observations on the same species, made by T. W. Vaughan from 1908 to 1915, yielded similar results, though none of the specimens observed by Vaughan showed quite as fast a growth rate as the most rapidly growing ones of Hoffmeister's observations.

7. A. G. Mayor, Papers From the Department of Marine Biology of the Carnegie Institute of Washington, Publication No. 340, v. 19 (1924), p. 17 and 24.

8. E. A. Shinn, "Coral Growth Rate, An Environmental Indicator," Journal of Paleontology, v. 40 (1966), p. 240.

9. A. G. Mayor, "Growth Rate of Samoan Corals," in Papers From the Department of Marine Biology of the Carnegie Institute of Washington, Publication No. 340, v. 19 (1924), p. 53 and 58.

10. Ibid., p. 60-61.

11. Vaughan found the average annual growth of healthy colonies of massive Porites in the Florida-Bahama region to be 6 mm. per year, as contrasted with Mayor's 17 mm. in Samoa. Ibid., p. 51

12. J. H. Johnson, Limestone Building Algae and Algal Limestones, 1961, p. 32-33.

13. Reef-forming corals will die if they are exposed to drying during low tides. Also, they can not grow if the water is of sufficient depth to prevent the penetration of enough light for the symbiotic algae which grow in the body walls of the coral polyps.

It is well known that reef-building corals can not make any appreciable growth if the water depth is greater than 300 ft., and that most growth occurs at depths of less than 100 ft. (E. J. W. Barrington, _Invertebrate Structure and Function_, 1967, p. 492.)

14. Hoffmeister, "Growth Rate Estimates," p. 356.

15. Mayor, "Growth Rate," p. 65.

16. Mayor, "Growth Rate," p. 64-65. This study was made on the Aua reef-flat, between Breaker Point, Pago Pago Harbor, and the southern end of Aua Village. The area of the reef-flat was 2,550,000 square feet. Mayor and his associates determined the number of coral heads (rounded masses of growing coral) which were on this entire area, and observed their growth for an extended period of time. They calculated the weight of mineral substance being added, by periodically collecting samples of the new growth and weighing and chemically analyzing them. The total number of coral heads growing on the test area was approximately 978,700. About 85% of them were of Genus _Porites_ and Genus _Acropora_--which are the two fastest reef-building corals. The calculations showed that the corals were adding about "2.8 pounds" (This should read 28 lbs.) of mineral deposit (limestone) to each square yard of the area per year. "Taking the specific gravity of limestone as 1.8, this would be equivalent to a layer of coral about 8 mm. in thickness per annum over the entire reef-flat" (p. 65). It is true, as mentioned previously, that massive _Porites_ coral colonies make an upward advance of about 17 mm. per year in the Pacific, but the reef surface is never comprised of one solid, continuous colony (just as a forest is never made up of a solid mass of tree trunks).

17. Ladd, "Drilling Operations," p. 863 ff.

18. The deepest layers of this atoll have been classified as belonging to the Eocene Epoch, which is usually placed at 35 to 50 million years ago by geologists and paleontologists, but we are not here attempting to defend these specific lengths of time.

19. Han-Lee Mao, "Bikini and Nearby Atolls, Marshall Islands, Physical Oceanography in the Marshall Islands Area," _U. S. Geological Survey Professional Paper_ 260-R, 1955, p. 681-682.

20. See Footnote no. 3 of Chapter 1 for an explanation of the expression "local stratigraphic column."

21. Ladd, "Drilling Operations," p. 873-895 and Plates 264 and 265.

22. E. B. Leopold, "Bikini and Nearby Atolls, Marshall Islands, Miocene Pollen and Spore Flora of Eniwetok Atoll, Marshall Islands," _U. S. Geological Survey Professional Paper_ 260-II, 1969, p. 1138.

23. _Ibid._

24. Ibid., p. 1145-1159.

25. The fact that wind or water transport from distant points could not have accounted for such high pollen counts in the ancient sediments was illustrated in the tests made by Leopold, on modern sediments. The modern sediments in those tests were taken from the shores of Ponape, an island slightly to the west of the Marshalls where large numbers of mangrove trees grow, and from the surface of Eniwetok and other nearby atolls. The largest pollen count found in the modern sediments from the shores of Ponape was 34,000 per gram of sediment. These samples were taken from the shallow bottom only a few yards from large clumps of mangrove trees. Samples from farther out yielded much lower counts, and modern samples from Eniwetok and neighboring atolls, where there are comparatively few pollen-producing plants, showed only very low counts. (Leopold, 1969, p. 1152-1156.)

26. Johnson, Limestone Building Algae, p. 26.

27. K. O. Emery, "Bikini and Nearby Atolls, Marshall Islands: Part I, Geology," U. S. Geological Survey Professional Paper 260-A, 1954, p. 2, and 128-131.

28. T. P. Scoffin, "Fossilization of Bermuda Patch Reefs," Science, v. 178, Dec. 22, 1972, p. 1280-1282.

29. Ibid., p. 1281.

30. The process of cementation in marine sediments involves the formation of many small crystals of mineral which fill cavities in the shells and build a sort of "bridge" between the small skeletal parts, shells, and other grains of sediment.

31. J. W. Wells, "Bikini and Nearby Atolls, Marshall Islands, Fossil Corals From Bikini Atoll," U. S. Geological Survey Professional Paper 260-P, 1954, p. 609.

32. Calcite is a crystalline form of calcium carbonate, differing somewhat from the original form of calcium carbonate found in marine shells and corals. The process of replacing the original calcium carbonate of a skeleton with calcite is called "recrystallization." Cementation and recrystallization are very similar processes.

CHAPTER 4

RECOGNIZING TIME IN NATURE'S RECORD

In Chapter 3 we began to examine a few types of time-indicating sedimentary strata as found in a coral reef. Now let us stop to consider the recognition of time in the stratigraphic record in somewhat more detail. Various types of limestone, as well as the great underground formations of rock layers in the oil fields, mountains, and ocean floors of the world, have a thrilling story to reveal to the inquiring Christian.

There are some Bible students who have the idea that there is practically no significant order in the sedimentary rock layers of the earth. They believe that during the Biblical Flood nearly all of the sediments were washed loose from their natural environment, tossed to-and-fro by huge, convulsive waves, and finally spread out in disorderly fashion over the face of the earth. But, though sincere in their beliefs, these persons are unaware of the marvelous and unmistakable, orderly characteristics of the sedimentary layers. They are also unaware of the development, since about 1955, of a whole new phase of geologic studies which identify and elucidate these orderly features much better than any previous studies have. This phase of study is what we call "carbonate sedimentology," the branch of geology which studies calcium carbonate and other limestone-type sediments. Advances in this discipline have been spectacular, enabling sedimentary geologists to identify a large proportion of the biological components of carbonate deposits and to understand the natural processes by which these deposits were so beautifully arranged. Many hundreds of excellent journal articles and books which describe and explain the carbonate sediments of the earth are now available.[1] In the chapters which follow, we will frequently refer to examples of the orderliness of great, thick series of these layers which show that they accumulated gradually as a result of biological growth, rather than by sudden, catastrophic processes. These layers, as well as other types of strata, are useful in learning the ages of geologic formations.

To find methods for assigning precise ages to various levels of the stratigraphic record is very difficult. Accuracy may not be so important for the average person; however, we do have a responsibility as citizens of God's kingdom, not to be arbitrary or careless in such matters. As seen in the previous chapter, we will not be doing justice to God's works if we fail to recognize enough time for the coral reefs and other natural structures to be formed.

Is there then any guide which we can use for learning the minimum amount of time needed for the formation of a particular stratigraphic record or column? The radiometric methods which have been worked out by professional geologists and paleontologists may be valid and useful. However, for practical everyday purposes, so that we can understand the stratigraphic and fossil records in relation to the Bible, we can use simpler methods for establishing some minimum ages. In a sense this is a return to some of the methods which were the mainstay of earth-science studies before the development of radiometric methods. But it should be remembered that most of these principles are still in use, and their meaning has been greatly extended by the discoveries of sedimentologists during the past 15 or 20 years. Therefore we have a number of good methods with which to investigate the record of God's works in nature, from a Christian point of view.[2]

Local Stratigraphic Columns

The most common type of natural record of life in the past which we find in the U. S. and Canada is a local stratigraphic column composed of sedimentary rocks which have been formed by water. This type of stratigraphic column is really just a sequence of layers of different kinds of sedimentary rocks lying one above the other at one specific location. Such a series of course always lies on a non-sedimentary base of igneous or metamorphic rock, which is easily identified when drilling operations reach to that depth. We speak of such a sequence of layers of rocks as a "column" because we see it as such when looking at the drilling cores which are removed while drilling through the layers, and also because it is convenient to picture it as a narrow column in books and journals, thus saving space. (See Figure 11 for an example of a part of a sedimentary column.) The reason we use the term "local" in describing such a column is to keep it from being confused with a "composite" column. Composite columns are often pictured in textbooks for the purpose of showing, in a rather general way, all the types and ages of strata found in the earth.

One of the reasons we can know that the rock layers of the sedimentary columns of the world were formed by water is that so many of these layers contain fossils of aquatic animals and (or) plants. It is the rule, rather than the exception, that sedimentary rocks contain recognizable fossils which belong to the same groups (phyla and classes) as the animals and plants of our time. Some of these are microfossils, but very often they are almost perfectly preserved, and are relatives of modern living microorganisms. (As mentioned in the previous chapter, some microorganisms produce hard shells or other skeletal parts for themselves, and thus are easily fossilized.)

Whenever we find fossils we can be sure that the sedimentary rocks in which they are located were formed after life was created on the earth. Christians usually agree that God did not create ready-made, buried fossils; for this would not be characteristic of the God we know. Because of the presence of these fossils one can not regard the sedimentary rock deposits as having been created "with appearance of age." It is possible that the doctrine of creation with appearance of age could be applied to some igneous rock deposits, but wherever we have a record of life mixed in with the rock layers, we know that this was formed after living things had become abundant in the earth. This is a fact which Leonardo da Vinci began to point out about the beginning of the 16th century, and which was then picked up in the 17th century by Robert Hook and Nils Steensen. (Steno, the latinized form of the latter name is

50

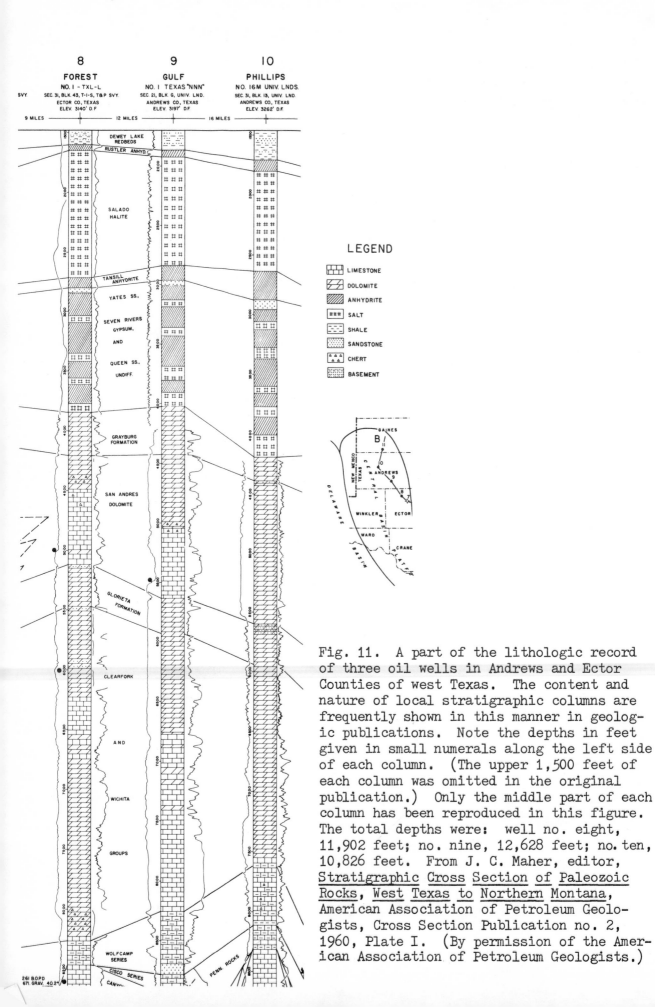

LEGEND

▦ LIMESTONE
▨ DOLOMITE
▩ ANHYDRITE
⊞ SALT
⊟ SHALE
▒ SANDSTONE
△ CHERT
▦ BASEMENT

Fig. 11. A part of the lithologic record of three oil wells in Andrews and Ector Counties of west Texas. The content and nature of local stratigraphic columns are frequently shown in this manner in geologic publications. Note the depths in feet given in small numerals along the left side of each column. (The upper 1,500 feet of each column was omitted in the original publication.) Only the middle part of each column has been reproduced in this figure. The total depths were: well no. eight, 11,902 feet; no. nine, 12,628 feet; no. ten, 10,826 feet. From J. C. Maher, editor, Stratigraphic Cross Section of Paleozoic Rocks, West Texas to Northern Montana, American Association of Petroleum Geologists, Cross Section Publication no. 2, 1960, Plate I. (By permission of the American Association of Petroleum Geologists.)

frequently used.) It is especially because of this record of life
mixed into the sedimentary rock that local stratigraphic columns
are so meaningful. When a certain part of a local column contains
an abundance of the fossilized skeletons from kinds of animals or
plants which are exclusively marine (rather than fresh-water), we
know that this layer was formed in some part of the ocean.[3] This
is especially true if the fossilized, exclusively marine animals
or plants are found in growth position, as is often the case. Examples of exclusively marine organisms are (a) the entire phylum
Echinodermata (starfishes and sea "lilies," and their relatives),
(b) all of the many species of corals, and (c) all of several distinct forms of calcareous green and red algae.

A Stratum of Coral in Indiana

        In the southern part of Indiana, a few miles north of the town
of Madison, there is an outstanding example of ancient marine organisms preserved in growth position. Along the new U. S. Route 62
is a terraced road-cut about 100 feet deep, which has exposed a
beautiful white layer of ancient, extinct corals of the Subclass
Tabulata, near the level of the road bed. The layer is approximately 12 to 18 inches in thickness, with the rounded clumps of coral
skeletons "sitting" in their original growth position. The layer
extends almost continuously and with uniform thickness for at least
one-fourth mile along the road. The coral layer is practically
horizontal, and appears on both sides of the highway. Immediately
above and below it are numerous distinct layers of siltstone and
shale. Here is the unmistakable record of a time when southern
Indiana was covered by ocean water for an extended period, allowing
these exclusively marine creatures to build a layer of skeletal
matter over the 4,000 feet of mainly marine sediments (mostly limestone and shale) which lay beneath. Then, without any major disturbance to break the continuity of the coral covering, a change
of environment brought in muddy waters which entombed the entire
coral community with a layer of siltstone, which then turned into
rock.

        On top of this layer, other distinct layers of marine sediments
(with marine fossils) were added. Just how many more hundreds of
feet of these sediments were added before the sea receded, we do not
know. By examining the immediate surroundings, and the depth of the
road cut, it is evident that at least a few hundred feet were added.
One whole side of the hill in which the reef was buried was removed
before the level of the coral was reached. There are marks of deep
erosion in that hilly area, indicating that the geologists who have
studied it are correct in saying that some hundreds of feet of thickness have been eroded from the covering of this beautiful Ordovician
"mini-reef." The studies of that geographic area also include test
drillings of the approximately 4,000 feet of sediments which lie
beneath the level of the reef. The records of these investigations
of the deeper parts of the stratigraphic column in this area are
still available, describing the alternating layers of fossil-bearing
marine limestone, shale, and dolostone. This is just a simple example of the great amount of information concerning ancient environments

which can be learned by a study of the fossils and of the many distinct layers which are revealed by earth-moving operations and drillings. These and other methods of study enable us to learn a great many specific facts about types of life which were present on the earth long before God placed man on this planet as an observer.

Extinct Fossil Species

Another time-indicating characteristic found in the drilling cores of local stratigraphic columns is that the cores from the deeper layers usually contain fossilized species which are now completely extinct. Furthermore, there is often a gradual fading away of a species as one proceeds upward in the column. For example, within a family or order of mollusks, bryozoans, or other marine animals, certain species very often appear in abundance in the deeper layers, then gradually become fewer in the higher layers, and are finally extinct in all the more recent strata. This is true even though the extinct kinds often differ from their modern relatives only in small details of structure, and have shells of the same shape and density.[4] So, here is a meaningful record of how some species of a presently-living family of mollusks or other marine animals once thrived, and then gradually disappeared from the earth.

This and related principles are used extensively by paleontologists and geologists for identifying and correlating strata in various geographic locations, and for determining the relative age category to which a particular set of sedimentary strata belong. For example, William Smith, in the early 19th century, in his detailed study of the strata of England, Wales, and Scotland, recognized that many of the kinds of fossils present in one set of layers were absent from those found in the set next above. That is, one geologic formation had a different "fossil assemblage" from that next above it, and beneath it. By using this principle he was able to relate one outcrop of sedimentary rock layers in a particular location to other outcrops in other parts of the British Isles, and to determine which were formed at approximately the same time.

Evidence of the genuineness of the "fossil assemblages" which geologists recognize is found in abundance on every continent. That these assemblages of kinds of fossils are very frequently the same natural groups which lived together is evident from the fact that many differing kinds of fossils are frequently found mixed together in the same rock layer. The types of fossils found in such a rock layer are usually completely independent of the density, structure, size, and shape of the original animals. Thus one regularly finds the highly contrasting kinds of organisms which usually grow together in a given environment, fossilized together in rock layers. For example, in the Ordovician and Silurian deposits of northern Kentucky and Indiana, one finds an abundance of heavy-shelled brachiopods and mollusks, from almost fist-size down to those of very tiny dimensions, mixed together with buoyant cephalopods and delicately branched crinoids and bryozoans. All these can be found on the same bedding plane in the deposit. This of course indicates that there was little or no selective sorting action by water at the time of burial.

By comparing the fossil assemblages of various outcropping sedimentary layers with each other William Smith was able to recognize the relation of one layer to another, and thus to learn the relative ages of the various sedimentary formations. This was a discovery which soon became useful in the understanding and commercial development of the coal beds and other mineral deposits of England. William Smith spent 24 years making this extensive study and compiling a geologic map of England, Wales, and part of Scotland. By the end of these investigations he was strongly impressed with the wonderful order and regularity of the geologic strata, so that he wrote the following in 1815, as a part of the introduction to the map he was publishing:

> (The) arrangement must readily convince every scientific or discerning person, that the earth is formed...according to regular and immutable laws, which are discoverable by human industry and observation, and which form a legitimate and most important object of science.[5]

At about the same time that William Smith was using fossil types to identify and correlate strata in England, Georges Cuvier and Abbé Giraud-Soulavie were observing the order of arrangement of fossils in France. Because of Cuvier's extensive knowledge of biological details, he noticed and was impressed with the systematic extinction of many of the species of animals, as one progresses to higher strata. By combining Cuvier's accurate observations of the systematic dying out of certain types of organisms (and the subsequent appearance of more modern fossil assemblages) with the geologic work of William Smith, geologists soon acquired the ability to compare and recognize detailed sedimentary sequences from widely separated localities. Sets of strata in two separate geographic locations can safely be considered to be of the same age if both sets contain essentially the same kinds of fossils, in the same order.[6] This type of comparison of fossils often makes it possible to determine the absolute age of a given stratum when such a stratum contains the same assemblage of fossils as does a layer of known absolute age. (The latter layer must of course be originally dated by some other method, such as sedimentation rate, growth rates of the fossils, or isotope ratios.)

Kinds of Fossils Which Appeared Late in Time

Another feature of nature's stratigraphic record, which enables us to recognize time, is the complete absence of some of the large and important groups of living organisms from the lower, older strata. Three of these great groups are (a) the diatoms, (b) the flowering plants which produce seeds enclosed in an ovary wall, and (c) the vertebrate animals (animals which have a backbone). Diatoms are microscopic, single-celled plants which make up a high proportion of the photosynthetic plant life in the oceans. They are so abundant that they are the major food source for many small marine animals. The diatoms are one of the great groups of algae, and are peculiar in that their cell walls contain a high percentage of silicon dioxide (the main component of glass). The glasslike walls of these organisms are extremely thin, but so durable that they are not appreciably affected by the chemicals of the ocean, nor by the digestive fluids of the animals which eat them. Because of this durability great masses of diatom shells are found in most parts of the sea floor,[7] and also in some marine sediments now exposed on land. Since these organisms are one of the very most abundant of the living things on the earth, it would seem that they should be found at nearly all levels of any stratigraphic column formed by marine deposition. However, such is not at all the case. In fact, they are never found earlier than the Triassic Period, which in many series of strata is rather near the top, with many thousands of feet of non-diatomaceous layers beneath. This distribution seems all the more remarkable when one considers the fact that the radiolarians (a kind of marine Protozoa, related to the amoeba) are extremely abundant in many marine sediments, even as early as the beginning of the Cambrian Period.[8] The shells of the radiolarians are composed of silicon dioxide, just as are the shells of diatoms, so it is practically certain that if diatoms had been living during the earlier geological ages, their shells would have been preserved, just as were those of the radiolarians. So this indicates that there were long periods of time when life flourished on the earth, before the appearance of diatoms.

When we come to the flowering plants we find a similar situation. The remains of many kinds of simpler plants appear in the early strata of the fossil record, but we do not find the flowering plants which produce an enclosed seed (Class Angiospermae) until Jurassic times. The lower marine strata contain the remains of numerous kinds of lime-secreting algae, and early terrestrial coal deposits contain an abundance of ferns and other lower land plants; but in none of these strata are the higher flowering plants found. There are at the present time approximately 200,000 species of these higher flowering plants known (more than all other known kinds of plants combined). So the absence of these higher plants in the early strata, contrasted with their abundance in the later deposits, seems to tell us that God created the flowering plants much later than the algae and other lower forms of plant life.[9]

In the case of the vertebrate animals we have much the same arrangement as with the flowering plants. There is no trace of vertebrate fossils in the strata of the Cambrian Period, and no vertebrates other than fishes until the last part of the Devonian Period. There is a great abundance of fossils representing most of the types of invertebrate animals in the Cambrian deposits, and later, but not even fishes until the middle of the next Period. In other words, there were long periods of time when the oceans were teeming with many kinds of animals and plants, but the vertebrates had not yet appeared. If someone suggests, as mentioned in a footnote above, that all the kinds of animals lived together from the beginning, and that the fossils were all buried and formed within a short period of time, then why are there no remains of vertebrate animals, higher plants, and diatoms in the Cambrian

layers? In some local stratigraphic columns the Cambrian strata
have a total thickness of more than 20,000 feet, but not even the
teeth of any vertebrate animals are found mixed in with the abundance of other fossils. It is a well known fact that sharks shed
large numbers of teeth during their lifetime, and many of the
beaches of the world are practically strewn with fossilized shark
teeth; but none of these dense, highly durable objects are found
in the lower strata of the fossil record.

We are thus forced to conclude that many earlier kinds of
animals and plants lived, thrived in abundance, and became sealed
off in the lower strata before the vertebrates, flowering plants,
and diatoms came into existence. (Then we believe that man, the
highest of the vertebrates, was created later than any of the organisms we have been discussing.) The facts concerning the earlier
organisms speak to us of long periods of time, and have greatly
aided geologists in understanding the fossil record and the sedimentary deposits of the earth.

The Forming of Rock Layers

It is very generally known that most sedimentary rocks are
formed in or at the edge of bodies of water. The most common types
of sedimentary rock are sandstone, conglomerate, siltstone, mudstone,
shale, limestone, dolostone, and evaporite. We will here restrict
our discussion of age to these types, and not deal with igneous and
metamorphic rocks. When one encounters a stratigraphic column composed of sedimentary types of rocks (as is often the case), an
approximate age for the column can be obtained by adding together
the minimum formation times for the various layers present, and
allowing appropriate additional time if unconformities are found.

In order to obtain an idea of the minimum age of such a column,
one must take into consideration the types of rock, and also the
thickness and number of layers of each type. For example, sandstones
and conglomerates, being composed of rather large particles, are
usually laid down by moving water which carries the particles along
for a time and then drops them as the water movement decreases somewhat. Considerable thicknesses of deposits, to form sandstones and
conglomerates, can be laid down within a matter of days. (This often
occurs on slopes of the ocean floor, as a result of what are called
"turbidity currents" sweeping down the slope.) Similarly, a layer
of siltstone might not take any great length of time to form, since
its particles are large enough to settle out fairly rapidly. After
the deposition of these layers of sand, gravel, or silt, the particles will eventually be converted into sedimentary rock, if they
continue to lie in an aquatic or other water-soaked environment.
The conversion into rock requires a considerable amount of time
because of the changes which must take place. One of these necessary changes consists of an extensive process of cementation, in
response to the circulating of mineral-laden water through the pores
of the rock mass. This causes the formation of many hard crystals
of minerals between the sand or silt particles, with the aid of at
least slow water circulation around the particles. These processes

of cementation are being observed today, as on the reefs described
in the previous chapter, and are much better understood than formerly.

In contrast to the sometimes rather rapid laying down of layers
of sand, gravel, and silt, the depositing of layers of shale in the
earth is a slow process. This is because the particles (mainly clay)
from which shale is formed are very small, being only 4 microns or
less in diameter. (There are approximately 25,000 microns in an
inch.) The clay particles from which most marine shales are formed
do not readily cling together in clumps, and thus they settle only
very slowly. However, in places where fresh water is coming into
contact with salt water (as at a river mouth) the clay particles
sometimes clump together and settle more rapidly. In either case
the water must be relatively calm for the settling to occur, just
as the clay and mud particles which we commonly see in mud holes in
the road do not settle out, so long as passing cars frequently
agitate the water.

Thus we begin to see that varying amounts of time, and the right
kinds of conditions, are necessary for the formation of sandstones,
conglomerates, and shales. We will wait until later chapters to
point out the thicknesses of these deposits in various places, and
something of the length of time required for their accumulation and
cementation.

Limestone and Dolostone Formation

Limestone and dolostone are familiar to practically all of us--
at least in the crushed form, as road building material. Many
recent studies, mostly made by petroleum geologists, have shown
that most beds of limestone were formed gradually, in shallow marine
environments, with the aid of marine organisms such as algae. This
process of limestone formation, with the aid of algae to serve both
as a secreting organism and as a binder for the calcium carbonate
particles, has now been observed in numerous shallow marine environments off the coasts of North America and Asia, and in the Caribbean
Sea. The buildup of such limestone deposits is thus dependent on
the rate of growth of the algae.[10]

The remains of the algae which aided in the building of ancient
limestone layers are still discernible in some limestone beds. Thus
J. H. Johnson, in 1961, could describe numerous examples of such
limestones;[11] and since that time a whole array of descriptive reports of algal limestones has been published in geological journals.
The idea that the vast limestone beds of the world were formed
rapidly is shown to be erroneous, not only by the characteristic
algal laminations now seen in many limestones, but also by the fact
that the calcium carbonate content of sea water is too small to
provide the material for rapid formation by precipitation. These
and other aspects of limestone and dolostone formation will be taken
up in Chapter 7. (Dolostone is a modified form of limestone, containing magnesium combined with the calcium and carbonate. The
pure form of the mineral is called "dolomite," with the formula
$CaMg(CO_3)_2$.)

The formation of dolostone is even more certainly a slow process than the formation of limestone. The only source of magnesium for the making of dolostone is the ionic magnesium which is dissolved in the water. Most dolostone has been formed by the conversion of calcium carbonate sediments, as is evident from the presence of dolomitized fossils in it. (Marine animals and plants do not form dolomite skeletal parts.) The conversion of the skeletal materials and sediment particles to dolomite requires an extensive process of water circulation in the sediment mass. This has to be accomplished while there is still an abundance of pores, and while magnesium-rich water is available. It is evident that dolostone not only forms slowly at the present time, but also that the formation rate of at least most deposits of it has always been slow. This is due to the fact that the magnesium content of sea water, and of other natural waters, is very low, and the laws of solution and ion replacement have been stable as long as the seas have existed. Even in those parts of the world where there is evidence that the magnesium content of the water was at times increased by volcanic-hydrothermal activity, we still can not postulate a truly rapid formation.[12] One can then safely regard the many thick, layered deposits of limestone and dolostone as indicating long periods of time.

It is true that the types of age indicators which we have been considering are not as precise as the counting of growth rings on a clam shell, but they are based on valid scientific principles of observation. For example, we take into consideration the rate of settling of the particles for shale as contrasted with those of sandstone; and we contrast the formation of most limestones with both of these, because they are formed by an entirely different process. These methods of estimation result in dependable (though not precise) minimum ages. Such minimum ages can be a very useful, simple aid to understanding God's works in nature; though for more elaborate scientific investigations more precise methods must be used.

Reliability of Many Geologic Observations

In the preceding pages we have seen some examples of how specific meanings can be derived from rock layers, and we will encounter more such cases as we take up other types of sedimentary deposits. Sometimes those who are unfamiliar with the types of rock layers, and the distinctive characteristics of them, doubt the ability of man to learn past history in this way. Some even go so far as to say that we can know only what has been observed while the process is taking place. Actually this is an unreasonable position to take, because we all realize the validity of some conclusions which do not have a direct observational basis. When we find an empty clam shell which has washed up on to the seashore by incoming waves, we have no trouble in believing that the shell was built by a clam. It is true that we have no historical record of that clam's life, and no way to fully prove that it ever lived. Nevertheless, by the reasoning and observational powers which God gave us we know that this clam shell once harbored a living clam animal. We have seen other clam shells of this type which did have living clams in them, so we can accept the validity of the empty shell we find on the beach. (Of course our observations in this case would need to include microscopic or chemical examination to verify the shell's composition.) To say that this empty shell may have been formed by some other way is to distrust the natural laws and processes which God created.

Another illustration of this principle can be considered. We know that a redwood tree forms one double growth layer (ring) of its trunk each year, except in years of very abnormal weather when this may vary slightly. We realize that this is a natural law which we can trust, and do not assume that before the time of Columbus' discovery of America this was different. We have studied the growth habits of this and other trees, and know that we can rely on the consistency of the natural processes, even though no one was watching the trees grow during the Middle Ages. To say that they may have formed 30 or 50 rings per year during that time would be to disregard the divinely established consistency of nature.

A slightly different example of our legitimately accepting a precise explanation for an unobserved event is the following: If lightning strikes a tree in a lonely forest when no one is there to observe, it will nevertheless leave the marks of the event (unless the area is set ablaze by the lightning). A trained forester coming upon the tree somewhat later can easily recognize what has happened, and describe it thusly: "A relatively small bolt of lightning has recently hit one of the upper branches of the tree, following down the north side of the trunk, leaving a streak of peeled bark as it passed down to the ground. At the edge of the peeled bark one can observe the characteristic splintering effect of the lightning as it passed along the tree trunk. A shallow hole one foot in diameter was left at the base of the tree where the lightning made contact with the earth."[13] The forester knows that it was a small bolt of lightning, because it has only peeled the bark and produced splinters in a narrow path; large bolts split a tree into many pieces. He also knows that the event took place recently, because the exposed wood is not appreciably discolored or covered with fungus growth. (Or he could fairly accurately date an older event by the amount and type of fungal growth on the decaying wood.)

It would be possible to doubt the judgment of the forester in such a case, and say that some other unknown combination of forces had produced all the likely signs of a bolt of lightning. However, if we call in several foresters, each of whom has examined numerous known cases of lightning striking trees, and find that they agree that the damage was produced by lightning, we can be safe in accepting their judgment.* The reason we can be safe in this is that the rational God has created a rational world, and has given man some of His own rationality for interpreting the creation.

Is it not thus true that God has endowed man with the necessary intelligence to evaluate many natural events properly and correctly without the benefit of direct observation of the event at the time

* What if they were all trained with the same presuppositions

when it occured? Is it not much better that we go ahead and admit
the accuracy of man's evaluation of such natural events, rather than
to stand off and say that knowledge is impossible without direct
human observation of the event? Certainly it would appear that God
intends for us to trust in our ability to make such evaluations,
rather than to maintain an unwholesome attitude of skepticism, as
some heathen philosophies do. It is true that one must guard against
going on to make unreasonable claims as to just how hard it was
raining when the lightning struck the tree; but let us not reject
the basic facts just because some details are not determinable.
Just so, man should not reject the validity of basic geologic processes and events of the past, merely because certain details are
obscure.[14]

The Past Compared to the Present

The fact of God's intending that we place a reasonable amount
of confidence in man's ability to observe and evaluate conditions
in nature should apply to the study of the strata of the earth.
Geologists have been carefully observing the processes by which
strata and rocks are formed, for at least a century. During this
time, data have been collected on many different types of rock-
formation processes, and many microscopic and chemical similarities
between recently formed rock layers and older layers have been observed. These men have consequently come to the logical conclusion
that a high percentage of the sedimentary layers of the earth have
been formed by approximately the same processes as we observe today.[15] They also find some layers which were obviously deposited
more rapidly than others. Occasionally the record of a catastrophic
event, such as a landslide, earthquake, volcanic eruption, or rapid
flooding is found.[16] Such formations are readily distinguishable
from the normal shallow-marine deposits and deep-sea sediments which
are so abundant in the stratigraphic record. Thus we are recognizing
both the slow and the rapid processes which have occurred in nature.
Any uniformitarianism which would attribute all formations of the
geologic record to slow processes is not acceptable. This fact is
now recognized by practically all geologists.

When we recognize older rock layers as similar to those which
we find being formed slowly today, we are of course assuming that
conditions and processes on the earth were somewhat similar in the
past to what they are now. We will have to admit that this type of
assumption is reasonable when we realize that we can readily accept
such processes as digestion and reproduction in mammals, and photosynthesis and water absorption in plants, as having remained the
same ever since mammals and plants were created. Why then should
the sediment and rock-forming actions of an aquatic environment not
have been similar in early times to what they are now? The principle
of the stability of God's natural laws, which we considered in
Chapter 2, assures us that it is right that we accept these as essentially the same.

True, we allow for catastrophic events which have perhaps had
a large part in forming mountains, lakes, and seas; but still, when

we observe the thick and extensive sedimentary deposits which give every evidence of having been formed slowly, we must accept them at their face value. We are here referring to types of deposits which are not producible by catastrophic events. A great flood can pile up masses of rock and debris, and even lay down some beds of sorted layers of gravel, sand, or mud; but this is very different from building a circular coral reef on top of an old volcanic cone, or forming a multitude of orderly layers of dolostone on a carbonate platform or shelf around the Bahama Islands. Floods can move great quantities of sediments, but they can not carry out the intricate chemical and physical processes necessary for the production of the many types of rock we find in the sedimentary deposits which are so widespread over North America.

If one should try to explain the complexity of the series of sedimentary layers by appealing to God's miracle working power, we must consider God's reasons for performing miracles. In the Bible we find God using miracles only for the benefit or judgment of the persons whom He has created. He opened the Red Sea, dried up the Jordan, and did other miracles for his people; but to rapidly form intricate layers of fossiliferous rock by a miraculous process would have been pointless. Furthermore, the forming of such would have been out of harmony with God's characteristic of truthfulness.[17]

Actually, when we look at the processes which are going on today in nature, and include such catastrophic events as have occurred within human history, we have an adequate explanation for practically all that we see in the geologic record. Even though the great majority of the sedimentary strata are of such a nature that they could not have been formed by one or even several floods, the Biblical Flood probably could have been responsible for numerous alluvial deposits which are close to the surface, major changes in climate, and the onset of the most recent period of glaciation. Almost certainly involved in the Flood were a rapid change in sea level, and some movements in the earth's crust, with consequent elevation or lowering of certain geographic areas. These are illustrative of types of actions which could be produced during such a catastrophe as the Flood seems to have been.

It is reasonable to accept certain large destructive actions as having been produced by the Flood, but we should also recognize the thick deposits which are of an entirely different nature as having resulted from the slow processes which are still producing those kinds of deposits today. This is basically the position which was taken by a large percentage of the evangelical scholars and ministers in America near the beginning of this century. They recognized the responsibility of Christians to accept the parts of the geologic record which obviously had to have been produced by slow processes in pre-Adamic times, as well as to accept the Biblical Flood which carried out great destructions in at least parts of the earth. They repudiated the tendency of some Christians to place their personal preference for a particular view above the factual data relating to the natural processes of the past.

These men (rightly) held to the absolute trustworthiness of the Scriptures, yet saw that these holy writings do not contain dogmatic statements concerning the amounts of time which transpired prior to the creation of man. Thus the eight editors of the Scofield Reference Bible, published in 1917, recommended that we take note of the places in the early chapters of Genesis which allow for indefinite amounts of time.[18]

A recognition of such principles as these serves as a valuable guard against any particular group of Christians setting up its own view concerning natural processes and events of the past as a mandatory theological issue. Since the Bible does not state the amounts of time which transpired in the past, such matters can be only an academic issue, not a theological one. God is timeless (not limited or controlled by time) and certainly does not encourage us to think of Him or his works as being time-bound (II Peter 3:8-10).

The Complexity of North American Sedimentary Deposits

One of the main reasons that there is so much misunderstanding among Christians concerning God's record in nature, is the fact that the average person never sees much of the total record in a given area. We drive through a highway cut, note some of the rock layers, and do not think about the fact that this 200 or 300 foot bank of rock is usually only about 1, 2, or 3 percent of the total sediment column at that spot. No amount of study of the rock layers at the surface can give us reliable information as to the nature and age of the fossil-bearing layers which lie deeply buried beneath.

With the advent of deep-well core drilling, the study of the stratigraphic record beneath what we normally see became possible. If one were to lay the drilling cores from a two or three-mile-deep oil well, out end-to-end, on the surface of the ground, and walk the entire length of the aligned cores, examining them as he went, he would be impressed with both the extent and complexity of the local stratigraphic column from which they came. He would find that the drill had not been passing through a monotonous mass of similar layers, but through an extremely complex and variegated series. In nearly all cases, the series contains numerous layers of rock types which, because of their chemical and physical nature, could not have been formed by rapidly moving water. (A number of these will be described in the chapters which follow.)

Were it not for the fact that such sedimentary columns usually contain identifiable fossils almost to the bottom, we might postulate that the series was a part of God's original creation, and that we were only viewing an appearance of age. But since the fossils are present, the Bible-believing Christian is left with only three alternatives. First, to accept the existence of these deposits as information which God has allowed man to discover by investigation and observation, just as God allowed man to finally find out that the earth was not a flat, four-cornered structure. Second, to admit that the deposits are there, but to say that God put them there with their fossils ready-made. Third, to take the position that, even though the evidence for greater age is there, we should ignore its existence, and not try to demonstrate an agreement between the Bible and the observed conditions in the strata. Concerning the latter position, one must ask if it is ever right for a Bible student to ignore the strata merely because they contain information which would disturb his own preferred system of Bible interpretation. Does not such a policy make one guilty of refusing to examine a part of God's creation?

All three of the above alternatives are in use by Christians of various beliefs today. However, it certainly seems evident that our Christian testimony in the world can be best carried out by adopting the first of the three alternatives, as many of the evangelical leaders in the early part of this century did. In recognizing the deposits as a meaningful record of life in the past, these men found their faith and appreciation of God to be strengthened.[19] Those of us who want to increase our appreciation for the majesty of God can surely do so by contemplating the larger displays of time which are found in the geologic record. To attempt to realize the magnitude of God's universe as it has existed through vast eons of time is to increase one's conception of God. In Psalm 102:25-27 we find the writer making use of his understanding of time in the past, to express God's greatness: "Of old Thou didst found the earth; And the heavens are the work of Thy hands. Even they will perish, but Thou dost endure...But Thou art the same, And Thy years will not come to an end." Many Christians have found it much more meaningful to contemplate the activities of God in his organized universe throughout a long past, than to think of his work as having been only recent. Some would consider the extent of this work of God to be only slightly over one hundred human life spans; but, to a lot of us, a really long time span of God's work is much more awesome.

Might it not be that God gave us the records of huge time spans in the past primarily as an object lesson of his immensity? It is common to hear Christians speak of the immense amounts of matter and space in the universe as a demonstration of God's greatness; why not then also recognize the unfathomable time spans as an expression of God's immensity? Space and time are certainly complements of each other in the realm of thought. We can never really comprehend the eternity and timelessness of God, but it is at least helpful to exercise one's mind to think back into the incomprehensible expanse of time in the universe; and then to realize that God was _before_ all that.

Methods of Dating and the Bible

The Christian may ask, "Does not the Bible give us a method of exact dating for the earth and for the various phases of creation?" The answer is in the negative. It is true that the Bible gives us the general impression that God's works in the material universe go far back into time, but there is no suggestion of the precise limits. Certainly if God had wanted to tell us how long ago the various phases of his creation took place, He could have done so, but it appears that this is one of the mysteries which He chose not to reveal.

He has left us to observe his creation and to use our reasoning power in a responsible way for understanding it.

We do not propose to assert the correctness of any one of the usual methods of "finding" sufficient time in the Bible for life in the past, but surely the Bible does encourage us to find such. In Genesis 1:1 we have God telling us that the heavens and the earth were created "in the beginning," but not definitely when that was. In Psalm 90:1-4 we hear the author (probably Moses) speaking to God by the inspiration of the Holy Spirit saying:

> Lord, Thou hast been our dwelling place in all generations.
> Before the mountains were born,
> Or Thou didst give birth to the earth and world,
> Even from everlasting to everlasting, Thou art God.
>
> Thou dost turn man back into dust,
> And dost say, "Return, O children of men."
> For a thousand years in Thy sight
> Are like yesterday when it passes by,
> Or as a watch in the night.

In II Peter 3:3-4 and 8-9 the suffering Christians are reminded that, even though God's persecuted people are inclined to think that the events in God's program should proceed rapidly, God does not always work as fast as man visualizes. Christians are to realize that God does carry out his works in due time, and that Christ will finally return, even though it may seem to be an unreasonably long time. Thus this passage gives us the realization that in the Bible a "day" can be a longer period of time than 24 hours. Similarly in Genesis 2:4 we find the expression "the day" (yom) being used of the entire period of creation of the "earth and heaven."[20] Also, most conservative Bible scholars admit that the period of time designated by the word "day" in the expression "day of the Lord," and "day of Christ" is much longer than an ordinary day. So, it may be that at least some of the days of creation of Genesis chapter one were long periods of time. At least there seems to be nothing to prevent our taking them as long periods and assuming that the fossil record of earlier plants and animals was formed during the third, fourth, fifth, and early sixth "days."[21]

Evolution and Time

In a chapter on the recognition of time in nature, it is probably necessary to mention the frequently encountered suggestion that one can not recognize large amounts of time without adopting an evolutionary position. This idea is false on two counts. First, there is no necessary or logical reason that the two must be associated. Why should a belief that God created numerous kinds of animals and plants, and let them live for a long time "to fill the earth," be an evolutionary concept? It is false logic to say that this demands an evolutionary origin for the groups of animals and plants involved. Second, a belief in long periods of time was held by most of the founders of fundamentalism in America during the

first part of this century. This belief did not cause these men to
adopt evolutionary ideas, nor keep them from vigorously denouncing
the doctrine of evolution within their denominational circles, and
elsewhere. They were able to visualize the dinosaurs and many other
prehistoric animals and plants as having lived and become extinct
long before the creation of man--all in the great plan of God.

The Present Flow of New Evidences

Before leaving this chapter we wish to remind the reader that
the increasing demand for mineral products of the earth has, within
the past decade, produced a vast increase in the amount of geological exploration being carried out. This is revealing an unprece-
dented amount of information concerning the crust of the earth, the
sediments of the ocean, and natural processes which go on in the
ocean depths. Off-shore drillings by the oil industry have brought
many new facts to light concerning ancient marine life, and sedimentation processes in early carbonate environments.

An even greater source of new information concerning the past
is coming from the deep-sea drillings being carried out under the
auspices of the National Science Foundation. In 1968 the drilling
ship, the Glomar Challenger, set out in its first exploratory
cruise. The main object has been to drill deeply into the ocean
floors at many points, taking up thousands of feet of sediment
cores, in order to determine the nature of the sea floor and of
the processes which have occurred in it. This drilling ship is
equipped far more adequately than any previous exploratory vessel,
and has equipment for collecting chemical and biological data along
with the several types of geologic information it is bringing back.

By October 1975 the Glomar Challenger with its highly trained
crew had completed 44 cruises, with major drillings made in the
ocean floor at 392 sites. Drillings were made in all of the oceans
of the world, from the Aleutian Islands in the north to Antarctica
in the south. Many of the "holes" penetrated to a depth of over
3,000 feet into the sea floor, and such drillings were carried out
even where the water is three and one-half miles deep.[22]

All of this is bringing to light a vast amount of information.
Most of the data of each cruise are being published by the U. S.
Government Printing Office in a series called Initial Reports of
the Deep Sea Drilling Project. As of May 1977, thirty-six large
volumes, with an average of approximately 1,000 pages per volume,
have been published and are available in many libraries. These
cover the first 35 cruises and the 38th. In addition to these, a
great deal of supplementary information on the drilling cores is
being published by various geological laboratories and agencies.

Thus we are living at a time when more information on geologic
structure and processes is coming to light each year than was reported in either the decade of the 1940's or that of the 1950's.
Practically every month brings exciting new data, and much of it
contains important indications on age. Some of these will be

mentioned in the sections dealing with marine sediments in the succeeding pages of this book.

So, we are by no means in a position of having to struggle to find evidence for great age in the earth. There is a veritable avalanche of such evidence, from many types of careful scientific observation. The main problem is to get the "news" out, and encourage Christian people to examine, appreciate, and use the evidence.

FOOTNOTES

1. See Depositional Environments in Carbonate Rocks, G. M. Friedman, ed., 1969, p. 1 and 4, for a brief summary of the great progress which has been made in the field of carbonate sedimentology.

2. See the Preface for more explanation concerning our choice of the simpler methods of recognizing time.

3. In the sciences, the word "marine" refers only to the oceans, in contrast to inland bodies of fresh water.

4. It has often been said that perhaps the reason that there are no trilobite fossils in the upper, more recent strata of the earth is that their skeletons were so dense that they sank down into the lower strata during the Flood. Actually such an explanation could not be accurate because (a) the skeletons of these animals were not very dense, and (b) many of the strata in which these animals appear were permanently hardened (lithified) long before the upper strata were produced. With regard to the composition of the trilobite skeletons, a significant proportion of the skeletal content was the very light, strong, organic material which is called chitin. Recent electron microscopic studies of fossilized trilobite skeletons have borne this out, and have shown the skeletal material to be similar to that of modern crabs, which belong to the same phylum as trilobites. In both cases the skeleton is much less dense than the shells of modern clams, so if any kind of remains of organisms had been going to sink to lower levels, the shells of marine clams would have been among the first to go down. However, the shells of modern and Flood-time clams are found only in the upper layers of sedimentary deposits.

5. As quoted in J. S. Shelton, Geology Illustrated, 1966, p. 291.

6. Ibid., p. 292-293.

7. See Chapter 9 for further information on the presence of diatom shells in marine sediments.

8. H. E. Harper, Jr., and A. H. Knoll, "Silica, Diatoms, and Cenozoic Radiolarian Evolution," Geology, v. 3 (1975) p. 175-177.

9. The Biblical account of creation states that "grass,"

66

"herbs yielding seed," and "fruit trees" were formed on the third "day" of creation. However, the Bible does not state that these were the first plants.

10. G. V. Chilingar, et al., in Developments in Sedimentology No. 8, Diagenesis of Sediments, G. Larsen and G. V. Chilingar, 1967, p. 193-194.

11. J. H. Johnson, Limestone Building Algae and Algal Limestones, 1961, p. 118-289.

12. M. Ilich, "Hydrothermal-Sedimentary Dolomite," American Association of Petroleum Geologists Bulletin, v. 58 (1974), p. 1331-1347. A careful reading of this article, on the influence of hydrothermal activity in the formation of certain dolostone deposits, reveals several reasons why this activity could never have caused a rapid buildup of the large beds of fossil-bearing dolostone which exist in so many parts of the world.

13. The terminology of this description may not be fully correct from the standpoint of the action of an electric discharge, but it is in the generally accepted terminology which is usually used.

14. There are some creationists today who question the validity of all geologic research concerning the prehistoric past. In doing this they sometimes say that science can not demonstrate anything about the past because there is no way to set up a repetition of the time spans of the past. This argument is invalid because of the divinely recognized validity of human observation of God's (stable) laws, as we have been pointing out, and also because we are observing many of the kinds of sedimentary rock-forming and fossilization processes going on today. In other words, we are now in the midst of a repetition of a great number of the geologic processes which went on in the past. It is unfortunate that those who discount science's observations concerning the past have usually not had opportunity to study these rock-forming processes. Because of this they are dependent upon nonobservational means of supporting their position.

15. Dr. Douglas Block states that, almost without exception, each rock formation found in the sedimentary deposits of the world "has its counterpart in some present environment, and is subject to detailed comparison with current geologic processes." Christianity and the World of Thought, Hudson T. Armerding, editor, 1968, p. 240.

16. Dr. Paul Tychsen states, "If one examines the geologic record, he will find that specific periods of geologic time were characterized by very extensive floods, which covered considerable portions of entire continents." Rock Strata and the Bible Record, Paul Zimmerman, editor, 1970, p. 195. This multiplicity of floods in the past is one of the reasons that neither scientists nor Bible scholars have ever been able to definitely identify any particular

stratum in North or South America as having been formed by the Biblical Flood.

17. See Appendix II for a discussion of God's attribute of truthfulness.

18. C. I. Scofield, et al., The Scofield Reference Bible, Oxford University Press, 1917, p. 3 and 4. (The same principles are stated on p. 1 and 2 of the 1967 edition.)

19. One of these men, Dr. W. B. Riley, founder of Northwestern Schools in Minneapolis, stated: "In a recent published address we called attention to the fact that the verse with which Genesis opens, 'In the beginning' lays no time limit upon the creative acts of God, and presented an elaborate defense of the elastic use of the word 'day' both by Ancient and Modern, and proved by the Book itself that Scripture students were not shut up to the solar day in interpreting any of the acts of God recorded in Genesis, but that God's days are geological days, as extensive in time as the rocks will require when once the truth of their creation is clearly known.

"Here then we have Genesis and Geology speaking together concerning the formless and nebulous state of our original world; and they are clearly together when order emerges from chaos in answer to the Word of God, ..." The Bible of the Expositor and the Evangelist, v. 1, "Genesis," 1926, p. 31-32.

20. Those who attempt to say that this statement refers only to "Day one," and that the sun, moon, and stars had not been created until "Day four," find themselves in a dilemma. (If the sun, moon, and stars had not been created until the fourth day, any statement that the heavens were created on Day one would be erroneous.)

21. See Appendix I for further comments on the length of the days of creation.

22. Winterer, E. L., et al., 1971, Initial Reports of the Deep Sea Drilling Project, v. 7, Washington (U. S. Govt. Printing Office), 1757 p.
Geotimes, v. 21, February 1976, p. 23-26.

CHAPTER 5

UNDERGROUND REEFS IN CANADA

The existence of reefs deeply buried far inland from the oceans
may come as a surprise to some. However, these are very common on
the North American continent and in parts of Europe. They are one
of the exciting time indicators which have come to light as a result
of man's search for oil and minerals deep in the earth.

A Discovery in Alberta

Before the 1940's the Canadian oil industry was very small,
due to lack of known oil reserves. Most of the vast central part
of Canada has very few sedimentary deposits for producing oil, because the sediments were long ago eroded off, leaving exposed igneous
and metamorphic rock. But the western part, expecially the province
of Alberta, is underlain by several thousands of feet of various
kinds of sedimentary rock. The knowledge of these deposits led
Canadian oil prospectors to drill test wells in various parts of
Alberta in hopes of finding oil-bearing sediments.

During the cold month of January in 1947, well drillers of the
Imperial Oil Company of Canada were drilling a few miles southwest
of Edmonton, the capital of Alberta, and had reached a depth of
almost 5,000 feet. At this level the drill passed from the siltstone in which it had recently been, to a layer of dolostone. Soon
the drill cuttings from this porous dolostone began to show small
amounts of crude oil stain.   The drilling crew immediately changed
to a core-type drill with which they could remove the remaining
footage of the well for careful study. (This would be of aid in
understanding the underground strata of the area, so that more wells
could be drilled, in case this one proved to be   successful.)
Within the next few feet a better concentration of oil was encountered in the dolostone, and by the time a depth of 5,049 feet had
been reached, the coveted crude oil was flowing to the surface.
Thus, what is known as the Leduc oil field came into the history
of Canadian oil. More producing wells were soon drilled in that
vicinity, and large amounts of oil were (and still are being) obtained from that field.

By studying the drilling records and cores from these wells,
the petroleum geologists who were assigned to this oil field soon
learned that the oil reservoir beneath them was a large mass of
ancient, marine, carbonate rock layers (limestone and dolostone).
This is one of the most common types of oil-retaining rock, and is
the "hope and joy" of every petroleum geologist.[1] Approximately
50% of the obtainable oil reserves of Canada are in porous carbonate reservoirs. Because of the large number of fossils present in
these carbonate layers, and because of the dissolving out of tiny
pockets in the rock layers as they were long exposed to sea water--
and sometimes to fresh water--a great many pores and small cavities
were produced. These pores could then become the storage place for

the oil which was formed in that vicinity in ancient times (probably from decaying animal and plant matter).

It was finally learned that the underground carbonate reservoir of the Leduc oil field was only one of several such reservoirs in Alberta and western Saskatchewan. Numerous very profitable oil fields are now in production in several parts of these provinces. Further studies of the drilling cores which were obtained greatly enhanced the discovery of the new fields.

Reefs in the Oil Fields

Two of the outstanding facts which soon came to be known from the petroleum geologists' studies were that (a) numerous ancient, fossilized reefs are present in the carbonate, oil-bearing layers, and (b) the oil-bearing layers are, in many areas, covered over with layers of marine evaporites which have served to prevent the oil from escaping from the porous carbonate rock body. The term "evaporite" is used for any of the kinds of salts which precipitate out of sea water when it is evaporated. These include mainly common salt (sodium chloride), anhydrite (calcium sulfate), and gypsum (calcium sulfate with water molecules bound to the sulfate). These salts form layers which can not be penetrated by the oil. A large percentage of the oil and gas reserves of the world are found in large carbonate bodies of porous limestone and dolostone, beneath evaporite strata which retain the petroleum.[2]

The reality of the fossilized reefs in Canada can be more readily visualized when we consider their use in the discovery of oil. In Alberta especially, one of the main guiding principles in oil prospecting has been the locating and following of ancient buried shorelines. One of the most prominent distinguishing features of these shorelines was found to be the presence of several long series of ancient reefs. The drilling of test wells, and the careful use of the drilling records from earlier producing wells, enabled petroleum geologists to construct reliable maps of the underground coasts, reef trends, and basins. The search for oil in Alberta became successful through the use of these maps, combined with a knowledge of the fossils and sediment types seen in the drilling samples. Thus geologists were able to reconstruct an accurate picture of the ancient environments of that geographic area, and to plan for the drilling of wells in the particular areas which once had an environmental history conducive to the formation and storage of petroleum. A large part of this remarkable success in understanding the ancient environments of that area has of course been due to the fact that we now know a great deal about the natural requirements for the growth of coral and algal reefs. So, the western part of Canada is a geographic area where the process of comparing modern reefs and other modern carbonate deposits with the ancient has yielded spectacular results in predicting the best drilling sites.

The facts which have been learned concerning the buried masses of carbonate rock, with their ancient reefs and evaporite coverings,

70

are of great interest to the Bible student because they speak of time--time required for growth, time for the evaporation of the sea water, and time for the final covering layers to be deposited above. Let us first consider the length of time needed for growth of the reefs.

In Chapter 3 we saw that the process of growing a thick reef in the Pacific requires at least many hundreds of thousands of years. Now it is obvious that a coral reef which is buried deeply in the middle of a continent is likely to be even older than the reefs which are still in the process of growth. Just as we saw in the case of the Eniwetok and Bikini reefs, the preserved remains of the many species of marine animals and plants which make up the ancient, buried reefs have an extensive history to reveal to those who will take the trouble to study them.

The type of organisms present is an important source of information. If strictly marine animals are present, then we immediately know that the reef was formed in some part of the oceans, or in a bay or sound which was connected with a body of sea water. As we saw in Chapter 4, the sea urchins, starfishes, sea lilies, and corals are all animals which are found only in sea water. This is because the chemical nature of their cells requires the abundant minerals which are present in sea water. River or lake waters can not supply this amount of minerals. The contrast between the mineral content of sea water and that of fresh-water lakes and streams is spectacular. For example, average sea water contains approximately 3.4% of dissolved minerals by weight. Most fresh-water streams and lakes contain less than 0.04% minerals. The Columbia River in the northwestern United States has an average of only 0.012% total dissolved minerals, and the very "hard" water of the Colorado River has only 0.076%.[3]

There are numerous present-day species of "sea lilies" and other echinoderms, and a great many species of modern corals, in the world today; but none of them are found in fresh-water environments. The physiological characteristics of such marine animals are "set" at much different levels than are required for enabling an animal to live in fresh water. Thus the abundance of corals and echinoderms in the Canadian reefs shows that some part of the ocean once covered that area. The presence of ocean waters in that region is also demonstrated by other marine organisms which are present, and by the chemical nature of the strata which surround the reefs.

Marine Strata and Reefs in Northwestern Alberta

One of the most informative oil producing areas of Canada is in what is called the "Rainbow area" of northwestern Alberta. (It is named for the town of Rainbow Lake, Alberta.) This area was opened up for oil production in 1965. The drilling records from the great number of wells, together with detailed seismic studies of the underground formations, present an unusually complete picture of the stratigraphic nature of the entire district. The first producing well encountered a dense layer of anhydrite, the most common evaporite associated with oil in that area, at a depth of about 5,600 feet.[4]

After passing through this evaporite deposit, the drill contacted oil in the thick body of porous dolostone which lay immediately beneath the evaporite layers. Since this well was being drilled for information as well as for oil, its depth was increased to see how many feet of oil-bearing rock lay beneath. At a depth of 5,866 feet the drill entered the top of an ancient reef.[5] This reef, like most ancient reefs, was found to be a very good oil reservoir, because of its high degree of porosity. This was the first of many such reefs to be penetrated by wells drilled in the Rainbow area within the years which have followed. See Figure 12 for a map showing where some of these reefs are located, and Figure 13 for a vertical section of the Middle Devonian strata in which they are embedded.

During the first two and one-half years following the discovery of the first reef "oil pool" in the Rainbow area, 55 more reefs were found in the same area--most of them within a 15 mile radius of the original "discovery well."[6] Most of these lie at a depth of between 5,000 and 6,000 feet below the surface. Many other similar reefs are now known in adjacent Middle Devonian oil fields in northwestern Alberta. Also, there is a whole series of these underground reefs, arranged along SW-NE lines, forming barrier reefs in the oil-bearing strata of that region, as shown in Figure 12.[7]

Reef Foundations

For understanding the significance of the oil-bearing reefs, note should be taken also of the fossil-bearing sedimentary layers which lie beneath them. We will here briefly describe some of these layers, then the make-up of the reefs themselves, and finally the strata which surround and cover them.

The lower layers of sedimentary rocks, which form the foundations on which the reefs of this region rest, consist of several kinds of marine sedimentary deposits. The thickness of this body of foundation sediments ranges from about 600 feet in some places to less than 100 feet in others.[8] Some parts of this deposit contain an abundance of marine fossils.[9] The arrangement and nature of these foundation sediments give unmistakable evidence that they represent a long period when a shallow sea covered the area. The entire 600 foot thick series consists of many alternating layers of shale, siltstone, anhydrite (calcium sulfate), limestone, and dolomite.[10] All of these, except perhaps the siltstone, represent kinds of sediments which require a considerable period of time for the laying down of even a thin layer. In the lower two-thirds of the series, fossils are not abundant, giving further evidence that these layers were formed slowly in a sea that was so quiet that most of the fossil shells were either dissolved or broken into fine grains before being covered over. Thus we find this to be a significant part of the ever-present time record which God has left in the earth.

72

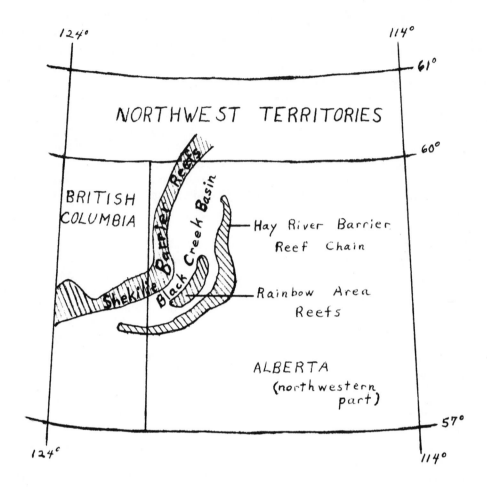

Fig. 12. Location of some of the ancient, coral and algal
reefs which are now reservoirs for petroleum in the northwestern part of Alberta, Canada. These reefs are of Middle
Devonian classification. Redrawn from M. E. Hriskevich,
"Middle Devonian reef production, Rainbow area, Alberta,
Canada," American Association of Petroleum Geologists Bulletin, vol. 54, 1970, p. 2260-2281, Figures 5 and 7.

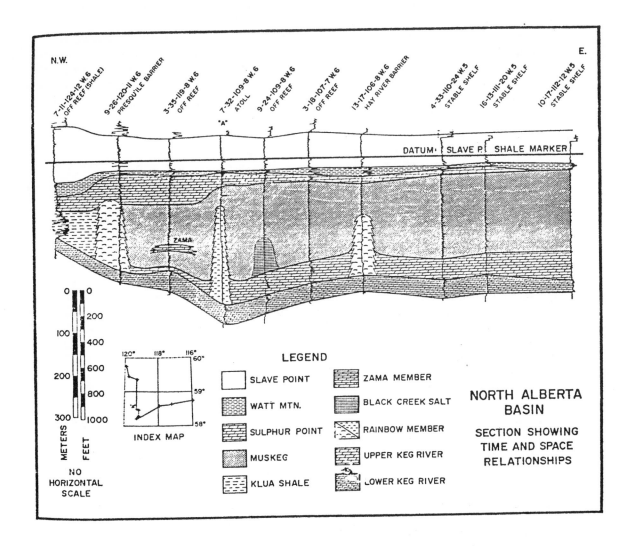

Fig. 13. A vertical section through the deeper rock layers of one of the Rainbow area oil fields in Alberta, Canada. Note the three reefs, shown as white towers with small, curved stipple marks. (These reefs and the beds which surround them are vertically exaggerated in the diagram, in order to show them more clearly.) Ten wells are shown penetrating this vertical section, and are also shown on the small map in the lower part of the figure. Note that the reefs are embedded, primarily in evaporites of the Muskeg Formation. A part of this thickness is laminated anhydrite. From D. L. Barss, et al., in Geology of Giant Petroleum Fields, M. T. Halbouty, ed., American Association of Petroleum Geologists, Memoir 14, 1970, p. 29, Figure 9. (By permission of the American Association of Petroleum Geologists.)

Also, a very meaningful part of this particular time record
is the set of layers of evaporite material (in this case anhydrite,
as mentioned above). They are found interspersed in between the
layers of shale, silt, and dolomite at various points in the local
stratigraphic column. These evaporite layers are of much the same
types as those which are presently being deposited in the shallow,
brinish waters in some parts of the Persian Gulf, Caspian Sea, and
on the coast of Baja, California, south of San Diego. Therefore,
we can only conclude that they were formed in relatively shallow,
evaporative basins of the ancient inland sea. Each recurring
evaporite layer of anhydrite which appears in the well cores, as
one progresses up the stratigraphic column in that geographic area,
undoubtedly represents a period of time when the amount of water
flowing into this inland sea was restricted (as is also true in
modern evaporite-forming seas). This reduction of supply of water
occurs as a result of islands or other barriers along the coasts,
a lowering of the ocean level, the sinking or rising of the land,
or merely because of the tidal cycles. With one or more of these
factors restricting the supply of water, the sun and wind concentrate the brine until the remaining water is unable to keep all the
salts in solution. The surplus salts then precipitate, sinking to
the bottom as sediment. This is of course a slow process, and many
years are required for building up an appreciable thickness of deposit.

The recent observation of such processes as the evaporative
formation of anhydrite, and of the production of various types of
limestone and dolomite, has done wonders in helping us to understand the ancient strata found in oil fields and elsewhere. In
fact, the value of comparing modern marine environments with these
ancient environments has become so obvious that the large oil companies now send their best geologists to various coastal areas to
study modern sedimentary processes. This has resulted in a much
better understanding of the marine strata found deep in the oil
fields, and thus enables the petroleum geologist to estimate the
position of other oil reservoirs which lie at various distances
from the test wells. An example of such close correlation between
the ancient and the modern is that of the similarity between the
large area of carbonate, oil-producing strata in Alberta and the
modern carbonate "Florida-Bahama Platform." This is discussed by
several recent authors.[11]

Composition of the Rainbow Area Reefs

The reefs of the Rainbow oil fields, to which we referred above,
grew in rather shallow water in Middle Devonian times. Growth conditions were apparently favorable, as numerous of the reefs grew in
the familiar forms (shapes) seen in the thriving Great Barrier Reef
area of Australia.[12] The organisms which produced these Canadian
reefs were typical marine animals and calcareous algae. The fossils
of these are abundant in the bodies of the reefs, and numerous places
in the reefs have the fossils still in undisturbed position. J. R.
Langton and his associates made a detailed study of drilling cores
from forty-five wells which had been drilled into these reefs in the

Rainbow area. They carefully examined 15,000 linear feet of well
core slabs under low-power microscopes (as well as studying some
of the sediments under higher powers). In this study they were able
to identify scores of kinds of fossils, and also to note which cores
contained types of fossils which normally grow in the forereef, the
lagoon, and the basins beside reefs, respectively. Numerous parts
of the reefs were found to be still intact, having been built by
wave-resistant organisms, including both colonial septate corals,
and the extinct tabulate corals.[13]

Several of the reefs of the Rainbow area have relatively steep
sides, arising sharply above the floor of the earlier "foundation
sediments." Some rise to a height of approximately 800 feet.[14]
The different forms (shapes) of these structures are significant
as evidence of their similarity to modern reefs. In order to determine the forms, Langton and his associates combined the results
of extensive seismic (earth-shock) studies of the area which had
been previously made, with their own investigations of the well cores
and drilling records. (The well cores are of course carefully cata-
loged as to the exact position and depth from which each was taken
from the well.) As a result of this study the team was able to
classify the reefs into four types, namely, "large atoll," "crescent
atoll," "small pinnacle," and "large pinnacle." The term "pinnacle"
is perhaps somewhat misleading, as the sides are not nearly so
steep as what we usually think of as a pinnacle. Their name is
derived from the fact that they are in the shape of a practically
symmetric cone with a circular base, tapering toward the top.
Since they do arise to nearly 800 feet above the surrounding sediment layers, the name is perhaps permissible. These could not
properly be called atolls as they have no lagoon in the center.
With a diameter of often less than 2,000 feet near the top, there
was not room for a lagoon to form there.

The fact that the pinnacle and atoll reefs grew in a normal
marine environment, and were not disturbed by unusual catastrophic
conditions is indicated, not only by their normal, reef-like form,
but also by the distribution of the fragments which lie around them.
The deposits of fragments which wore off the reefs (often called
"reef debris") during the time they were growing are found near the
bases of the reefs, not scattered widely over the bottom of the basin.
This shows that each reef grew as a distinct entity and retained
its position and shape until it was later covered over and became
an oil reservoir.[15]

Perhaps of   greatest interest are the large atoll and crescent atoll types, which resemble some of their modern counterparts
north of Australia, as mentioned above. One typical large atoll
of the Rainbow oil-bearing strata is four miles long and two and
one-half miles wide. A lagoon, with typical fine-grained, lagoonal-
type reef sediments, is present in the center. The total thickness
of this atoll at its rim is 800 feet, which of course means that
many thousands of years were required for its development. The
crescent atolls are similar to the large atolls, except that they

76

average only one-half the length and breadth of the latter, and the
outer, organic reef rim of each is higher and more pronounced on
the northeast side. This greater development of the strongly cemented rim on the northeast side indicates that the prevailing wind
direction was from the northeast at that time.[16] (Reefs develop
most on the side toward the wind, as the wind keeps bringing waves
with fresh supplies of oxygenated water and food.)

The Death and Burial of the Reefs

After a long period of flourishing growth, "hard times" came,
and most of the reef organisms could no longer grow. The usual
unrestricted flow of food-and-oxygen-laden water which is so vital
for reef growth gradually became less and less. The layers of
evaporite minerals with which most of the reefs are covered give
testimony to the condition of stagnation and increased salinity of
the water. The fact that the larger reefs became heavily dolomitized (changed to dolostone), as their burial progressed, is further
evidence of the slow change to more saline (salty) water. The
dolomitization which is observed in the well cores of these reefs
is of the type expected in an intertidal and supratidal (just above
the tide) environment. This type of environment brings about the
death of reefs, and if there are increased evaporative conditions,
the increase in magnesium content of the water provides the magnesium ions to slowly convert the reef material to dolostone.[17]

It is possible that the briny water was considerably deeper
at some times than others, but in either case the reefs were dying
and being fossilized right in the broad marine basin which had
fostered their growth.[18] This change was undoubtedly brought about
either by an altering of the sea level, or by a rising of the floors
of the inlet channels through which water was supplied to the basin
from the ocean. In fact, the sedimentary record which has been left
in the basin tells us clearly that there were numerous changes of
this type (or of both types), which left an elaborate series of
evaporitic sediments in the basin around the reefs, and over the
tops of the same.

There is much evidence that there were, in this basin, long
periods of time when the evaporating water was deep; whereas during
other periods it was shallow, as we have just described. Evaporite
mineral layers can be deposited in deep water if the basin is stagnant, with extensive evaporation occurring from the surface. However,
an absolute requirement for deposits of the type found here is that
there be time and proper conditions for the concentrated brines to
be produced by the evaporation. This requires many years for each
foot of evaporative sediment formed.

The evidence for the shallow-water condition during a part of
the reef's history consists not only of the shallow-water types of
mineral deposits mentioned above, but also of the remaining marks
of weathering processes. Bebout found these remaining effects in
the reef limestone and dolostone at numerous levels on the sides of

the Rainbow reefs, and also in the reefs of nearby subbasins which are buried at similar depths. He refers to this as vadose (above the water level) weathering.[19]

There is considerable variety in the evaporitic covering layers which fill the spaces between the reefs, lap up on to their sides, and finally seal them over. Figure 14 is a diagrammatic representation of these different coverings, as they encroach upon the sides of the reefs, and finally cover them. Note that the first of this series (designated no. 1 in the diagram) is a thick deposit of finely layered ("laminated") anhydrite, which is as much as 80 feet thick in some places. More details on the nature of this significant deposit will be given a little farther on in this chapter. The thickness and characteristics of this and the succeeding coverings were learned partly through seismic surveys, but mainly as a result of wells drilled into the basin, as shown in Figure 13, both beside the reefs and into them.[20]

Next above the laminated anhydrite layer is a covering (no. 2 in Figure 14) of approximately 70 feet of a distinctly laminated dolostone. (The term "laminated" always refers to thin layers, often much less than one-fourth inch thick.) Each of the laminations represents at least a slight change in environment--probably an annual or seasonal change in most cases. (Similar layers, representing present-day, seasonal deposition, are common in numerous parts of the world. Such layers are often called "varves.") It is also of interest to note the presence of a five-foot layer of shale near the middle of the thickness of this 70 foot covering of dolostone. The shale represents a time when there was a more distinct change in environment for a period of time, with fine clay sediment being brought in to form the shale. The clay particles were of course brought in by water currents, but the extremely small size of the particles shows that these currents were of a slow and gentle nature, and that there were quiet, non-turbulent periods which gave the particles time to settle out to form the shale.

Above the dolostone covering unit just described, is found a much thicker deposit of alternating anhydrite and dolostone layers (no. 3 in Figure 14). The maximum thickness is 500 feet. This is of sufficient thickness to completely cover the tops of the reefs in some places. In some wells this blanket over the reefs is encountered when a depth of about 4,500 feet is reached. Many of the thick layers of anhydrite and dolostone in this deposit are made up of thin laminations.

Microlayers in the Covering

The nature of the layering and lamination in all of these coverings is of great significance for an understanding of the types of environment which dominated the Rainbow area in the milleniums which followed the death of the reefs. A careful study of the evaporite series which we have been discussing has recently been made by G. R. Davies of the Institute of Sedimentary Petroleum Geology in Calgary, Alberta.[21] He and S. D. Ludlam, his associate,

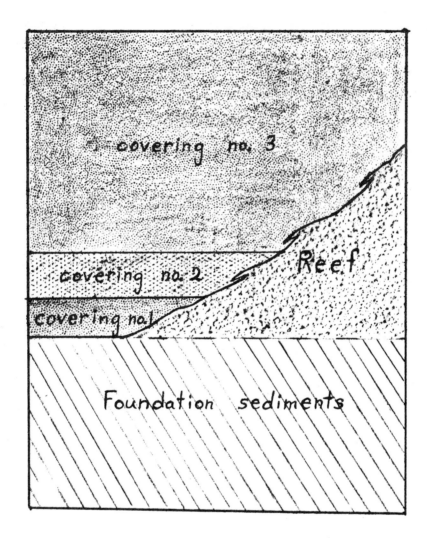

Fig. 14. Diagram of a buried Canadian atoll reef, with evaporite coverings. No. 1--laminated anhydrite (80 feet), no. 2--laminated dolostone (70 feet), no. 3--anhydrite and dolostone in alternating layers (500 feet thickness). These coverings belong to the Middle Devonian Period. See text of chapter 5 for further description.

focused their attention particularly on the lower layers of the covering series. This study provides a very reliable and meaningful insight into the history of the large, relatively shallow marine basin of Alberta, during the period of time which immediately followed the growth of the reefs.

One incontrovertible part of this history, recognized not only by Davies and Ludlam but also by all geologists who have studied the area, is that evaporative conditions dominated this period of time. It is also widely agreed that a part of the influence which brought on evaporative conditions was the growth of the barrier reef which extends for more than 150 miles in a SW-NE direction across the northwest end of the large basin in which the pinnacle and atoll reefs lay (as shown in Figure 12). The gradual upward growth of this linear, barrier reef not only slowed the flow of water over it from the main ocean which lay to the north and west, but undoubtedly helped to further cut off the flow of fresh sea water in times when uplifts of the land occurred, or when the sea level dropped.

The first evaporite layers (no. 1 in Figure 14) which began to cover the reefs show very thin, alternating layers in the drilling cores. These laminations (microlayers) are composed mainly of anhydrite, but some of the thinner ones are of relatively pure calcium carbonate (called "calcite" in the geologic literature); and some are of dolomite (similar to calcium carbonate but including magnesium). The anhydrite laminations range from less than one millimeter to a few millimeters in thickness. They closely resemble the thin layers of the "banded anhydrite" from the Delaware basin of West Texas, shown in Figure 19. There is regularly a very thin, dark layer of organic material between each anhydrite layer. This is taken to be the remains of the microscopic organisms which were living in the water before it reached such a high salt concentration that they died.

We must here pause to reflect on the meaning of these laminations. What can thin layers of anhydrite, calcium carbonate, and organic matter tell us about the lengths of time which elapsed? As stated earlier, each of the laminations must represent at least a seasonal change in the environment. This is evident from the fact that it takes time for a body of water to develop a new population of organisms for formation of the organic layer. It is also evident from the known length of time required for evaporating enough water to form calcite and anhydrite layers of this thickness.

The anhydrite (and probably also the calcium carbonate) for producing the evaporative layers usually comes out of the mineral-laden water by precipitation, the minute particles of precipitant settling to the bottom.[22] In order to bring about the precipitation of the calcium carbonate ($CaCO_3$), normal sea water has to be evaporated to a concentration of about one-half of its original volume. Then, if evaporation continues until the volume is only about one-fifth of the original, this forms a sufficiently strong brine to begin the precipitation of anhydrite ($CaSO_4$). When a volume of about one-tenth of the original is reached (if evaporation continues to that extent), ordinary salt (NaCl) begins to precipitate. These relationships are shown in Table 1. The fact that these three minerals each precipitate out at such definite, but widely differing, brine concentrations provides us with an unusually good opportunity to learn some of the past conditions under which laminated sedimentary deposits were formed. In other words, when we see layers of precipitated calcite and anhydrite, we know that the water which precipitated the calcite was not as concentrated as later on when the anhydrite layer just above it was produced. Likewise, if there is a layer of common salt just above the anhydrite, this shows that the brine became at least ten times as concentrated as normal sea water.

In the case of the laminated deposits around the reefs, the water did not usually reach sufficient concentration to precipitate common salt. However, in the layers higher up, there are relatively thick beds of salt alternating with thin layers of anhydrite, in the oil fields to the east of the Rainbow area.[23]

Summarizing the Significance of Microlayers

A close examination of the thin mineral layers in the basin in the Rainbow area reveals important information about past conditions there. First is the recognition that, since there are several thousands of these alternating layers, there obviously had to be a radical change of concentration of the sea water from low to high, and back, recurring many times. We need also to remember that there is no doubt that many of the times of low salt concentration were sufficiently dilute for marine animals and plants to grow. Otherwise they could not have left fossilized remains sealed beneath the precipitated layers. (Organic materials can not be produced from sea water without life, for the sea water is only a mixture of inorganic elements and compounds.) Then, on the other hand, we have to recognize the reality of periods of high salinity caused by a gradual evaporation from the surface of the sea; for there is no other known or conceivable way by which the orderly series of mineral laminations could be produced.

Of interest also is the fact that strata of soluble salts such as anhydrite and common salt could not have been formed in the presence of moving water. There must be reasonably long, quiet periods for undisturbed settling of the precipitating salt; and besides that, moving water would only redissolve what salts had been precipitated.[24]

When Davies, and also some earlier geologists who had studied these laminated deposits in Canada, investigated the similarity of the individual microlayers at any particular depth in the ancient basin deposit, they found further evidence of the orderly and uniform deposition process which we have been describing. This evidence consisted of the fact that particular sets of couplets of microlayers could be recognized and identified in the drilling cores of two or more wells located at various distances from each other. This shows the remarkably quiet condition of the sea bottom at the

TABLE 1--Amounts of calcite, anhydrite, and halite obtained by evaporation of one liter of sea water (as the evaporation proceeds).

Amounts (in grams) of materials precipitated by evaporation of one liter of sea water.

Density	Volume	$CaCO_3$		$CaSO_4$*		NaCl	
1.0258	1.000	–		–		–	
1.0500	0.533	0.064	Range of	–		–	
1.0836	0.316	trace	precip-	–		–	
1.1037	0.245	trace	itation	–		–	
1.1264	0.190	0.053	of $CaCO_3$	0.443	$CaSO_4$ precip-	–	
1.1604	0.145	–		0.445	itated before	–	
1.1732	0.131	–		0.144	NaCl begins	–	
1.2015	0.112	–		0.127		–	
1.2138	0.095	–		0.040		3.261	
1.2212	0.064	–		0.117		9.650	Range of
1.2363	0.039	–		0.055		7.896	precip-
1.2570	0.030	–		0.011		2.624	itation
1.2778	0.023	–		–		2.272	of NaCl
1.3069	0.016	–		–		1.404	

Total deposit		0.117g.		1.382g.		27.107g.	
Amount in last bittern		–		–		2.589g.	
Total		0.117g. (i.e. sea water is 0.0117% $CaCO_3$)		1.382g.		29.696g.	

*Given by Clarke as $CaSO_4.2H_2O$ but recalculated here as $CaSO_4$.

From:

Petrologic and Geochemical Variations in the Permian Castile Varved Anhydrite Delaware Basin, Texas and New Mexico. By Walter E. Dean, Jr., Ph.D. dissertation, University of New Mexico. 1967, p. 84 a. Data of Usiglio, 1849; modified from Clarke, 1924, p. 220. (Explanatory notes added in the table by D. Wonderly.) Used by permission of the author, W. E. Dean, Jr.

time the calcite, anhydrite, and organic material were deposited.
This ease of correlation of layers also shows that the amounts of
material settling out of the water in any one season (or period of
time between changes of environment) were very uniform throughout
the evaporative basin. In fact, from cores brought up from a depth
of 4,475 feet, a short distance to the east of the Rainbow oil
fields, Davies and his associates were able to correlate laminations from two wells which are spaced at 25 kilometers (15.5 miles)
apart.[25]

Another time-indicating feature of these covering layers which
we have been considering is that there is such a large number of
dolomite microlayers. There is no possible way for large amounts
of either dolomite or of calcium carbonate to rapidly precipitate
from sea water, because the magnesium and calcium content of the
water is very small (much less than the sodium chloride content).
However, since it is obvious that the microlayers of these had to
come from the dissolved calcium and magnesium in the sea water, the
only conclusion which can be reached is that each thin layer of the
calcite or dolomite mineral represents at least a few months of
precipitation time. Most geologists and oceanographers believe that
each dolomite layer was first a layer of calcite, which then was
gradually changed to dolomite, as magnesium ions were supplied from
the water circulating around the calcite crystals. Whether the
dolomite layers were formed in this manner or precipitated directly
is of no great importance for our purposes here, as the process
could not have been rapid in either case, due to the low amount of
magnesium ions in the water.

Thus we are again reminded that the earth has had a long history,
with many kinds of slow processes going on to form the intricately
organized series of deposits in the thick sedimentary blanket which
covers most of the earth. Truly our God has not been miserly in
his establishing of a sufficient number of physical and biological
processes upon the earth!

Periods of Water Turbulence

Now, after emphasizing the long, non-turbulent periods during
which the precipitating minerals were able to settle to the bottom
of the marine basin in Alberta, we must take a moment to pursue a
very different line. Davies reports that the laminated sedimentary
deposits which were studied (no. 1 in Figure 14) contain a number
of levels at which there were interruptions because of water turbulence. In each such case the turbulence left a layer of moderately
fine-grained, sandy sediments, before allowing another series of
anhydrite and organic laminations to be added. The layers of sediments left during these periods of water turbulence vary in thickness
from only about one-fourth of an inch, to over one foot. Two exciting features about these "graded beds," as they are called, are
(a) the fossils they contain, and (b) the fact that they also contain
a record of what happened at the beginning of each period of turbulence. At intervals there is a slightly, but definitely, eroded
upper surface of the anhydrite series of microlayers. The erosion

by the turbulent water broke up the top layer or two of thin anhydrite and dolomite laminations, moving and agitating the thin, flaky parts from the layers enough to break them into small irregular fragments. These fragments of the microlayers are now found mixed in with the other sandy materials of the entire layer deposited during turbulence. With them in the sediment are found a small number of recognizable pieces of foraminifera shells and ostracod skeletons. Then at the top of each such graded layer, the point of contact with the next series of anhydrite laminations is nearly always smooth and conformable, showing that the rapid movements of the water had ceased, allowing quiet periods of precipitation to resume.[26]

When we take into consideration the total thickness of the many laminated series, and the periods of mild erosion due to turbulence, we will soon see that we here have a clear record of much more than 100,000 years, during which the approximately 650 feet of these anhydrite, calcite, and dolomite covering layers were being applied to the reefs.[27] Thus were the fossiliferous carbonate reefs and their fossil-bearing foundation layers sealed off, making valuable storage reservoirs for the petroleum which man would need in the future.

The Upper 4,000 Feet

What have the Canadian oil drillers found in the more than 4,000 feet of rock layers which lie above the evaporite "cap" which covers the ancient reefs? The main kinds of rock layers are shale, siltstone, limestone, dolostone, and hard sandstone (quartz-chert sandstone). The uppermost part of the stratigraphic column in northwest Alberta is composed of glacial gravel, sand, and clay. The amount of each kind of rock layer and glacial layer varies somewhat between wells, but Table 2 gives an average amount as found in several wells in the Rainbow fields and nearby areas. This table does not list the many thin subdivisional layers or beds which make up each section of the local stratigraphic column, but it does give one a general idea of their make-up. It should also be kept in mind that the different wells from which these averages were made vary somewhat in depth, because of the differing amounts of glacial material at different well sites, and because some of the deep layers underwent more subsidence or uplift at one geographic location than at another.

One should realize that the majority of the rock layers listed in Table 2 are of marine origin, indicating that the area remained as a part of the ocean for long periods of time following the burial of the Rainbow reefs. (The presence of many crinoids and other exclusively marine fossils at some depth levels in these upper layers is a part of the evidence for their marine nature.) Some of the siltstones and shales could well have been deposited at times when the water was much deeper than it had been during reef growth.

Desert Cycles in Canada

For several decades oil geologists were puzzled by a strange repeating series of layers which they were finding in some of the evaporite beds. Drilling samples from the series included laminated

TABLE 2. Summary of deposits which lie above the evaporite coverings of the reefs of oil fields in northwestern Alberta. The thicknesses given are averages for several wells in the area. Each section shown in the table is actually an elaborate series of layers or beds of varying thickness--usually from a few inches to a few feet--and differing somewhat in composition from each other. (Based on J. Law, "Geology of Northwestern Alberta and Adjacent Areas," American Association of Petroleum Geologists Bulletin, v. 39, 1955, p. 1927-1965.)

Geologic Period	Thickness in feet	Description of strata (beginning with the uppermost, ground-level deposit)
Pleistocene (an epoch)	100 ft.	Varied layers of glacial till, gravel, sand, silt, and clay
Cretaceous	700	Thin layers of shale; and small to considerable amounts of layered sandstone, layered limestone, and ironstone
Mississippian	300	Limestone, shale, and siltstone, with some chert nodules (many alternating layers)
Upper Devonian	700	Limestone (several different types and grades)
	600	Silty limestone (Some layers alternate with thin deposits of calcareous shale)
	1600	Shale, with intermittent layers of siltstone and limestone
Middle Devonian	300	Limestone (often laminated), with some interstratified dolostone, shale and sandstone
	700	Evaporite coverings (Muskeg Formation)

carbonates and several forms of gypsum and anhydrite. Some of the
anhydrite was in the form of nodules such as have been recently
described on the desert coasts of Arabia. Finally, oil geologists
began to study desert coasts as a possible aid in interpreting the
above mentioned underground series of sediments.

On the Arabian side of the Persian Gulf, near the southern end
of the Gulf, is a shallow-water coast line where the water temperature is very often above 90° F. (sometimes above 100°), and evaporation takes place at a rapid rate. This 200 mile long area is known
as the Trucial Coast, and is studded with a series of low islands a
few miles off shore, which restricts the circulation of water in
the long lagoon which lies between them and the shore. Corals and
other tropical marine organisms form a great deal of carbonate (limy)
sediment which is deposited in the lagoon and on the shore. Evaporation along the shores leaves layers of anhydrite and salt during
most of the year, and salty mud flats abound. (See Figure 15.)

All in all, the Trucial Coast is an inhospitable place to set
up a research station. Nevertheless, by 1963, petroleum geologists
had combed the salt-covered beaches and flats, taken hundreds of
shallow sediment cores and other samples, and had solved many of
the mysteries about that area. It soon became evident that several
of the mysteries of the underground strata in the oil fields in
various parts of the world could be solved by relating them to the
environments of the Persian Gulf's shores. Further research on the
Trucial Coast by numerous other petroleum geologists bore out the
truth of this discovery.

In the preceding parts of this chapter we described some of
the evaporite sediments which cover the reefs in the oil fields of
Alberta. In the upper parts of those covering layers (no. 3 of
Figure 14) are several repeating series of sediments which have
much the same order, texture, and chemical content as the layers
on the Trucial Coast. The underground strata can now be much better
understood and traced because a modern desert-shore environment,
in which the repeating series was produced, has now been studied
and described. This has enhanced oil exploration, not only in Canada, but in other parts of the world where these series of sediments
are found. Since the salty mud flats along the Trucial Coast are
given the Arabian name "sabkhas," this is the name by which such a
series of deposits is called, even when discovered at great depths
in oil wells.

The Sabkhas of the Persian Gulf

A modern sabkha, such as is seen on the Trucial Coast, is a
salt-encrusted flat, lying a short distance inland from the usual
water's edge. It is at an elevation just above the high tide, except that it is flooded over occasionally due to higher water
resulting from storms. These inundations supply salt water which,
when evaporated, adds to the sabkha's thickness. Also, there is
some lateral seepage of salt water from the shore inland. In some
places these "coastal sabkhas" are rather wide, extending inland

86

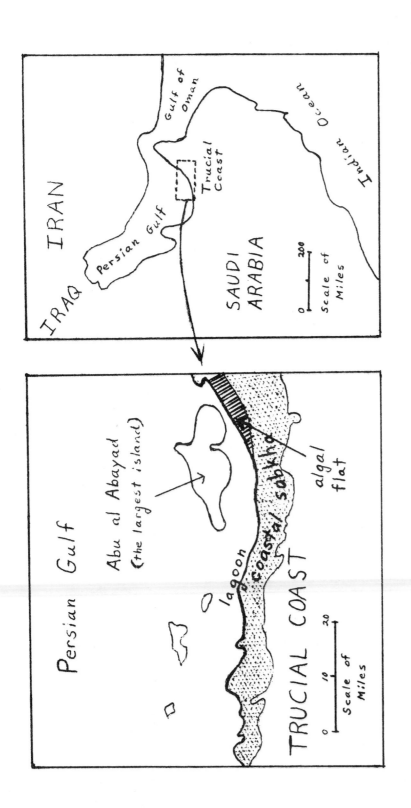

Fig. 15. Location and structure of the Trucial Coast, where extensive studies of modern evaporite formation and dolomitization have been made. In the larger figure, the coastal sabkha is a broad band along the coast, which lies just above the high-tide level. Redrawn from D. J. J. Kinsman, "Modes of formation, sedimentary associations, and diagnostic features of shallow-water and supratidal evaporites," American Association of Petroleum Geologists Bulletin, vol. 53, no. 4, 1969, Figure 2; and other sources.

as much as 8 or 10 miles. Also, there are older salt flats farther inland with a width of as much as 60 miles. At one time they were nearer to the sea, but the production of carbonate sediments by the corals and other calcium-secreting marine organisms has now added some miles of width to the shore. The present rate of this horizontal seaward movement ("regression") of the shoreline is from 3 to 6 feet per year. The sabkhas which are presently next to the coast are thus believed to have been formed within the past 4,000 to 5,000 years.[28]

A typical coastal sabkha (salt flat) contains several kinds of sediments and minerals which have been modified by the brine which saturates the sediments just beneath the surface. This brine is produced and concentrated down among the sand grains as evaporation occurs from the surface of the sabkha. The brine is kept from sinking to any great depth by the layer of hard rock which lies beneath, all along the coast, in this part of Arabia. Since the brine can not escape to lower depths, it keeps the main body of sediments of the sabkha saturated. The upper level of the brine is usually only a few inches beneath the surface. It becomes more concentrated as the hot sun and wind continue to "draw" water out of the sediments and evaporate it. As a result, the brine becomes concentrated enough to do two primary things, (a) form crystals and nodules of the calcium sulfate minerals gypsum and anhydrite (evaporites), and (b) slowly convert the calcium carbonate sediments to calcium-magnesium carbonate (dolomite) in the lower zone.[29]

Thus the sabkha becomes a sort of "layer-cake" composed primarily of layers of gypsum crystals and various sizes of anhydrite nodules, with a deeper layer of rather fine-grained dolomite. The anhydrite nodules are sometimes as much as two and one-half inches in diameter. The entire sabkha series of layers is usually only a few feet in thickness.[30] The lower zones contain a high proportion of sand-sized particles of carbonate skeletal materials from the marine animals and plants which grew in the lagoon. A very distinctive characteristic of these lower zones is that they contain left-over, algal-mat layers which retain their identity even after the sea regresses from them and they become converted to dolomite. Thus a bed of dolostone, with what are called "algal laminations," can eventually be formed at the bottom of the salt flat.

One must realize that all of the flat area of the sabkha, as it lies a short way back from the coast, was once at the water's edge, with an abundance of fine, filamentous strands of algae growing over the surface of the wet sand. These filaments of algae produce a protective slime for themselves, that later becomes mixed with the finer beach sand which washes up over it as the tide comes in. Thus a thin, rather durable layer is produced, and a thickening series of successive layers (called a "laminated algal mat") is formed as the algal filaments continue to grow. Since these mats have a high percentage of carbonate sand, they are eventually converted to a layer of laminated dolostone, if they are exposed to strong brines on the sabkha for a considerable period of time. Much of the algal, laminated dolostone which is found so commonly in the

88

oil-bearing strata of many parts of the world is thus a record of
the sea coast growth of the algae, and of the formation of algal
mats.

The Present as a Picture of the Past

The reason we have considered the process of sabkha formation
in some detail is that processes very similar to this were going
on along numerous ancient arid coasts. In fact, the layers of
evaporite coverings which lie above the Canadian reefs often contain
not only one sabkha series of layers, but several. This is a strong
indication that there was enough change of environment at various
times during the burial of the reefs, that a whole new sabkha layer
series was formed on top of the old.

Since sabkhas on our modern coasts are often several miles in
width, it is not surprising that the ancient ones likewise cover
broad areas. In the Rainbow oil fields of northwestern Alberta,
wells drilled into and around one of the large atoll reefs passed
through a set of 20 recurring sabkha-type cycles. Some of them are
continuous for a distance of more than six miles across and beyond
the reef. (Their layers can be matched from well to well.) Actually, these sabkha-type layers are widespread in Alberta, being
found at least as far north as the Zama area oil fields (60 miles
north of the large atoll reef mentioned just above), and also in
the oil and gas fields much farther south.[31] Evidently the sea had
dried up in various parts of the area, giving opportunity for the
sabkhas to form along the edges of the remaining bays and lagoons.
J. G. Fuller recently observed and described a series of 13 sabkha
cycles in 50 feet of core from a well near Calgary, Alberta.[32]

In the study of the cycles in the Rainbow area, Bebout found
that each cycle usually has a thickness of from two to four feet.
Those cycles which are complete are made up of four zones or layers
which are similar to the zones of the modern Trucial Coast deposits.
(See Figure 16 for a drawing of these, accompanied by a description
of the contents of each zone.) The cycles recur, one upon another,
their combined thickness in the Rainbow area being approximately
150 feet, including some layers of salt. In most of the cycles the
sediment-laden algal mats of the ancient coast were converted to
laminated dolostone, which lies in the lower part of the cyclic
deposit. Some of the cycles are incomplete, having one or another
of the four zones missing.[33] However, this is to be expected, since
the natural changes of climate which have occurred in the past could
easily alter the sedimentation processes which were going on in the
sediments of the salt flats.

Immediately above the series of 20 sabkha cycles are 15 more
cycles which are similar, but less complex. These are made up of
two main components: nodular anhydrite layers alternating with
dolostone. Their total thickness is somewhat more than 100 feet.[34]
It should be noted that nodular anhydrite such as this (with large
nodules) is a very reliable indication of coastal deposition.
These nodules form at or very near the surface of the salt flat

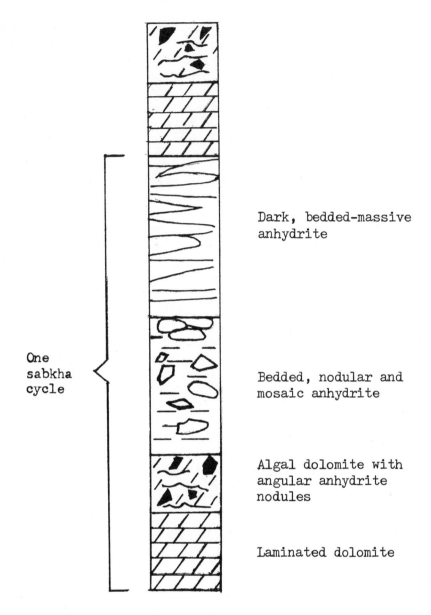

One
sabkha
cycle

Dark, bedded-massive
anhydrite

Bedded, nodular and
mosaic anhydrite

Algal dolomite with
angular anhydrite
nodules

Laminated dolomite

Fig. 16. Diagram of the layers of a sabkha cycle of the
type found in the Rainbow area of Alberta, Canada, at
depths of slightly more than 6,000 feet. Adapted from
D. G. Bebout and W. R. Maiklem, "Ancient anhydrite facies
and environments, Middle Devonian Elk Point basin, Alberta," Bulletin of Canadian Petroleum Geology, vol. 21,
no. 3, 1973, Figures 3 and 24.

which is exposed to the wind and sun.

These two sets of cyclic, evaporite layers which have been described should be related in one's mind to our description of the evaporitic coverings given earlier in this chapter. They are actually in the upper part of the 650 foot series of evaporitic strata which we previously described as sealing over the Rainbow reefs. All of these evaporitic strata are combined together in the bottom section of Table 2, to which we have already made reference.

Some Time Calculations

If one asks how much time is represented by the sabkha series of cycles in the upper part of the evaporite coverings (Figure 14), a meaningful response can be made. First, we must recognize, as we did when considering the lower, laminated parts of this 650 foot deposit, that the deposition of gypsum, anhydrite, and dolomite are necessarily slow. (See the earlier parts of this chapter for the factors which limit the rate of deposition of these minerals.) Second, we must take into account the rate at which a salt flat with the sabkha-cycle organization is formed. It may be that the rate of formation was somewhat faster or slower in ancient times than now--or probably faster at some times and slower at others. Nevertheless, the very nature of the sedimentary components of the cycle demands a period of at least a few thousand years for forming such a salt flat, of even six miles width. According to the studies made by D. J. Kinsman on the Trucial Coast of Arabia, to which we referred earlier, the present rate of shoreline regression (increase of land) would broaden the sabkhas approximately one mile each 1,000 years. He estimates that the flats which are six miles wide have required about 5,000 years for their formation. These six-mile expanses of organized salt flat are only one or two sabkha cycles thick.[35]

So when we think of the 20 cycles which lie above the reefs in the Rainbow area, we will realize that the sabkha-forming process had to progress laterally over the area several times. As pointed out above, the sabkha deposits of the Rainbow area are considerably broader than the six-mile circle in which Bebout studied them. Now, even if we were to take them as only eight miles wide, this would require something like 7,000 years of coastal deposition to form just one or two of the sabkha cycles. Since the progressing desert coast line had to sweep over the area numerous times to form the 20 cycles observed by Bebout, at least 70,000 years were thus required for the actual forming process, for the entire series. In addition to this we must allow extra time for the necessary coast-line subsidence (sinking), or rise in sea level, before the beginning of each new cycle of deposition. One of these two kinds of processes has to take place before the sea begins to build another sabkha on top of the old one. Since land subsidence and sea-level elevations are both very slow processes,[36] we will have to at least double the amount of time just stated, in order to provide for the formation of a 20-cycle deposit 8 miles in width. (And let us remember that these make up only about 150 feet of the 4,000 to 5,000 feet of varied sediments which cover the reefs.)

Now suppose that someone were to postulate that these cycles of evaporites did not form as salt flats along a coast line, but formed in some other manner? There *are* variations of opinion as to exactly how these sabkha layers were accumulated in the oil field deposits, but all who have studied them agree that they are the result of evaporative processes. The soluble minerals of the sea water must become concentrated before they can be deposited, and evaporation is the only possible way by which such a concentrating could occur. So all agree that the sabkha cycles in the oil fields are a record of long periods of time. And this is a part of God's time record in nature.

Thus our realization of the antiquity of the oil field strata in Alberta is not based merely on the gross thickness of the strata through which the oil drills pass. It is based on (a) information concerning the time required for forming the fossiliferous, foundation strata on which the reefs grew, (b) an understanding of the time which was necessary for growth of these reefs which now serve as sources of oil, (c) a knowledge of the characteristics of the sea water which furnished the minerals for the evaporite coverings, (d) an understanding of the processes by which the thinly laminated anhydrite, calcite, and dolomite of the first evaporite coverings were deposited, (e) the study of the rates of formation of sabkha cycles, and (f) a knowledge of the rates of formation of the many kinds of limestone and other rock layers which lie above these. (Some rates of formation of limestones will be taken up in a later chapter.)

FOOTNOTES

1. Not nearly all limestone and dolostone are sufficiently porous to serve as a reservoir for petroleum.

2. D. G. Bebout and W. R. Maiklem, "Ancient Anhydrite Facies and Environments, Middle Devonian Elk Point Basin, Alberta," Bulletin of Canadian Petroleum Geology, v. 21 (1973), p. 287.

3. P. K. Weyl, Oceanography, 1970, p. 324.

4. This level of depth is in the Muskeg Formation of the Middle Devonian geologic period.

5. M. E. Hriskevich, "Middle Devonian Reef Production, Rainbow Area, Alberta, Canada," American Association of Petroleum Geologists Bulletin, v. 54 (1970), p. 2279.

6. J. R. Langton and G. E. Chin, "Rainbow Member Facies and Related Reservoir Properties, Rainbow Lake, Alberta," American Association of Petroleum Geologists Bulletin, v. 52 (1968), p. 1925 and 1927.

7. Hriskevich, "Middle Devonian," p. 2260-2281.

8. These sediments are in the lower part of the Devonian System (actually Lower Middle Devonian), and rest on Precambrian strata throughout most of the area. The uppermost of them (just below the base of the reefs) is called the Keg River Formation. (D. L. Barss, et al., "Geology of Middle Devonian Reefs, Rainbow Area, Alberta, Canada," in Geology of Giant Petroleum Fields, 1970, p. 23-25.)

9. The main kinds of fossils found there are crinoids, brachiopods, sporadic corals, and some stromatoporoids. These are found in interbedded layers of limestone and dolostone of the lower part of the Keg River Formation. (Ibid., p. 25.)

10. Ibid., p. 24.

11. John C. Kraft, "Carbonate Analogs--Modern and Ancient," in Field Guide to Some Carbonate Rock Environments, Florida Keys and Western Bahamas, 1971, p. 134-136.

12. Barss, "Geology of Middle," p. 34-35.

13. Some of the other fossils which were found are, an abundant amount of stromatoporoids (the growth habit of which was important in building the wave-resistant parts of the reef), brachiopods, crinoids, gastropods (aquatic snails), ostracods, and several kinds of limestone-building algae. (Langton and Chin, "Rainbow Member," p. 1933-1943; and S. Machielse, "Devonian Algae and Their Contribution to the Western Canadian Sedimentary Basin," Bulletin of Canadian Petroleum Geology, v. 20 (1972), p. 204-206, 212, 220.)

14. Langton and Chin, "Rainbow Member," p. 1930-1942.

15. Barss, "Geology of Middle," p. 35.

16. Ibid., p. 34.

17. Langton and Chin, "Rainbow Member," p. 1943.

18. G. R. Davies and S. D. Ludlam, "Origin of Laminated and Graded Sediments, Middle Devonian of Western Canada," Geological Society of America Bulletin, v. 84 (1973), p. 3541-3543. The entire, large basin in which these changes were taking place is usually called the "Elk Point Evaporite Basin." It is then divided into subbasins, such as the Rainbow subbasin, for convenience in discussing local parts of the oil fields.

19. Bebout and Maiklem, "Ancient Anhydrite Facies," p. 298-301, 314-321.

20. Approximately the first 650 feet of the covering layers we are discussing here belong to what is called the Muskeg Formation. A brief but good description of them is given in J. G. McCamis, and L. S. Griffith, "Middle Devonian Facies Relations, Zama Area, Alberta," American Association of Petroleum Geologists Bulletin, v. 52 (1968), p. 1907-1912, 1915-1919.

21. Davies and Ludlam, "Origin of Laminated," p. 3527-3546.

22. Under some circumstances thin layers of calcium carbonate are formed as a result of the action of microscopic forms of algae. However, the amount of layer thickness which can be formed in one season in this manner is not essentially different from the amount which can precipitate inorganically under ideal conditions.

23. A. M. Klingspor, "Middle Devonian Muskeg Evaporites of Western Canada," American Association of Petroleum Geologists Bulletin, v. 53 (1969), p. 928-938.

24. The origin of salt domes (composed of common salt) by being pushed up out of the deeper layers of the earth's crust is entirely different from the production of a series of alternating salt, calcite, and organic layers in a marine basin. In the many ancient marine basins of the world which have such deposits, the fact that the common salt is in thin uniform layers, alternating with anhydrite--or with anhydrite and calcite or dolomite--is more than adequate proof that the layers originated by slow precipitation, rather than by being pushed up from beneath. And, because of the fact that fossiliferous carbonate strata underlie them, we know that they were formed after the creation of life on the earth.

25. Davies and Ludlam, "Origin of Laminated," p. 3528, 3532, 3534-3535.

26. Ibid., p. 3535-3537.

27. Davies does not state the total number of laminations and other layers in this deposit; but even the lower 80 feet, which contains approximately 40 feet of very thin laminations, must have required at least 10,000 years for its formation. This is allowing for normal rates of evaporation from a stagnant body of water, and taking into consideration the fact that the amounts of calcium carbonate and anhydrite which are present in the water awaiting precipitation are small. The amount of water which evaporates from ocean or lagoon surfaces annually in the most arid and hot regions of the world rarely exceeds 5 meters depth, and is usually only about one-half that amount. Even the 5 meters of water has only enough minerals to produce a layer of calcium carbonate 0.5 mm in thickness, and a 2.2 mm layer of anhydrite (W. B. F. Ryan, et al., Initial Reports of the Deep Sea Drilling Project, v. XIII, 1973, p. 1214). These quantities are for "normal" or average sea water. It can be seen from Table 1 (which is also based on normal sea water) that even if the water were completely saturated with respect to $CaCO_3$, only about 90% more calcium carbonate could be precipitated per unit of water. Thus in the above case the amount of calcium carbonate precipitated from 5 meters of water would still be less than 1 mm.

28. D. J. Kinsman, "Modes of Formation, Sedimentary Associations, and Diagnostic Features of Shallow-Water and Supratidal Evaporites," American Association of Petroleum Geologists Bulletin, v. 53 (1969), v. 53 (1969), p. 832, 839.

94

29. The latter process is made possible by the increase in percentage of magnesium ions in the water, due to evaporation and to the precipitation of the calcium sulfate, which raises the magnesium/calcium ratio in the water.

30. C. G. St. C. Kendall, and Sir Patrick A. D'E. Skipwith, "Holocene Shallow-Water Carbonate and Evaporite Sediments of Khor al Bazam, Abu Dhabi, Southwest Persian Gulf," American Association of Petroleum Geologists Bulletin, v. 53 (1969), p. 854, 858-861.

31. Bebout and Maiklem, "Ancient Anhydrite Facies," p. 302, 304, 322-324.

32. J. G. C. M. Fuller and J. W. Porter, "Evaporite Formations with Petroleum Reservoirs in Devonian and Mississippian of Alberta, Saskatchewan, and North Dakota," American Association of Petroleum Geologists Bulletin, v. 53 (1969), p. 910-913.

33. Bebout and Maiklem, "Ancient Anhydrite Facies," p. 289-291, 322-324.

34. Ibid., p. 305, 326-327.

35. The modern sabkha areas which are usually described are only one cycle in thickness; however, Butler has described one on the Trucial Coast which is 8 miles wide, and is two cycles in thickness. (G. P. Butler, "Modern Evaporite Deposition and Geochemistry of Coexisting Brines, The Sabkha, Trucial Coast, Arabian Gulf," Journal of Sedimentary Petrology, v. 39 (1969), p. 71-72.)

36. It is of course very likely that there was a sudden change in sea level at the time of the Biblical Flood. This, however, was too recent an event to have been one of the sea level changes which took part in producing these coverings which are found deeply buried beneath 4,000 feet of well organized strata.

CHAPTER 6

TIMEKEEPERS IN TEXAS

Most people in the United States automatically associate the
words "Texas" and "oil." By 1949 the oil fields of Texas were producing 42 per cent of the oil of our nation. Since the petroleum
industry is one of our major sources of information concerning deep
underground deposits and local stratigraphic columns, it is not
surprising that the many oil fields in the various parts of Texas
have supplied us with a great deal of information about the past.

The area from which our best stratigraphic time records come
is that of western Texas (and southeastern New Mexico). During the
1940's this part of Texas became the leading oil producing district
of the state.[1] One of the major oil reservoirs there consists of
an ancient, buried organic bank or reef which has a porous texture
similar to that of the Canadian reefs. We use the term "organic
bank" because some geologists feel that the scarcity of coral fossils in it makes it advisable to avoid the term "reef." Nevertheless,
this organic bank is usually called the "Capitan reef," and gives
every evidence of having grown in the ancient shallow sea which
formerly covered that part of the United States. The word "organic"
in the term "organic bank" refers to the fact that the bank or reef
is made up almost entirely of materials produced by organisms. Many
of the marine organisms which produce the calcareous fecal pellets
and skeletal parts, of which a bank such as this is largely composed,
can not produce strong, wave-resistant structures like the coral
reefs in the oil fields of Alberta. These organisms can, however,
produce enormous amounts of skeletal debris as they live and die
generation after generation. Some of the kinds of organisms which
are found embedded in the drilling cores taken from the Capitan reef
are calcium-secreting sponges, bryozoans, crinoids, hydrozoans,
brachiopods, and foraminifera. The hard, limy deposits of various
kinds of encrusting algae are abundant among these other organisms.
Such algae are very effective in binding and stabilizing reefs, as
we regularly observe in the reefs of Bermuda and of the south Pacific.
Also, some hydrozoans of this early geologic period built hard crusts
which probably gave further aid in producing the necessary wave resistance.

It is significant that large numbers of (well preserved) sponges
and bryozoans are found in their original growth position (in situ)
in the reef.[2] The sponges are very similar to some of our modern
sponges. As they grow they secrete thousands of tiny, needle-like
"spicules" in their body wall. These calcium carbonate needles give
the sponge support and protection in life; and, when the animal dies,
either the needles drop down and contribute to the sediments, or
else the whole sponge is fossilized in place. The bryozoans are
tiny marine animals which grow in large colonies. Each individual
animal forms a calcium carbonate tube surrounding it, for its protection. All the tubes join together in branching fashion to form

a colony, which has somewhat the appearance of a clump of moss.
When the colony dies, the calcareous tubes are often fossilized,
becoming a permanent part of the reef. The presence of these, and
of the sponges fossilized in growth position (rather than inverted
or scattered about), shows that the Capitan reef did actually grow
in its present position, rather than having been built out of sediments washed in from elsewhere.

As geologists studied the drilling records and seismic surveys
of the Capitan area, the immensity of this ancient underground organic bank became evident. It is buried beneath parts of 7 counties
of Texas, and 2 of New Mexico, forming almost a complete circle.
(See Figure 17 for its position and extent.) This reef is situated
as a relatively narrow band around the rim of a great underground
depression, which is known as the Delaware basin. This basin is
approximately 90 miles wide and 160 miles long, being somewhat oval
in shape, with one end of the oval protruding northward into New
Mexico. Most of the basin is now covered with several thousands
of feet of sedimentary rock layers, which must be penetrated by the
oil drillers to reach the oil-bearing layers of the depression, and
of the reef which lies around the edge of it.

Near the northern end of the basin, parts of the reef project
above the level of the basin itself and have now been exposed by
erosion in some of the canyons of the Guadalupe Mountains. The
famous Carlsbad Cavern is actually in the ancient Capitan reef (that
is, the cavern is an underground area of the reef limestone which
dissolved away). However, the eastern parts of the reef are buried
much deeper than in the Carlsbad area, apparently because that side
of the basin sank considerably before the final covering process
took place. By using drilling records, petroleum geologists have
now learned the exact position, thickness, and depth of nearly all
parts of the reef, as well as its composition. The total length
of this structure, as it extends around the Delaware basin, is
slightly over 350 miles.[3] In ancient times this bank was growing
in the shallow water around the edge of the basin, which contained
sea water at that time, and was probably an actual part of the ocean.
The reef itself has a total thickness of more than 1,200 feet in
some places, but in other places is as little as 400 feet thick.[4]
There is now an abundance of underground maps of the basin and of
the Capitan reef which surrounds it. These maps show both the lateral extent and the thicknesses of these structures. (Figure 18, to
which we will refer later, is a portion of one of these which is
designed to show thicknesses.)

Length of Time for Growth

In Chapter 3 we saw that growth rates of coral reefs are very
slow, and that even in the most favorable latitudes in the Pacific,
reef-forming organisms add only approximately one-third of an inch
of thickness per year. In the case of the Capitan reef, many of
the same kinds of organisms are present, but the fact that only a
small percentage of them are corals is an indication that growth
of this reef-like bank was slower than that of a true reef. Even

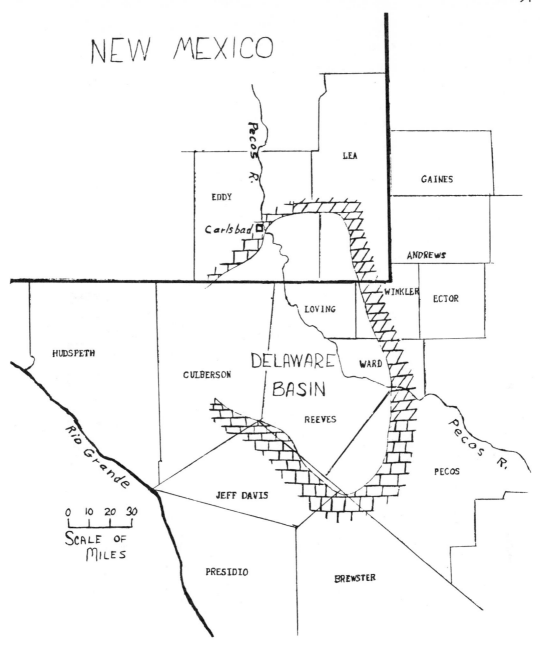

Fig. 17. Location and position of the Delaware basin and Capitan reef of west Texas and southeast New Mexico. The position of the reef is shown by the large curved structure which practically surrounds the Delaware basin. The depth of burial of the reef is not shown, but all except the northwest part of it is deeply buried, as explained in the text. In the figure, brick-like units are used for indicating the reef because this is the usual type of symbol for designating limestone and dolomite. Adapted from J. E. Galley, "Oil and geology in the Permian basin of Texas and New Mexico," in Habitat of Oil, a Symposium, L. G. Weeks, editor, American Association of Petroleum Geologists, Tulsa, Oklahoma, 1958, Figure 41; and other sources.

98

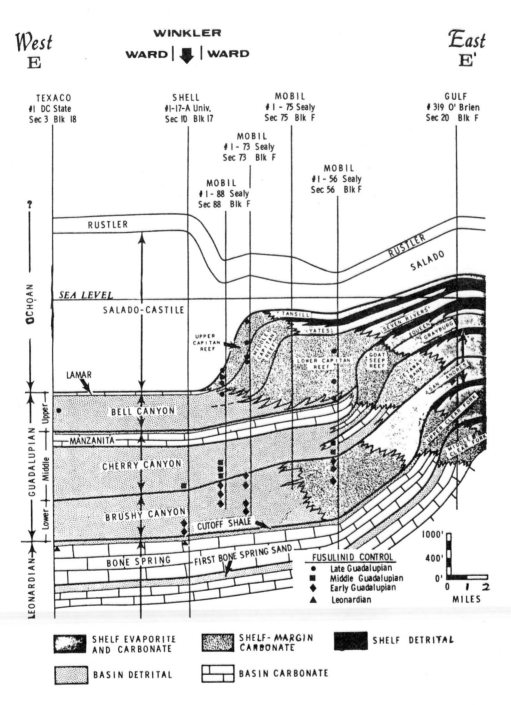

West
E

WINKLER
WARD ⬇ WARD

East
E'

TEXACO
#1 DC State
Sec 3 Blk 18

SHELL
#1-17-A Univ.
Sec 10 Blk 17

MOBIL
#1-75 Sealy
Sec 75 Blk F

GULF
#319 O'Brien
Sec 20 Blk F

MOBIL
#1-73 Sealy
Sec 73 Blk F

MOBIL
#1-56 Sealy
Sec 56 Blk F

MOBIL
#1-88 Sealy
Sec 88 Blk F

?

OCHOAN

RUSTLER

RUSTLER

SALADO

SEA LEVEL

SALADO-CASTILE

TANSILL

UPPER
CAPITAN
REEF

MIDDLE CAPITAN REEF

YATES

SEVEN RIVERS

QUEEN

GRAYBURG

LAMAR

LOWER CAPITAN REEF

GOAT SEEP REEF

GETAWAY BANK

SAN ANDRES

Upper

BELL CANYON

GUADALUPIAN

MANZANITA

UPPER CLEAR FORK

Middle

CHERRY CANYON

MIDDLE CLEAR FORK

Lower

BRUSHY CANYON

CUTOFF SHALE

1000'

400'

0'

LEONARDIAN

BONE SPRING

FIRST BONE SPRING SAND

FUSULINID CONTROL
• Late Guadalupian
■ Middle Guadalupian
♦ Early Guadalupian
▲ Leonardian

0 1 2
MILES

SHELF EVAPORITE
AND CARBONATE

SHELF-MARGIN
CARBONATE

SHELF DETRITAL

BASIN DETRITAL

BASIN CARBONATE

Fig. 18. Diagram showing a vertical section through the Capitan reef which lies just east of the Delaware basin in Ward and Winkler Counties, in west Texas. This profile of the reef is shown from the perspective of an observer standing in southern Ward County, looking north at the line of oil wells which are shown in the diagram, and at the cut end of the reef. The basin is seen to the left of the reef. Note the thickness scale at right, and the position of the sea-level line. The wells penetrate approximately 2,750 feet of sediments above the sea-level line, which are not shown. The limestone and dolostone of the reef are termed "shelf-margin carbonate" in this diagram, and the names of the geologic formations are given in blocks in the beds of the basin and "shelf." From B. A. Silver and R. G. Todd, "Permian cyclic strata, northern Midland and Delaware basins, west Texas and southeastern New Mexico," American Association of Petroleum Geologists Bulletin, vol. 53, no. 11, 1969, p. 2223-2251 and Figure 13. (By permission of the American Association of Petroleum Geologists.)

if it were possible for it to grow as rapidly as a modern reef, more than 50,000 years would be required for development of the main 1,200 foot thickness. In fact, nearly 50,000 years would have been required, even without any interruptions of growth, or any spreading and leveling effect of waves. But the Capitan reef has numerous unconformities which represent periods of time when there were long delays in its upward growth. It also has large deposits of fossil-iferous reef debris on the sides, which were evidently washed off from the upper parts of the reef as it grew. Thus at least several hundred thousand years must have been required for its formation. This of course does not include the very long periods of time which were required for the subsequent covering of the entire area with thousands of feet of sediments, which will be discussed below.

Another reason that such a long period of time is represented here is that what is spoken of as "the Capitan reef" is actually a series of reefs which grew parallel to each other. The newer reefs were farther from the shore, growing next to the fresher water in the large central basin, as is seen in Figure 18. As each new reef grew, it partially buried its predecessor. Thus a horizontal, as well as upward, reef growth was achieved. The reason for this horizontal advance was that reef-forming organisms thrive only on the side facing the sea, which brings oxygen-and-food-laden water. The water in the lagoon area (between the growing reef and the shore) is usually too stagnant to support active reef growth. The multiple structure of the Capitan reef, which resulted from these conditions, left a broad band of overlapping reefs around the Delaware basin. Obviously it took much more time to grow such a series of reefs than a single one, growing only upward, would have required.[5]

Another meaningful time indicator in the vicinity of the Capitan reef is the extensive series of alternating layers of evaporites and dolostone which extends landward from the reef. In Figure 18 the thick deposits which are labeled "Tansill," and "Yates," extending shoreward from the reef, are the formations which contain these inter-bedded evaporite and dolostone layers. At certain times while the reef was growing, and for a long period of time afterward, evaporative conditions existed next to the shore, and in the sediments on shore, just above the tide level. This resulted in the series of alternat-ing layers of anhydrite and/or gypsum, and dolostone which we find today on the outer perimeter of the reef. (Anhydrite is calcium sulfate, and gypsum is calcium sulfate chemically bound to water molecules.) These alternating deposits are similar to the ones which lie next above the 20 sabkha cycles which we described from the Rain-bow area in Canada. The alternating layers of anhydrite and dolomite in New Mexico and Texas evidently were formed on an arid shore in much the same way as those. This is especially indicated by the large nodules of anhydrite, the regular patterns of dessication cracks in the evaporite layers (due to periods of drying and sun baking), and the accompanying buried layers of windblown quartz sand.[6]

Regardless of the details of reef growth and arrangements of the parts of the Delaware basin, these features show that the deposits

100

which extend outward from the reef were formed by slow evaporative processes. Because of the fact that both anhydrite and gypsum are soluble in water, there is no possibility that these strata could have been formed by any aquatic activities such as floods or rapid inundation. Thus we have here another good example of a long series of cyclic changes of environment which produced interstratified layers of evaporite minerals and dolostone. Canada and the Delaware basin are only two of the many areas in the world where this type of cycle is present.

The Filling of the Delaware Basin

The length of time which the processes of reef formation required was only a small part of the total time represented by the deposits of the Delaware basin area. The thick deposits represented in Figure 18 by the white areas above the basin floor and reef are nearly all evaporitic deposits. Their extent and complexity are truly amazing to those who have studied them, and are one of the best sedimentary time records in the world. The entire basin, a part of which is shown on the left in Figure 18, is filled with very thin, alternating layers of calcium carbonate, anhydrite, and organic matter. These thin, evaporitic varves make up thousands of small cycles which represent periodic (probably annual) fluctuations in the environment. The environmental changes progressed each time from near normal sea water (when the organisms could form organic matter), to a concentration such that calcium carbonate could be precipitated, to a more concentrated brine from which anhydrite (calcium sulfate) could be precipitated. (Table 1 shows the sea-water concentrations necessary for the precipitation of these minerals.) Some of this evaporitic deposit in the deeper parts of the basin may have formed during the time the reef was still growing. In this case the brine would have been sinking into the bottom of the basin, because of its greater density, after having been produced by evaporation at the surface of some part of the basin. This kind of sinking of brines has been observed in modern marine environments in some parts of the world.[7]

Walter Dean, while at the University of New Mexico, made a detailed study of these thinly laminated deposits. By studying cores and drilling records from 415 wells of the Delaware basin, he found that there are more than 200,000 of these thin calcium carbonate-anhydrite-organic cycles, spreading over a broad area in the center of the basin. The total depth (thickness) of these 200,000 layers was found to be approximately 1,300 feet in most places.[8] This deposit makes up the main thickness of the sediments which filled the basin, and is part of what is known as the Castile Formation of that area. Geologists have been aware of this great body of thinly laminated sediments for several decades, calling them the "banded anhydrite" (because the thin layers, as seen in a well core, look like narrow bands on the core). There is a great deal of evidence that each of the thin cycles represents one year of deposition.

An examination of Dean's Ph. D. thesis, and the work which he later published on the same subject, will soon convince anyone who is interested in time-indicating strata, that this is a fabulous find. Some of the most significant facts concerning this laminated deposit are as follows:

1. The alternating microlayers of calcium carbonate and anhydrite are distinct from each other. This shows that a radical change in the concentration of the sea water occurred for each calcium carbonate-anhydrite pair. (These thin cycles are frequently called "couplets." Even though there is a third layer--the organic matter--in each cycle, the fact that this third layer is much thinner and less noticeable than the other two layers encourages the use of the term couplet.) As was explained in the section on the evaporites of northwest Alberta, calcium carbonate precipitates out of sea water before it becomes evaporated sufficiently to precipitate anhydrite (calcium sulfate). Since there is thus a distinct difference in sea-water concentrations at the times when the two chemicals precipitate out of the water, the calcium carbonate forms the first microlayer; and then the anhydrite is added later, after more evaporation takes place. Figure 19 is a photograph of three of the well cores of banded anhydrite studied by Dean. In the figure notice the thinness of the couplets, as judged by the scale of millimeters near the top. Dean found the mean thickness of the thousands of couplets he measured to be 1.1 to 2.0 millimeters.[9]

2. Horizontally, there is a remarkable uniformity of the couplet layers over a broad area of the Delaware basin. Some of the individual couplets can be traced laterally from well to well for a distance of 60 kilometers (37 miles), by noting the exact percentages of their chemical composition, and by correlating the thicknesses of the series of couplets immediately above and below.[10] This is an indication that the water which was precipitating the layers was uniformly concentrated over a broad area, and was very quiet (non-turbulent).[11] Further evidence of the calm nature of the basin during the deposition of these layers is found in the fact that the latter contain no large amounts of terrigenous (land-derived) sediments, and no evidence of volcanic activity.

3. The thicknesses of the microlayers of calcium carbonate and anhydrite were found to be in proportions very similar to those precipitated upon evaporation of ordinary sea water. Thus, in each couplet, the calcium carbonate layer is much thinner than is the anhydrite, as one would predict from a knowledge of the calcium carbonate and calcium sulfate content of sea water. (See Table 1 for "total deposit" amounts from one liter of sea water, and Table 3 for the actual thicknesses of some of the mineral layers in the drilling cores studied by Dean.) Dean lists the thicknesses of the microlayers in 12,800 couplets which he carefully measured.[12] This consistent proportion of the two minerals in the couplets is more than sufficient evidence that the layers were being formed by actual evaporating sea water, rather than by some other fluid mixture or solution.

4. The thin organic layer which exists in most couplets is

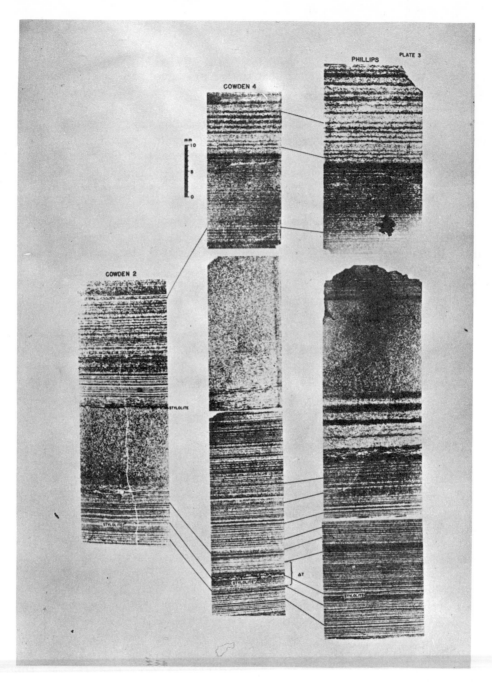

Fig. 19. Photographs of three vertical-column thin sections of the
well cores used by Walter Dean in his studies of the Delaware basin.
The strips of well core were ground thin enough for light to pass
through for photographing. The light layers are anhydrite, and the
dark layers calcite; thus many evaporitic couplets are seen in each
column. Note the scale bar near the top. (Its total length was 10
millimeters as the photograph was taken.) The slanting lines con-
necting the core sections identify the same couplet in two (or three)
wells. The wells, designated as "Cowden # 2, Cowden # 4, and Phillips," are approximately 6.5 and 15 miles apart, respectively, in
Culberson Co., Texas. From W. E. Dean, Jr., Petrologic and geochemical variations in the Permian Castile, varved anhydrite, Delaware
basin, Texas and New Mexico, Ph.D. dissertation, University of New
Mexico, 1967, 326 p., Plate 3. (By permission of the author.)

103

TABLE 3. A sample listing of thickness measurements of the banded anhydrite couplet layers from the Delaware basin. These are from the "D-zone" of the "Cowden no. 2 core," from the Cowden no. 2 well in Culberson County, Texas. W. E. Dean, "Petrologic and Geochemical Variations in the Permian Castile Varved Anhydrite, Delaware Basin, Texas and New Mexico," The University of New Mexico, 1967 (Ph.D. Dissertation), p. 279, 282, 285.

Couplet number	Thickness of calcium carbonate and organic layers (combined)	Thickness of anhydrite layer	Total thickness of couplet
1	0.20 mm	1.10 mm	1.30
2	0.30	0.80	1.10
3	0.30	1.30	1.60
4	0.20	1.30	1.50
5	0.20	0.70	0.90
6	0.30	1.10	1.40
7	0.40	0.74	1.14
8	0.20	1.24	1.44
9	0.30	1.12	1.42
10	0.30	0.92	1.22

evidently a record of the biological growth which was going on during the part of each year when the salinity of the water was lower. This was apparently a period of abundant growth of the smaller (microscopic) forms of plants and animals which ordinarily grow in the sea--just as occurred in the formation of the laminated anhydrite which is over the Rainbow reefs discussed in the previous chapter. It is possible that the growth was mainly that of floating organisms which settled to the bottom to form the organic layer each year. On the other hand, the organic layer could have been formed by microscopic size algae growing on the bottom, covering over the previously deposited layer of mineral.[13]

Dean's research included measuring the percentage of organic matter in the evaporitic couplets, by an oxidation process. He made this measurement on several hundred sections from the well cores. The percentage of organic matter in most couplets ranged from 0.15% to 0.60%.[14] This is a very significant amount, representing an abundant growth of microorganisms in the water each year. The layer of organic matter is usually found either just beneath, or mixed with, the calcium carbonate; both being beneath the layer of anhydrite of the couplet. This is the relationship which would be expected. The usual, expected order would be, first the dying of the microscopic organisms, due to rising salt concentration and (probably) rising temperature as the seasonal temperature increased. Next, or simultaneously with the death and settling of the microorganisms would be the precipitation of the calcium carbonate. Finally, when the water reached a salt concentration of five to six times that of ordinary sea water, the anhydrite could precipitate on top of the calcite and organic deposit which had been formed a few weeks or months before. This is the usual order found in the couplets.[15]

So, here in the Delaware basin we see a body of sediments which was laid down year after year in an orderly manner, constantly subject to definite natural controls. Evidently a major change in the concentration of the sea water took place 200,000 times, with the concentration coming back each time to at least very near the same value. This is somewhat comparable to the forming of rings in a tree trunk, in which case the laying down of the cellulose-lignin layers of which the rings are composed is under the definite control of natural laws. The laminated anhydrite series of the Delaware basin is, in the realm of precipitation, what tree rings are in the biological realm. It is true that we are not able to determine with absolute certainty that only one couplet of the laminated anhydrite was formed each year. But since the laws of precipitation of these same minerals are observed in operation today, and since the mineral content of the sea water was low enough for the growth of organisms during each cycle, we can be certain that no large number of couplets could have been formed in any one year.

Thus we can say that the microlayered anhydrite deposits which filled the Delaware basin are not only extensive and widespread, but are meaningful in their minute structure. They show the regularity of the periodic changes of environment which fostered the deposition, as well as the chemical nature of the water during this long period of time. We can also observe what the relationship of these deposits of banded anhydrite was to the reef which surrounded them. In most cases these deposits are found lapping up on to the sloping sides of the reef, showing that they were laid down after those parts of the reef had grown. So the deposition of the entire series of banded anhydrite layers most likely came late in the history of the basin.

Thicknesses and Their Meaning

Concerning the thickness of the entire series of evaporitic couplets, it was pointed out earlier that this was found to be approximately 1,300 feet, in the area of most intensive study. In the eastern and southern parts of the basin, the total thickness is often over 1,600 feet, and in at least one place is 2,600 feet. (In some places this includes layers of common salt which are interstratified with the anhydrite.)[16] It should be remembered that this Castile evaporite deposit extends over almost the entire Delaware basin.

The extent and thickness of this evaporite deposit brings up the question of how much sea water had to be evaporated in order to form it. In Chapter 5, footnote no. 27, we pointed out that five meters (16 feet) of sea water contains enough calcium carbonate to form a layer one-half millimeter thick, and enough calcium sulfate to produce 2.2 millimeters of anhydrite. Thus approximately 400 miles depth of water is required for producing even a 1,000 foot deposit of anhydrite. This means that the equivalent of at least that much depth of water had to flow into the Delaware basin (at times of high tide, storms, etc.) and evaporate, in order to produce such a deposit. Even at an evaporation rate of 16 feet per year, which is practically the highest marine evaporation rate known today, 135,000 years would be required for producing a 1,000 foot deposit of anhydrite. Dean took this evaporation rate into account in arriving at his conclusion that each of the couplets in the series of 200,000 represents an annual deposit.[17] Thus his estimate of the length of time is reasonable.

Therefore, since these broad, uniform beds of microlayers have all the characteristics of a series of natural deposits, produced by the well-known laws of concentration and precipitation in a quiet body of water, we can be sure they are "genuine." Because of the uniform nature of these microlayers over many miles horizontally, and throughout many hundreds of feet vertically, any possible speculation about such layers of minerals having emerged from mysterious, hidden storage depots deeper in the ground would obviously be out of order. If the calcium carbonate and anhydrite were found in huge, irregular masses, and without the layers of organic matter, such a speculation would be within reason. But when this orderly, natural depositional record is viewed as it actually exists, the Christian is instinctively led to think back to the principle of God's consistency in upholding the natural laws which He originally established. Actually, it is a thrilling experience just to realize that such splendid, dependable records of the past have been left undisturbed for our information in this century of scientific research. God is graciously allowing man to learn some of the mysteries which were once hidden in the earth's crust.

Deposits Above and Beneath

While considering the extensive sedimentary deposits which formed the Capitan reef, and filled the basin which it surrounds, we must not forget the significance of the fossiliferous sediments above and below. The reef and the banded anhydrite layers which we have described make up only from one-eighth to one-tenth of the local stratigraphic column in that area. Many of the wells have to penetrate more than 3,000 feet of sandstone, shale, dolostone, and thick evaporite layers before reaching the top of the reef. Most of these layers of contrasting sediments were applied by various processes within the sea water which continued to cover the area for long periods of time. Frequently these covering layers are in an alternating series similar to the covering layers in the Alberta oil fields; and a good number of the strata contains identifiable fossils. Some of the uppermost strata may have been deposited in a fresh-water environment, but most are marine. (See Tables 4 and 5 for a summary of the deposits which lie above and beneath the level of the reef. Note in Table 4 that a very high percentage of the covering layers consists of the evaporites anhydrite and common salt.) To this point, we have not made mention of these Salado and Rustler deposits, and will not take time to discuss them in this book.[18] They are similar to some of the evaporitic layers which lie above the tops of the Canadian atolls and pinnacle reefs which we described in the preceding chapter. Above the Salado and Rustler evaporitic layers in Texas are sandstones and shale as listed in the table. Both of the latter were laid down by water, but not in an evaporitic environment.

Perhaps we should mention here the possibility of a participation of the Biblical Flood in the formation of the upper layers covering the Delaware basin of west Texas and New Mexico. Of course none of the evaporites could have been deposited by the Flood, and not many, if any, of the shales. (The Flood was a period of great water turbulence and so could not deposit any appreciable amount of uniform layers of fine clay particles such as we find in these shales.) We must not forget that the Bible very explicitly tells us that the flood waters dried up within one year after the Flood began (Genesis 7:11 and 8:13-14). Thus the many months required for the settling out of enough clay particles to form even a few feet of shale were not present as a part of the Flood. And besides, a glance at Table 4 will soon reveal the fact that the shale layers are in the wrong place in relation to the conglomeritic sandstone, in order to have been laid down by the Flood. Sandstone particles are much larger than clay particles, so they settle out of suspension sooner than do clay particles. This would put the conglomeritic sandstone beneath the shale, instead of above it.

Now it is possible that the Flood could have deposited the final,

TABLE 4. The strata which lie above the level of the Capitan reef, at the site of the Socony Mobil No. 1 Moore well in the western edge of Pecos County, Texas. (Based on the map "Cross Section Through Delaware and Val Verde Basins, From Lea County, New Mexico to Edwards County, Texas," West Texas Geological Society, Publication no. 64-49, 1963.)

Geologic Period	Thickness in feet	Description of strata (beginning with the uppermost, ground-level deposit)
Quaternary (the most recent Period)	75 ft.	Conglomeritic sandstone
Triassic	125	Red shale
Upper Permian	550	Red sandstone
	125	Anhydrite (uppermost deposit of Rustler Formation)
	350	Dolostone interstratified with layers of anhydrite
	2,400	Salt (NaCl) interstratified with thick beds of dolomite anhydrite (the Salado Formation)

108

TABLE 5. The strata which lie beneath the level of the Capitan reef, at the site of the Richardson and Bass No. 1 Harrison-Federal test well, in Eddy County, New Mexico. (Based on P. W. Hughes, "New Mexico's Deepest Oil Test," in Fifth Field Conference Guidebook, New Mexico Geological Society, 1954, p. 124-130; and the map "Cross Section Through Delaware and Val Verde Basins, From Lea County, New Mexico, to Edwards County, Texas," West Texas Geological Society, Publication no. 64-49, 1963.)

Geologic Period	Thickness in feet	Description of strata (The beginning depth below the surface is 4,300 ft.)
Permian	700 ft.	Sandstone interstratified with layers of shale and limestone (This is the uppermost of the series given in this table, and is the upper part of the Bell Canyon Formation.)
	400	Limestone interstratified with sandstone layers and a few shale layers
	850	Sandstone interstratified with layers of shale and of limestone
	50	Limestone interstratified with shale layers
	1,500	Sandstone interstratified with shale layers (continuous sandstone for 90 or 100 feet of thickness in three parts of this segment)
	1,100	Limestone interstratified with shale layers (continuous limestone for 100 feet in one part)
	300	Sandstone interstratified with limestone and shale layers
	10	Dolostone
	900	Limestone interstratified with shale and sandstone layers
	120	Limestone
	60	Limestone interstratified with shale and sandstone layers
	90	Limestone
	200	Limestone interstratified with shale layers
	80	Limestone
	150	Limestone interstratified with layers of shale
	550	Sandstone interstratified with layers of limestone (continuous sandstone for 90 feet of the thickness in one part of this segment)
	1,900	Limestone interstratified with shale layers
	70	Shale
	400	Shale interstratified with a few limestone layers
	20	Limestone
Pennsylvanian	1,150	Limestone interstratified with shale layers
	450	Shale interstratified with layers of sandstone
Mississippian	370	Shale interstratified with layers of sandstone
	330	Dark gray to black shale
	100	Shale interstratified with limestone layers
	300	Limestone with small amounts of chert
	120	Shale
Silurian	70	Limestone
	1,100	Dolostone (the "Fusselman dolomite")
Ordovician	250	Limestone with small amounts of chert
	150	Limestone
	175	Shale interstratified with limestone layers
	50	Limestone
	125	Sandstone
	50	Shale interstratified with layers of limestone
	150	Limestone interstratified with layers of sandstone
	1,000	Dolostone (the "Ellenberger dolomite"). This lies directly on the igneous-metamorphic precambrian base (depth below surface, 19,800 ft.).

75 foot surface covering of conglomeritic sandstone, which is listed in Table 4. This is sandstone with various sizes of pebbles and other rock fragments mixed in with it. Both the sand and the larger fragments are dense enough to settle out of moving water, and thus could have been deposited by the Flood. Of course we have no proof of what happened in Texas at the time of the Flood, but if any part of the present local stratigraphic column in the western edge of Pecos County was formed by the Flood it was this 75 feet of sandstone. The 125 feet of shale beneath it is nothing like what a violent, short-lived flood could produce.

Now to return a moment to the deposits which are lower down in this stratigraphic column of west Texas. Those beneath the Capitan reef are even more impressive than those which are above--at least from the standpoint of thickness. In most parts of the Delaware basin this amounts to more than 12,000 feet of sedimentary strata, and in the southeastern part it is 20,000 feet. (Table 5 shows the layers which are present in the northern part of the basin.) As is also true of most of the deposits which cover the reef, the layers in these lower deposits are usually flat and regular (even), showing that the particles settled out slowly from water which was not in rapid motion. These layers, at most levels, have a very different composition from those of the reef. They also show that they were marine, rather than freshwater, by the types of fossils preserved in them. Some of the kinds of fossils present in the strata beneath the reef are: (a) different kinds of brachiopods (a "seashell-type" of animal, some of which resemble scallops in appearance), (b) several genera, and many species, of the order Foraminifera (small, marine animals, most of which in this case had thick shells), (c) ostracods (one group of crustaceans), and (d) fossilized plant spores of the genus Tasmanites.[19]

The fact that these are present assures us that the deep layers we are considering were formed after these creatures had been created and had had time to multiply.

So we see that when all the main types of sedimentary strata of the Delaware basin are considered, we have an extensive record of a large part of the biological growth in the seas since the original events of the creation of life took place.[20] The great deposits of limestone and dolostone which lie beneath the Capitan reef (Table 5) necessarily represent immense periods of time, because of the nature of these two kinds of rock. When viewing these we must of course realize that the deepest strata were formed first, and the layers above were formed in turn at later times. (It should be obvious that, because of the law of gravity, there is no way that a new layer of sedimentary particles could be "slipped in" underneath an older layer, out across the bottom of the sea.)

Then the main intervals of time which elapsed after the laying down of these deep strata are as follows (given in the order of their occurrence as one progresses up the stratigraphic column of that locality): (a) sufficient time for the growth of the reef, (b) the many cycles of climatic change necessary for producing the 200,000 microlayers of banded anhydrite, (c) the additional periods of evaporation necessary to produce the thick covering layers of anhydrite and salt above the reef, and (d) sufficient time for the application (depositing) of the top parts of the stratigraphic column in that area.

FOOTNOTES

1. K. K. Landes, Petroleum Geology, 1951, p. 425.

2. C. W. Achauer, "Origin of Capitan Formation, Guadalupe Mountains, New Mexico and Texas," American Association of Petroleum Geologists Bulletin, v. 53 (1969), p. 2317-2321.

3. N. D. Newell, et al., The Permian Reef Complex of the Guadalupe Mountains Region, Texas and New Mexico, 1953, p. 9.

4. Ibid., p. 38.

5. The Bible-science writers who have occasionally suggested that the Capitan reef might have been formed rapidly by means of the Flood have done so without investigating the major (buried) part of the reef, and without taking into account the many in situ fossils it contains, or the evaporite coverings which lie around and upon it. (Moving water dissolves evaporite minerals, rather than depositing them.)

6. C. G. St. C. Kendall, "An Environmental Re-interpretation of the Permian Evaporite-Carbonate Shelf Sediments of the Guadalupe Mountains," Geological Society of America Bulletin, v. 80 (1969), p. 2503-2521.

7. Some reef-forming calcareous algae have the ability to grow in brine which is concentrated enough to precipitate anhydrite, so the presence of these more mild brines would not necessarily kill the reefs entirely. (L. L. Sloss, "Evaporite Deposition from Layered Solutions," American Association of Petroleum Geologists Bulletin, v. 53 (1969), p. 779.) Even if the reef growth was entirely stopped at times by brines, this would only agree with the fact that there are unconformities evident in the reef, as stated above.

8. Walter E. Dean, Jr., "Petrologic and Geochemical Variations in the Permian Castile Varved Anhydrite, Delaware Basin, Texas and New Mexico," The University of New Mexico, 1967 (Ph.D. Dissertation). (Some of this same material can be found in R. Y. Anderson, Walter E. Dean, Jr., et al., "Permian Castile Varved Evaporite Sequence, West Texas and New Mexico," Geological Society of America Bulletin, v. 83 (1972), p. 59-86.

9. Dean, "Petrologic and Geochemical Variations," p. iii, and 71.

10. Ibid., p. 15, 73-75, 143-145.

11. Further evidence of the calm nature of the basin during the deposition of these layers is found in the fact that the latter contain no large amounts of terrigenous (land-derived) sediments, and no evidence of volcanic activity.

12. Ibid., p. 214-287. One will note that the ratios of calcium carbonate to calcium sulfate in these tables are not always exactly the same, nor do they exactly correspond to the ratio shown in Table 1. This is because of the fact that the sea water did not evaporate to exactly the same concentration for each cycle. Thus, in some cycles the sea water gave up more of its calcium sulfate than in others. A related fact which is of interest is that, on the eastern side of the Delaware basin, evaporation frequently reached the point at which common salt (NaCl) begins to precipitate, so that on that side of the basin there are salt layers interbedded with the banded anhydrite. (Ibid., p. 11-12.)

13. Gerald M. Friedman has recently reported finding algal mats growing on the bottom in brine that is precipitating calcium sulfate in the form of gypsum. This is forming alternating gypsum and organic layers in shallow water near the southernmost tip of the Sinai Peninsula. (G. M. Friedman, "Generation of Laminated Gypsum in Sea-Marginal Pool, Red Sea" (abstract), American Association of Petroleum Geologists Bulletin, v. 57 (1973), p. 780.

14. Dean, "Petrologic and Geochemical Variations," p. 29-32, 288-307.

15. In some couplets there are two organic layers close together, with calcium carbonate between. However, it is rather obvious that this merely represents two periods of prolific growth of aquatic organisms, with only a short interruption between. (Ibid., p. 66-67, 148-149.)

16. Ibid., p. 12-13, and Figure 7.

17. Since the calcium carbonate and organic matter make up only about 20 per cent of each couplet, there are approximately 1,000 feet of actual anhydrite in this 1,300 foot of banded anhydrite on the western side of the basin. Dean estimated that 200,000 years for forming this amount of anhydrite requires a marine evaporation rate (2 meters per year) which is very similar to that known for most arid regions of today (Ibid., p. 144).

18. For a description of the alternating layers of salt and anhydrite, of which the Salado Formation is largely composed, see W. B. Lang, "Basal Beds of Salado Formation in Fletcher Potash Core Test, Near Carlsbad, New Mexico," American Association of Petroleum Geologists Bulletin, v. 26 (1942), p. 63-79; and also "Cycle of Deposition in the Salado Formation of the Permian of New Mexico and Texas," by the same author, American Association of Petroleum Geologists Bulletin, v. 60 (1949), p. 1903.

112

19. P. W. Hughes, "New Mexico's Deepest Oil Test," in Fifth
Field Conference Guidebook, New Mexico Geological Society, 1954,
p. 130; R. F. Meyer, Geology of Pennsylvanian and Wolfcampian Rocks
in Southeast New Mexico, New Mexico Bureau of Mines and Mineral
Resources Memoir 17, 1966, p. 13-29; and S. P. Ellison, Jr., "Subsurface Woodford Black Shale, West Texas, and Southeast New Mexico,"
in Bureau of Economic Geology, University of Texas Report of Investigations no. 7, p. 12-15.

20. This is not to say that all time periods of the past are
represented in the local stratigraphic column at this geographic
location. A few periods, including the Jurassic and Cretaceous,
are missing. Either they were never deposited, or they were eroded
off into the sea, after having been laid down. If one should wish
to relate the depositional time periods of the Delaware basin area
to the Rainbow oil fields of northwestern Alberta, he may do so by
comparing Table 2 with Tables 4 and 5. It will be noted that the
Mississippian Period appears in both the fields of Alberta and those
of west Texas and New Mexico. This means that, judged by the close
similarity of the fossils in the Canadian strata to those of the
Mississippian deposits in the Delaware basin, the two areas were
being formed simultaneously.

CHAPTER 7

THE BAHAMA BANKS—LIMESTONE IN THE MAKING

In this age of rapid air transportation many people have become familiar with "The Bahamas" as a great recreation and vacation area. There are scores of beautiful islands, surrounded by warm, clear waters which attract people from all over the United States, Canada, and Europe. But a look at the map (Figure 20) will show that there is more than just a group of islands here. Note from the several small numbers indicating water depth (in feet) that there are great shallow-water areas stretching out for many miles from the islands. These are the upper surfaces of the Bahama Banks, which stand high above the ocean floor. The Great Bahama Bank is approximately 80 miles wide and over 300 miles long, and the Little Bahama Bank is 50 by 150 miles.

Perhaps the most remarkable feature of these banks is their flat-topped nature, and their very steep sides, which plunge rapidly to great depths. All across the platforms (tops) of the bank the water is only from 3 to 20 feet deep, but the sides then suddenly drop off, allowing the water to become over one-half mile deep on the west side of the Great Bahama Bank and approximately one mile in depth on the east. In fact, one needs to go only 10 miles east of the edge of the platform, in the region of Cat Island, to be in water which is nearly 3 miles deep.

The Banks as Geologic Structures

What then is the significance of these great, flat-topped, slightly submerged plateaus which tower above the ocean floor? The key to their significance lies in the types of carbonate sediments of which they are composed. So we will have to consider those types to get a full picture of these banks in relation to time. However, as a preliminary statement we can point out that the sediments, as well as the geometric form, of the Banks show that these great structures have not been hastily or haphazardly formed. They were built up from the bottom by the gradual accumulation of carbonate sediments such as those which are still being produced daily all across their upper surface. In fact, the Bahama Banks are composed almost entirely of pure carbonate sediments--some sand-sized, some smaller, and some larger. Most of these, except in the upper surface of the banks, are now lithified, and are thus limestone and dolostone. "Who" then are the builders? All the host of lime-secreting organisms, both animal and plant, which live there in the warm tropical waters.[1]

Types of Sediments Which Form the Banks

There are coral reefs on several parts of the Bahama Banks, and the corals and other organisms which grow with them have contributed a great deal of sediment ("skeletal sand"). However, the

113

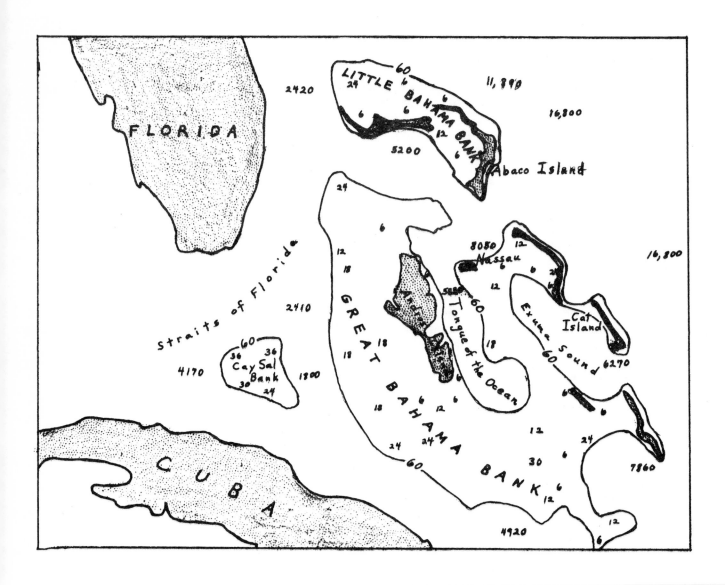

Figure 20. The Bahama Banks. The numbers are water depths, in feet,
at representative points. The 60 foot contour line is on the outer
edges of the Banks. Scale: 1 inch = approximately 75 miles.

sediments from the reefs make up only a small proportion of the total accumulation. There are broad stretches of shallow water with sandy bottom which are not near to any coral growths. The sand in these areas has a high proportion of fecal pellets, oöids, and other nonskeletal carbonate grains (that is, grains which are not actually pieces of the skeletons of animals or calcareous plants). These nonskeletal grains are now being formed continuously, and are present at numerous levels deep in the Banks, as revealed by deep core drillings.

Fecal pellets are formed by small marine animals, especially burrowing worms and snails, but also by several other types. These animals eat large quantities of the finer particles (lime mud), in much the same way that burrowing earthworms do in terrestrial soil. The marine worms, snails, crustaceans, etc. extract the organic food material from the mud, and then expel the leftover lime mud in compacted pellets. These pellets are held together for a time by the mucus which they derived from the animal's intestine, and are later cemented together by very fine crystals of calcium carbonate which form inside the pellet, and sometimes over its surface. A high proportion of these pellets permanently retain the ellipsoidal shape in which they were formed in the intestine. In a few parts of the Bahama Banks they make up as much as 30% of the total sediment covering the bottom.[2]

Oöids (sometimes called "oöliths") are another important type of sand grain found in abundance on many parts of the Banks. A mass of oöids together is called "oölitic sand," or "oölite" if it has been lithified to form rock.[3] Oöids are sand-sized grains which have one or more coats of microscopic-size, needle-like crystals of calcium carbonate around them. Sometimes the "nucleus" (original part which received the coatings) is a very small fragment of a marine shell, but it can be practically any small sand particle. When an oöid which has several coats of crystals is cut in two, the coats show as concentric rings (as in Figure 21). One remarkable feature is that the crystals of these layers are arranged in very orderly patterns. When they are viewed under high magnification the arrangement is often found to be radial (with the "needles" pointing outward from the center). These needle-like crystals are composed of one of the pure forms of calcium carbonate which is called aragonite.[4]

The formation of oöids is one of the many slow but orderly processes which goes on in the sea. However, they can form in only very special environments. There must be (a) warm, very shallow water, (b) a moderate amount of turbulence, such as is produced by a strong ocean current coming up over the western edges on to the Bahama Banks, (c) the proper amount of calcium carbonate and carbon dioxide, and (d) probably one or more kinds of organic action by algae or bacteria. When these conditions are present the crystalline coatings are gradually precipitated on to the grains as the ocean current causes them to roll back and forth on the bottom.

The final type of carbonate grains which we will mention here

116

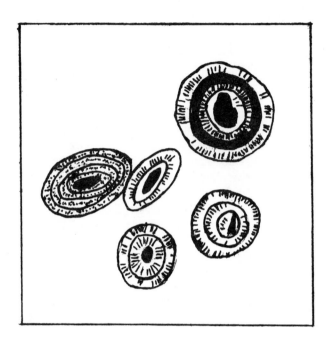

Fig. 21. Drawing of oöids (also called oöliths) which have
been cut and ground thin enough for light to pass through.
These oöids are composed of calcium carbonate, and the radiating lines in the layers are crystals of this mineral. Note
the dark center which in each case is a part of the original
grain around which the concentric layers were precipitated.
Oöids such as this are a major component of certain beds of
limestone, as in the Redwall Formation of the Grand Canyon.
They are also being formed today in many places; for example,
in parts of the Florida coasts, and on the Bahama Banks.
Magnification approximately 30X.

is the very small mineral crystals produced inside of some marine
algae. In the shallow water of the Bahamas, as well as off the
coasts of Florida, the alga Penicillus grows abundantly, forming
microscopic crystals of calcium carbonate within its tissues. Because of the abundance and rapid growth of this alga, great quantities
of the crystals are produced, forming an important component of the
"lime mud" part of the sediments.[5] Thus one should never think of
lime mud as a structureless or unimportant form of matter.

Let us then keep in mind that the carbonate components which
make up the Bahama Banks are of several types--some formed by the
slow processes of organic growth and others by gradual precipitation
of aragonite crystals. This fact becomes even more meaningful when
we realize that these are the processes by which the Bahama Banks
were built up.

The building processes which are now going on are readily observable in numerous locations. The accumulation of reef sediments
occurs mainly on the eastern sides of the Banks. There, the reef
organisms can benefit from the freshly oxygenated ocean water which
is brought in by the prevailing winds from the east. However, the
building of sand bars, cays, and other observable sedimentary structures occurs in many parts where there are no reefs to produce
sediments. An example of this is seen in the "pseudoatolls" which
are being formed to the north of Andros Island. These are circular-
to-elongate cays with a shallow lagoon in their centers. They are
composed primarily of oölitic sand, and project just above the water
level. They lie in the path of reversing tidal currents which deposit this non-skeletal sand in crescent-shaped ridges, first on
one side and then on the other.[6] This is one example of how effective
a sedimentary building process can be, even without the aid of any
reef-forming organisms. It also illustrates some of the processes
which undoubtedly participated in the formation of what are now the
deeper parts of the Bahama Banks, in the past.

Test drillings which have been made into the deeper layers of
the Great Bahama Bank show that the entire mass is composed of carbonate materials, part in the form of limestone and part in the form
of dolostone. Much of the limestone, and some of the dolostone,
contains large amounts of oöids, fecal pellets, skeletal fragments,
and Foraminifera shells which can still be identified. Therefore,
the drilling samples show us that the deep parts of the Bank were
formed from basically the same kinds of materials that are being
produced today. And the fact that, at various places in the Bahamian
stratigraphic column, there is a layer containing large quantities
of oöids, is an indication that each such layer was produced at
shallow depths (when the Bank was higher with respect to sea level).
It is also important to realize that nearly all of the sediments
of which the Bahama Banks are composed are very different from the
very fine-grain sediments (oozes) which make up most of the ocean
floors.

118

The Deepest Test Well

The region of the Bahamas is not a petroleum producing area, because no impervious layers such as shale and evaporites for retaining the oil or gas have been found. However, because of the close similarity between the Bahamian carbonate deposits and those located deep in some of the oil fields of the world, the oil companies have done a great deal of study of the Bahama Banks. They have done this in order to better understand those carbonate deposits which do have oil-retaining impervious layers covering them. The deepest of the test wells drilled in the Bahamas is the one made in 1947 by the Superior Oil Company, on Andros Island.[7] Andros is the largest island on the Banks. The deposits which are above sea level, making up the island itself, are composed chiefly of eolian dunes of limestone, old reefs, and old cemented beach ridges which mark the level at which the sea stood at various times in the past. The dune limestone has a very high percentage of oöids. These were piled up by winds, into dune formations. The winds carried them from the broad, flat, exposed upper surface of the Banks, as the sea level was lowering.[8]

The Superior Oil Company selected the northern end of Andros Island as the site for the deepest test well, and drilled to a depth of 14,585 feet. The drillers had expected to penetrate to the base of the Bank, but had to stop at this depth because of the loss of some of the drilling pipe in the bottom of the hole. To the very bottom they were cutting through various grades of limestone and dolostone. The cores and other samples of these have been studied in detail by numerous specialists in sedimentology, who have found them to be made up of shallow-water, marine sediment components very similar to those which are being formed today on the Banks.

The entire stratigraphic column is listed in detail by Goodell and Garman.[9] The types of rock, kinds of grains, and kinds of identifiable fossils are shown for the various depth levels. The entire list includes 62 descriptive entries. We have given a sampling of these entries from a few of the depth levels in Table 6. Notice in this table that almost every description gives the characteristics of the rock or other sedimentary material for at least 100 feet of depth (just as in the original table in Goodell and Garman).

It should be remembered that each 100 foot (or more) segment of rock in the well includes numerous subdivisional layers. Each of these many changes in the type of limerock or dolostone in the column represents at least a minor change in the environment in which the sediments of the layers were being formed. Such changes can include alterations in the water temperature, the water depth, the mineral and carbon dioxide content of the water, and the amount of turbulence. Each of these has a major influence on the type of sediment and rock which will be produced.

The Nature of the Deeper Layers

Numerous observers who have studied the drilling records and

TABLE 6. Representative samples of sections from the deepest boring into the Bahama Banks. (The items are quoted from H. G. Goodell and R. K. Garman, "Carbonate Geochemistry of Superior Deep Test Well, Andros Island, Bahamas," American Association of Petroleum Geologists Bulletin, v. 53 (1969), p. 533-536.

Depth from which cores and other samples were taken (in feet)	Description of cores and other samples
734-771	Microcrystalline to very finely crystalline dolomite with several fairly well-preserved, dolomitized fossils....
2,200-2,640	Fragmental limestone (composed mainly of fragments of micro-fossils). Matrix, where present, is dense microcrystalline calcite. Recrystallization is slight and there is no obvious solution.
4,270-4,335	Interbedded limestone, dolomitic limestone, and calcitic dolomite. Limestone is dense with included oöliths, pellets, and small microfossils. Irregular, discontinuous laminae of carbonaceous material are present....
4,830-4,940	Dense, calcitic dolomite with oöliths, pellets, and fossil fragments.
6,370-6,560	Microcrystalline, dolomite with vugs filled or lined with clear, very finely crystalline dolomite. A few fossils are present, but are poorly preserved because of replacement by very finely crystalline dolomite.
10,395-10,413	Limestone composed largely of microfossil fragments with soft, microcrystalline matrix....
10,413-10,617	No samples because of lost circulation.
10,617-10,640	Finely crystalline dolomite with a few patches of micro-crystalline limestone. A few fairly well preserved fossils and fossil fragments are present. Rock is relatively porous because of many small vugs and pores. Paleontology: miliolids, pelecypods.
14,575-14,585	Dense, calcitic dolomite with scattered small fossils. Dolomite is microcrystalline to finely crystalline with trace of intercrystalline porosity. No fractures are evident.

samples taken from the Superior Oil Company well have been impressed by the several sudden changes from limestone to dolostone, as one proceeds up or down this stratigraphic column. Also, within the bodies of limestone and of dolostone of the Bahama Banks there are abrupt changes to other varieties of these rock types. Any change from limestone to dolostone is highly significant, because it represents not only a change in the marine environment, but also a period of many years for converting the carbonate sediments to dolostone. This important principle will be explained in the latter part of this chapter.

We know that limestone is forming on the Banks, and on shallow sea floors in other parts of the world, by the cementing together of carbonate grains such as those described above. Whenever a particular, favorable set of environmental circumstances exists, a layer of one variety of limestone is formed from the carbonate sediments which are present. Later, a change in one or more factors of the environment results in the formation of a somewhat different variety of limestone.

A familiar example of a type of limestone which is now forming by the cementing together of carbonate sediment grains is what is called "beach rock." Beach rock sometimes forms within less than a human lifetime, on tropical and subtropical beaches, in some parts of the world. Sometimes pieces of it are found to contain man-made objects such as beer bottles.[10] However, such rapid limestone formation is unknown in other types of environments. Cementation proceeds very slowly except in an environment where the sediment mass can be exposed to rainwater at least part of the time. The process consists of a gradual forming of minute crystals of calcium carbonate mineral in between the pellets, oöids, and other types of grains of which the rock layer is formed. Figure 22 shows some of this type of crystal. Such crystals are easily observed in practically any limestone or dolostone, with a high-magnification petrographic microscope. (In order to observe the cement crystals, the piece of rock must be sawed and then ground so thin that light will pass through it.) Ancient sedimentary carbonate rocks, as well as young ones, show this cementation when examined microscopically.

The carbonate substance for the process of cementation is carried to the grains by the mineral-laden water which circulates between them. This type of cementation, if it is to occur, has to be accomplished while the proper type of water and water circulation are available. Deep burial usually cuts off the necessary type of water supply needed for cementation. This is one of the reasons why the Bahama Banks could not have been formed by any sudden or rapid piling up of sediments.

We should also mention here that geologists have found convincing evidence that some of these deep limestone layers of the Great Bahama Bank were lithified during periods of exposure. Apparently there were times when the upper surface of the Bank was even higher with respect to sea level than now, allowing exposure to rainwater.

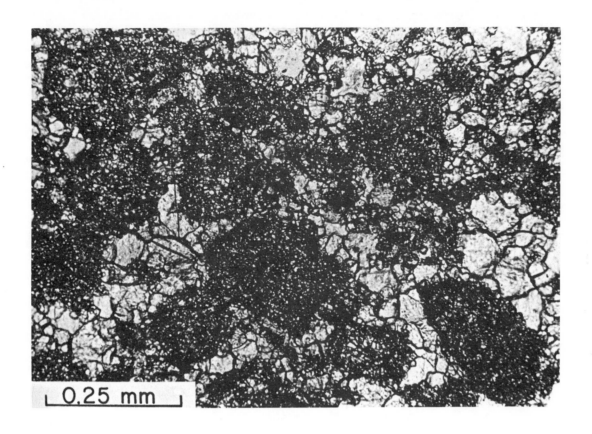

Fig. 22. Peloidal limestone from the Lost Burro Formation in east-central California (Middle-Upper Devonian).
This is a magnified view of calcium carbonate crystals
of cement, together with several peloids (or pellets)
which have been cemented together by the crystals. The
cement crystals are the white, angular blocks; the peloids
are the large dark masses. A considerable proportion of
the limestone deposits of the world show this type of
texture. Note the scale bar; thus the magnification is
approximately 150 diameters. Photomicrograph by D. H.
Zenger, Dept. of Geology, Pomona College.

During such periods fresh-water cementation of the carbonate grains could take place. (Cementation by fresh water just above sea level is a common occurrence.) One of the evidences for periods of exposure above sea level is the discovery of large "solution cavities" which have at one time been dissolved out of some of the buried limestone layers by fresh water. Since the sea water in low latitudes such as this is at or near the saturation point with respect to calcium carbonate, it does not dissolve limestone sufficiently for forming such cavities.[11]

Another line of evidence indicating that the Bahama Banks were formed very gradually, over a long period of time, is the almost complete absence of land-derived (terrigenous) sediments within the entire stratigraphic column in that locality. If the Banks had been built up from sediments brought in from elsewhere, it would have been impossible to have formed a 14,500 foot stratigraphic column of practically pure carbonate material. This is true especially in view of the fact that the North American continent is close by on the one side, and the large island of Cuba on the other. Both of these could have supplied huge quantities of non-carbonate mud and clay, if there had been any strong transporting force.

Then there is the fact of the extremely steep sides of the Bahama Banks, as an indication of slow formation. When water currents pile up sediments, the mounds they produce have a gentle, broad slope. In order for the steep sides to be formed there has to be lithification of the sediments to form stable rock layers before any appreciable thickness of steep escarpment can be accumulated. Otherwise the new sediments only slump down to low-angle slopes. Thus we can be sure that the Bahama Banks were formed by natural marine sediment production, rather than by some catastrophic means.

The Amount of Time Necessary

Careful measurements of the rate of sediment production on the Bahama Banks have been made. Thirty centimeters of thickness per thousand years is accepted as a close estimate.[12] Since this is very close to one foot per thousand years, one can easily see that 14,500 times 1,000 years would be required for producing the thickness of carbonate materials which was found in the deep test well which penetrated the Bank at Andros Island. We of course can not say that the time required for the formation of this stratigraphic column was exactly 14,500,000 years. Sediment production rates vary considerably with changes in the environment. However, because of the large part played by algae and marine animals in the production of the sediments, one can not postulate any enormously higher sedimentation rate than now exists.

Another factor to keep in mind is the existence of periods of time which were less favorable for the forming of sediments. At present, the conditions for such production on the Bahama Banks are extremely favorable, especially with respect to water depth. It is evident that subsidence of the Banks in the past has succeeded in maintaining a proper water depth for sediment formation, because all rock, even to the bottom of the deepest test well, is composed of shallow-water marine sediments. In the Superior Oil Company well, excellent oölitic layers were found at several levels, including some below 6,000 feet. (It will be remembered that the formation of oölitic grains requires a very precise shallow-water environment.)

However, during the times when the sea level was lower, and major parts of the Banks were exposed, sediment production was stopped, except around submerged edges of the Banks. Also there were times when the water was too deep for efficient sediment production. For example, during the interglacial period which immediately preceded the last glaciation of North America, when there was no longer a very great quantity of water stored as ice at the poles, the sea level was substantially higher in the Florida-Bahamas area than it is now. This is evidenced in the existence of the Florida "keys," which are old reefs which grew during the period of higher sea level, and then died when they were permanently exposed by the lowering of the water.[13] During periods when any great change of sea level occurs, carbonate sediment production rates are decreased. Just how many periods of lower sedimentation rates there were on the Bahama Banks, we do not know.

Now, to come back to the question of the age of the Banks, the rocks from the bottom of the deepest test wells have been classified as Lower Cretaceous by geologists. The Cretaceous Period is usually dated as much older than the minimum formation time we have stated above. We admit that these Banks could well be much older than the minimum time required for forming the sediments. As pointed out above, there were long delays due to environmental changes. We will allow the reader to choose between the minimal formation time stated above, and the older dates which can be found in standard geology textbooks. However, we do not see in such lengths of time the necessity of an evolutionary sequence such as is often visualized in the standard geologic timetable. This principle was discussed briefly in the subsection "Evolution and Time," in Chapter 4 above.

The Dolostone Sections in the Bahamian Stratigraphic Column

Now that we have seen some of the characteristics of a major geologic structure which is composed of limestone and dolostone, we should consider a few of the specific features of these two kinds of rock.

When the drilling records of the Superior Oil Company's deep test well in the Bahamas are examined, we find several very thick sections of dolostone, as well as considerable thicknesses of limestone. One of the dolostone sections is 3,600 feet in thickness.[14] It is of course somewhat layered, but there is very little material other than dolostone.

The exact method by which these thick deposits of sediment were dolomitized is not known. However, the familiar types of shallow-water sediments and fossils making up the dolostone layers tells us

124

that they were first laid down as calcium carbonate, rather than as
the calcium-magnesium carbonate of which they are now composed. The
conversion to dolostone most likely occurred progressively as new
layers of sediments were added to the Banks. In relation to this,
we should keep in mind that the animals and plants which produce
such a large proportion of the sediments do not have the ability
to secrete dolomite. In fact, most of the animals and plants which
produce skeletal components of limestones have only a very low proportion of magnesium in their shells or other hard parts. Thus
most of the magnesium for dolomitization must be brought into the
sediment mass by water, from elsewhere.[15]

During the past 15 years sedimentary geologists have located
and extensively studied numerous seashore areas where dolomitized
sediments are being formed.[16] One such area, the Trucial Coast of
the Persian Gulf, has already been described in Chapter 5. Another
is on the western shores of Andros Island in the Bahamas. Still
other sites where present-day dolomite formation is taking place
are southern Australia, the Netherlands Antilles, and the Florida
Keys.[17]

There is strong evidence that some dolomite has been slowly
forming by direct precipitation from natural waters, in certain
specialized environments. However, this is an even slower process
than the sediment formation we have described for the Bahamas, and
of course could not form fossils or fecal pellets.[18]

Goodell and Garman cite several types of evidence to show that
the conversion of the Bahama Bank sediments to dolostone occurred
at shallow depths, though not in the exact manner in which the supratidal dolomites are formed today.[19] At least 3 basic facts are
evident: (1) The dolostone was formed from carbonate sediments
similar to those being formed today on the Banks. (2) The fossilized and cemented sediments in the dolostone layers are in natural
proportions, without any appreciable admixture of non-carbonate
materials. (3) The process of conversion of the sediments to calcium-magnesium carbonate (dolomite) was dependent upon (at least
slowly) circulating water for the necessary magnesium ions.[20]

The last point is one to which we have briefly referred in
previous sections, where dolostone was mentioned, but it is so fundamental and universal that overstressing it would be difficult to
do. A large supply of magnesium ions must be carried, in solution,
to every sediment grain which is to be converted to dolomite. Even
if the water is circulating as rapidly as possible through the
sediment mass, there is no really rapid delivery of ions to the
sites of dolomitization. This is true even if the relatively small
magnesium content of natural sea water has been supplemented by
evaporitic conditions or by volcanic-hydrothermal sources such as those
mentioned in Chapter 4. As the water passes through the sediment
mass the supply of magnesium ions is constantly depleted in the
multitude of small channels through which the water is moving. In
each such channel the grains nearest the source of water supply

effectively reduce the magnesium content of the water before the more isolated parts of the sediment mass are reached. Furthermore, the process of ion exchange in the conversion can occur only as the ion-carrying water penetrates and circulates through the sediment grains themselves. This is true, whether the process of dolomite formation is occurring in a submarine location, at the tide level, or above the tide level. Even though there are elements of doubt and disagreement among geologists concerning the details of formation of the ancient deposits of dolostone, there is an almost universal agreement on the necessity of circulating, magnesium-carrying water and ion exchange.

A related process which we must recognize in connection with the conversion of carbonate sediments to dolostone is that of dolostone cementation. By means of this process cement crystals are formed in between the grains of sediment, either after or as the grains are converted to dolomite. The crystals of mineral cement are precipitated from the water which circulates between the grains. Some of these crystals in a mass of dolostone are composed of calcium carbonate, and others of dolomite, depending on the environmental conditions at the time of their formation. Also, a great many of the grains themselves, for example fecal pellets, have internal cement crystals built into them, as was mentioned earlier in this chapter. The cement crystals, both inside of dolostone grains and between the grains, can be observed with a high-magnification petrographic microscope. They are often arranged in beautiful, symmetric patterns.[21]

All of this of course leaves us with the realization that there is no possible way of forming fossiliferous dolostone in a rapid manner, and that large amounts of time have been involved in producing such dolostone deposits. The laws of solubility, dissolution, and ion exchange which God established have been stable since the time of their creation, as have his other physical laws. Thus, our discovery that large sections of the stratigraphic column in the Bahama Banks are composed of dolomitized, biologically formed sediments is one of the proofs that the Banks were formed very slowly, on their present location. Similarly, within many of the deep layers of dolostone in the oil fields, the presence of cemented pellets, oöids, animal fossils, and algal-mat layers in growth position, show us that long periods of time were required for the formation of those deposits.

FOOTNOTES

1. It is likely that inorganic precipitation contributes some to the building process, though not as much as was formerly believed.

2. L. V. Illing, "Bahaman Calcareous Sands," American Association of Petroleum Geologists Bulletin, v. 38 (1954), p. 24-25.

3. The usage of these terms is not uniform in the geologic literature. We will try to use them as outlined by Curt Teichert

126

in the "Discussion" section, _American Association of Petroleum Geologists Bulletin_, v. 54 (1970), p. 1748.

4. J. E. Sanders and G. M. Friedman, "Origin and Occurrence of Limestones," _in_ _Developments in Sedimentology no. 9A, Carbonate Rocks_, 1967, p. 187.

5. R. G. C. Bathurst, _Developments in Sedimentology no. 12, Carbonate Sediments and their Diagenesis_, 1971, p. 139.

6. N. D. Newell and J. K. Rigby, "Geological Studies on the Great Bahama Bank," _in_ _Regional Aspects of Carbonate Deposition, A Symposium_, 1957, p. 25.

7. H. G. Goodell and R. K. Garman, "Carbonate Geochemistry of Superior Deep Test Well, Andros Island, Bahamas," _American Association of Petroleum Geologists Bulletin_, v. 53 (1969), p. 513-536.

8. Newell and Rigby, "Geological Studies," p. 26-27.

9. Goodell and Garman, "Carbonate Geochemistry," p. 520-521, 533-536.

10. Bathurst, _Developments in Sedimentology no. 12_, p. 367-370.

11. Newell and Rigby, "Geological Studies," p. 28.

12. Goodell and Garman, "Carbonate Geochemistry," p. 527-528.

13. R. Carson, _The Edge of the Sea_, 1955, p. 195.

14. Goodell and Garman, "Carbonate Geochemistry," p. 520, 533-536.

15. H. Blatt, et al., _Origin of Sedimentary Rocks_, 1972, p. 414.

16. Excellent summaries of the methods by which dolomite formation occurs are found in D. H. Zenger, "Dolomitization and Uniformitarianism," _Journal of Geological Education_, v. 20 (1972), p. 104-124; and D. H. Zenger, "Significance of Supratidal Dolomitization in the Geologic Record," _Geological Society of American Bulletin_, v. 83 (1972), p. 1-12.

17. Bathurst, _Developments in Sedimentology no. 12_, p. 517-535.

18. _Ibid._, p. 539-542.

19. Goodell and Garman, "Carbonate Geochemistry," p. 527-529.

20. H. Blatt, et al., _Origin of Sedimentary Rocks_, p. 484-486.

21. G. V. Chilingar, et al., _Developments in Sedimentology no. 9A, Carbonate Rocks: Origin, Occurrence and Classification_, 1967, p. 187-189, 279.

CHAPTER 8

LIMESTONE REVEALING THE PAST

Most people in North America have long been familiar with limestone as it comes from the many quarries which are found in most of the United States and Canada. An occasional person notices the presence of some fossils in the pieces he examines, but those who have been sufficiently inquisitive to wonder about the origin and nature of this form of rock have been all too few. Information on the nature of both limestone and dolostone is almost completely missing from current Bible-science writings. These types of rocks are often thought of as having been formed merely by the rapid piling up of huge numbers of seashells and other skeletal materials by flood waters. Some, not knowing the extent or fossiliferous nature of the deposits of these rock types in the earth, have even suggested that they were rapidly precipitated out of the water during the Biblical Flood. Neither of these methods could produce even a small proportion of the limestone and dolostone which we know exists in the crust of the earth. The latter method (rapid precipitation) is not only completely inadequate to produce the known quantities of rock, but could not form the many very pure deposits which exist. Pure layers of rock can not be precipitated out of muddy flood waters, nor can fossils be formed in this manner. There are occasional, small deposits of precipitated limestone known, but these give every evidence of having been formed in very clear, quiet water, over considerable periods of time. (This variety is called "lithographic limestone," because of its uniform and pure nature, which makes it suitable for lithographic printing.)

Both the wide distribution and the abundance of limestone and dolostone upon the earth are truly amazing. Most of us know of at least a few places where "limerock" is obtained from open pit quarries, but we usually are oblivious to the fact that there are thousands of feet of thickness of it deeply buried underneath large parts of the continents and in parts of the sea floors. It is appropriate at this point to explain that the term "limerock" is commonly used for both limestone and dolostone, in industrial and agricultural circles. However, the chemical difference between the two, which has been pointed out in previous sections of this book, is significant.

Numerous calculations of the abundance and distribution of carbonate rocks (limestone and dolostone) have been made during the past half-century. These estimates are based largely on the amounts which are observed in limestone outcrop areas, and in deep-well drilling records. Sanders and Friedman give the following informative statement (using "limestone" in the general sense which includes dolostone):

Limestone occurs in all parts of the world and at all levels in the stratigraphic column, though probably it is less common in ancient Precambrian strata. Limestones have been

estimated to comprise 19 to 22% of available measured stratigraphic sections.[1]

The percentage of limestone and dolostone is similarly stated by
B. B. Hanshaw of the U. S. Geological Survey, as "20% of the sedimentary record." He also explains that "carbonate rocks contain
about 50% of the world's known petroleum reserves."[2]

The 19 to 22%, to which these authors refer, means far more
thickness of limerock than most people imagine. For example, when
one considers the entire area of the United States east of the
Rocky Mountains, he finds an average of approximately 4,500 feet
of sedimentary rock above the Precambrian base.[3] This means an
average of nearly 1,000 feet of thickness of limerock underneath
the surface, for the larger part of our country. Pettijohn cites
research which determined that the average thickness of sedimentary
rock and other sediments for the entire earth is approximately
2,400 ft.[4] It is probable that this figure will be somewhat revised after all of the Deep Sea Drilling Project reports are in,
but it is not likely that the revision will be to a lesser thick-
ness--at least not for carbonate deposits.

We have already referred, in Tables 2 and 5, to some of the
thousands of feet of thickness of fossil-bearing limestone and
dolostone in certain oil fields, and could cite many more areas
where similar thicknesses exist. In fact, these amounts of fossiliferous carbonate sedimentary rock are very representative of what
is found in Europe, Africa, Asia, and under some parts of the sea
floor.

Such huge amounts of carbonate rock can only mean that in the
past, marine organisms have had at least some millions of years to
live, grow, and produce the "biogenic" components of the sediments
which became limerock and dolostone. (It will be remembered that
a very high percentage of the components of nearly all known deposits of these rocks is made up of skeletal sand, fecal pellets,
calcium carbonate needles, and other types of biogenic particles.)
Obviously there was never any one time when enough skeleton-producing
animals and plants lived contemporaneously--or even within the same
ten-thousand year period--to produce this much limestone and dolostone. To hypothesize, as some have, that thousands of feet of
limerock thickness were produced by the rapid piling up of skeletal
matter is meaningless without sufficient available animal and plant
skeletons. Most of the animals and plants which produce thick
skeletons grow on ocean bottoms or on rock surfaces along the coasts.
These could never have lived crowded upon one another in great,
thick layers such as would be required for producing this much
skeletal matter within a short time. The great bulk of shell-producing marine organisms are bottom-dwelling. Such animals require
room to live and be in contact with the water, which provides life-
supporting oxygen for them.

The Lack of Compaction

Still another reason why it is impossible to conclude that any significant proportion of the limestone sediments was deposited within a short time is that most limestones show that they were formed without significant amounts of compaction. (Compaction is the compressing together of sediment particles which occurs when considerable weight of sediments above presses down upon them.) The internal structure of nearly all known limestones shows that the sediments and fossils were not greatly compacted before they became lithified. (Lithification is the sum total of the processes which result in the transformation of the sediments into rock.) When samples of the limestones are examined with a petrographic microscope, the sediment grains and fossils are not packed together tightly as they are in rock which was compacted as lithification took place. In fact, the amount of pore space between the grains, plus the volume of the cement crystals which have formed in between the grains, is commonly found to total 40 to 50%.[5] In the case of ancient limerock which now has 10% internal pore space, the amount of cement will thus be 30 to 40% of the volume of the rock. Evidently, in a given layer of sediment, a large proportion of the cement crystals was built in before any great weight of sediments was added on top of the layer.

Even the skeletons of very delicate fossilized animals are frequently found unbroken, because the cementation of the sediments immediately surrounding them protected them from the weight of heavy deposits added later. The cement crystals themselves are delicate, and are known to form only very slowly; but eventually they do provide sufficient rigidity to prevent further compaction, and to maintain the 10% porosity mentioned above, even though a mile or more of other rock layers are added on top of the limestone. Bathurst and others have calculated from known cementation rates that 80,000 to 90,000 years are often required for normal filling in of the spaces between the sediment grains in a given limestone layer.[6] Certainly, at least 25 to 40% of this cementation had to be accomplished before thick deposits were added on top. Otherwise, what cement crystals had already formed would have been crushed, and would not be seen to be intact when examined with the petrographic microscope.

Workers Boring and Building

We have frequently referred to the fact that a great deal of the marine limestone which is found, both deep in the earth and near the surface, is in separate layers. We speak of these rock deposits as being "bedded." The divisions between layers in such deposits are caused by a number of factors, including a change in the currents on the sea bottom, and chemical changes in the environment which may bring about a cessation of the carbonate deposition process.

When one goes to a limerock quarry and pulls or pries some of the bedded layers apart, examining the upper surfaces of the layers, he sometimes finds the record of both boring and building processes. These processes formed various markings and raised areas on the surfaces before those surfaces were deeply buried under other layers. The marks, most of which were formed by creatures of kinds similar to those known today, show that the particular rock surface in question was exposed to the action of water and organisms on the sea bottom for a considerable time <u>before</u> <u>being</u> <u>covered</u> <u>over</u>. Since lithified limestone strata often form within the first few inches of sediments on the ocean bottom, it is easy to see that a slight change in bottom currents could expose the upper surface of the rock layer, making it available to the work of boring and building organisms.

Animals and plants which bore holes in the limestone surfaces, in nearly all cases do so by a slow dissolving process carried out by acid which they secrete. Certain kinds of algae, sponges, and snails are among the most common boring organisms. Frequently the holes and channels formed by these organisms are so distinct that the observer using magnification sees that the ends of invividual, previously cemented sediment grains were cut off. Thus, the bored channel shows the ends of the grains in much the same way as they would be seen after having been bored with a mechanical drill. This is definite evidence that the rock had hardened before the marine organisms carried out their boring process on it.

Along with, or following, the boring and partial disintegration of the limestone surfaces, encrusting organisms--including oysters, clam-type mollusks, bryozoans, lime-secreting marine worms, and sessile foraminiferids--frequently attach themselves to the rock surface.[7]

Whenever we find limestone layers which have their upper surfaces showing this boring and encrusting, we of course know that <u>each</u> such surface was exposed for an appreciable length of time before the layer was covered by other sediments. No noticeable amount of boring or of building of encrusting deposits could be accomplished in less than several months of time. The <u>extensive</u> results of these processes which are often found certainly must have required much longer than that for each surface showing the boring and encrusting. So wherever we find limestone showing such layers, we have to recognize not only the many years for the deposition and cementation of each carbonate layer, but also the additional periods for boring and encrusting.

One of the types of geologic deposit in which the bored and encrusted upper surfaces of the limerock layers can be observed is the Cretaceous chalk beds of the British Isles. Here the soft layers of chalk can be easily removed from the numerous, repeating hard layers which have the fossilized encrusting organisms built on to their surfaces. Similar series of encrusted layers of limerock are found in many other parts of the world. (These flat, hard layers are often called "hardgrounds.") A typical example is found in the Turonian chalk beds of England. The thin, hard layers, when they are removed and cleaned, show on their <u>upper</u> surfaces the work of various boring organisms; and are also encrusted with the shells of mollusks, the calcareous tubes formed by annelid worms, and the skeletons of bryozoans.[8]

It is thus obvious that during the formation of the chalk beds each hard layer was exposed to the sea water long enough to be bored by organisms, and then encrusted by the animals which attached themselves. After the encrusting organisms of any particular surface had built their structures, the layer was finally covered over with a deposit of soft chalk upon which another hard layer was then formed. The chalk, as well as the hard layers, is highly fossiliferous. The chalk itself is composed primarily of carbonate ooze from the ocean bottom. A high percentage of its composition consists of the fossilized shells and calcareous cell walls of floating ("pelagic") marine organisms of various kinds.[9] The loose, uncemented deposits of these surround and enclose the fossilized encrusting organisms which lie attached to the hard layers, leaving us a clear record of the biological growth which accompanied the formation of the chalk-bed series. This is of course also a record of the passage of many thousands of years of time, even in the case of the lesser chalk-bed deposits.

Plants That Make Rocks

We have previously made several brief references to the participation of algae in the formation of certain limestone and dolostone layers. Some very small filamentous algae growing in layers on beaches, such as in the Persian Gulf, collect and bind fine grains of carbonate sediment, forming algal mats which later become cemented into laminated rock. Such hardened algal-mat layers are very frequently found in oil-bearing strata, as in the Rainbow area in Canada. Algal limestone similar to this will be discussed below, under "Algal Layer-built Rocks." Some of the larger forms of algae, such as Halimeda and Penicillus, secrete great quantities of plate-like particles and minute needles of calcium carbonate which fall to the bottom. These make up a very significant part of the sediments which eventually become limerock on the shallow sea floors. Such algal components are frequently found in deeply buried, as well as surface, deposits of limestone. Still other kinds of algae, mostly belonging to the group we call the "red algae," build calcareous encrusting layers over dead or broken masses of coral in reef areas, as was mentioned in Chapter 6.

In the deposits of ancient limestone on the continents we find the record of all of the above types of algal building processes. In some formations of these rock layers the fossilized algal structures are very pronounced and obvious when observed with the naked eye or with a hand lens; for others, a microscope of higher power must be used. Here we wish to briefly describe two of the more readily visible types of algal remains which are fossilized in ancient deposits of limerock.

The first of these is what is called the "phylloid" algal limestone. This is limestone in which many fossilized, leaf-like blades of lime-secreting algae have been preserved. (The word "phylloid"

comes from the Greek phyllon, which means "leaf.") There are numerous species of this form of algae found in ancient limestones. The
leaf-like blades are commonly found to be 1 to 6 inches long, and
the fossilized plants show indications of having been 6 to 8 inches
in height. These plants are very abundant in the mound-like deposits
of calcareous sediments in which they grew. The blades had a calcareous skeleton of their own, and thus could maintain their identity until they were covered over by more sediment and preserved.
They are found in natural burial position, slumped down in the
sediments. Because they were rather broad (resembling broad leaves)
they frequently sheltered small empty spaces beneath them.[10] Most
of these cavities were later partially filled with crystals of calcium carbonate, but a large proportion of them retained small spaces
which, in the oil field strata, serve as recesses for the retention
of oil in the rock.

The discovery of algal mounds with these blade-protected cavities shows us that they were buried in a rather calm environment,
and that they were not covered over with heavy weights of additional
sediment until long after their original burial. The building in
of enough calcium carbonate cement crystals to support even a few
feet of additional sediments requires centuries. So the lack of
compaction in these limestones is an indicator of the long periods
of time which passed before the additional sediments were deposited.
For example, a thick bank of phylloid algal limestone, showing the
characteristics we have been discussing, is found at a depth of
about 6,000 feet, in one oil field in southwestern Colorado.[11] The
broad-bladed algal plants found in the drilling cores show that
they were only mildly compacted. So in this case also, long periods
of time passed before most of the sediments above were added. Figure 23 shows the approximate shape and position of one of the algal
banks found in this oil field. (The name Ivanovia seen in the figure is the generic name of the most common broad-bladed alga in
that geographic area, and the names across the top of the figure
are the names of oil wells.)

In addition to the phylloid algal deposits just described, there
are many other similar ones in Utah, New Mexico, Oklahoma, Missouri,
and Kansas. Some of these deposits are near the surface, and are
seen in road cuts, while others are found deeply buried in oil
fields.

A good example of the phylloid algal limestone in Kansas is
that of Greenwood County in the southeastern part of the state.
Core samples from this 90 foot thick deposit, collected by the
Marathon Oil Company from a depth of approximately 1,400 feet, contain a very high proportion of broad, phylloid algal blades. Some
of the blades in these samples show the effects of slight compaction.
However, the weight of the sediments above was not great enough to
obliterate nearly all of the cavities beneath the blades. A vivid
testimony of this fact was recorded in the groups of calcium carbonate cement crystals which now lie in regular patterns in most
of the cavities. These finally filled the spaces sufficiently to
support the 1,400 feet of sediments which were to be added above.

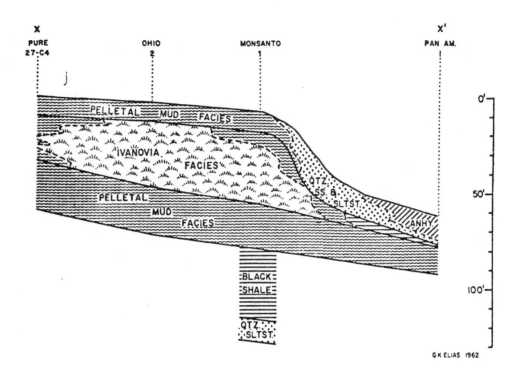

Fig. 23. Vertical section through a bank of phylloid algal limestone, located at a depth of approximately 6,000 feet in the oil-bearing strata of southwestern Colorado. The part labeled "Ivanovia Facies" is the bank which was built up by algal growth. Note the thickness scale, in feet, to the right, and the names of oil wells above. From G. K. Elias, "Habitat of Pennsylvanian algal bioherms, Four Corners area," in Shelf Carbonates of the Paradox Basin, Four Corners Geological Society, Fourth Field Conference, 1963, p. 189-196, Fig. 6. (By permission of the Four Corners Geological Society.)

The structure of this limestone, and also the microscopic cellular structure of the algae which are present in it, are described in detail by J. L. Wray.[12] Numerous deposits of phylloid algal limestone which are close enough to the surface to be exposed in road cuts and river banks are described by P. H. Heckel and J. M. Cocke.[13]

Algal Layer-built Rocks

Another type of algal limestone in which the effects of algal growth are readily visible is a certain laminated limestone which consists of stromatolites. Stromatolites are of various shapes, but the best known ones are rounded structures which are made up of thin layers of hardened sediments. In most cases each layer of the stromatolite was formed by a thin mat of fine, filamentous algae which collected sediments from the water. This is the same process by which the fossilized algal mats of sabkha deposits are formed, as described in Chapter 5. However, in the case of stromatolitic limestone, the mats form rounded or roughly spherical structures up to more than one foot in diameter. Figure 24 shows a photograph of one such structure, a stromatolite, in limestone of the Belt Series of Montana. The laminations which were produced by the successive generations of algal growth can be clearly seen in this and in many other beds of ancient stromatolites. Many of these are found in the United States, Canada, Europe, Asia, Africa, and Australia.[14]

These stromatolitic structures were largely a mystery to geologists of the earlier part of this century, but about 1930 biologists and sedimentary geologists made the exciting discovery that modern stromatolites are now in the process of growth on the coasts of islands in the Caribbean, and of the Persian Gulf and Australia.[15] During the last 15 years, many other places where these are currently being formed have been discovered, and the processes of their development have been studied in detail. In each case it is found that the stromatolites, and similar carbonate layered structures, develop only in shallow water or in the tidal zones where they are exposed intermittently.

The formation of stromatolites and related structures is basically a process of accumulation of calcium carbonate sediments on thin, growing mats of filamentous algae. There are numerous species of algae which have the ability to produce stromatolites by this process, most of them belonging to the group called blue-green algae. The majority of these do not secrete calcareous skeletons, as the encrusting red algae do, but instead, they form a sticky, mucilaginous layer over their surface. The sticky surface traps sediment grains which wash up over it as the tide comes in, and also traps small amounts of calcium carbonate particles which precipitate out of the water. After a thin coating of calcium carbonate sediments has accumulated, more algal filaments grow up over the coating, produce more mucilage, and collect another layer of carbonate sediment.[16] This process results eventually in the formation of thick beds of laminated calcium carbonate, which later lithifies to become hard limestone or dolostone.[17]

Fig. 24. Photograph of a stromatolite which is located in
Glacier National Park, in Montana. The many thin layers of
this and similar stromatolites were built up in ancient
times by successive generations of algal growth. The size
of this structure can be estimated from the size of the hand
rock hammer which is seen in the upper left of the photograph.
From R. Rezak, "Stromatolites of the Belt Series in Glacier
National Park and vicinity, Montana," U. S. Geological Survey
Professional Paper no. 294-D, 1957, p. 127-154, Plate 19,
Figure 2.

Thickened parts of such beds are called stromatolites, which are often found in great abundance, both in ancient limestone, and in modern coastal areas where evaporative conditions have alternated with tidal flooding. Figure 25 is a photograph of an Australian coastal area which is covered with modern stromatolites. Geologists are careful not to assume that all ancient stromatolites were formed under exactly the same environmental conditions as those being formed today. However, the similarity of the modern and the ancient in this case is unmistakable, and in some ancient ones, identifiable algal filaments are preserved in the laminations.[18] These, together with the many similarities of lamination patterns and of sediment particles, give more than sufficient evidence of the relationship of the modern and the ancient stromatolites.

The ancient deposits of stromatolitic limestone are both widespread and extensive in volume. They are present in carbonate rocks of all geological periods, especially in the Precambrian, Cambrian, Ordovician, and Pennsylvanian Periods. In the United States, the best known of the great beds of stromatolitic limestone which are exposed (outcropping) are in Montana, Arizona, Michigan, Vermont, New York, and Pennsylvania.[19] The stromatolites and other algal-mat structures are regularly found in growth position, closely resembling the manner in which they are distributed in modern stromatolite beds.

In the Rainbow Lake area of Alberta, Canada, extensive stromatolite-containing deposits are found at depths of from 4,000 to 5,000 feet. These are found in the oil-bearing strata next to, and also cemented against, the sides of some of the better-known atoll reefs in the Rainbow oil fields. There are up to 25 feet of thickness of stromatolitic limestone found in the well cores from this particular area.[20]

It is significant that almost all of the stromatolites in these Devonian deposits are associated with evaporative sequences. (It will be remembered from Chapter 5 that the Rainbow reefs are covered by many layers of evaporite minerals, and that some of these are in sabkha sequences.) This is in agreement with the fact that many of the stromatolites of today are formed on arid coasts where evaporative conditions exist. Another important fact concerning these Canadian stromatolites is that, while some of them are found along the sides of the cone-shaped reefs, none are found interlayered with the reef limestone. The stromatolites are found in growth position about one-half way up the sides of the atolls. The conditions under which laminated algal mats can form are not the same as those which are conducive to reef-growth. Thus a time sequence is evident, in that the reef rock was formed before the stromatolitic limestone along its sides.[21] Then of course the entire reef structures were later covered by evaporative minerals.

All of the limestone which has been formed by algal mats, which we have been discussing, is of significance as a time indicator. No bed of limestone which contains stromatolites in growth position

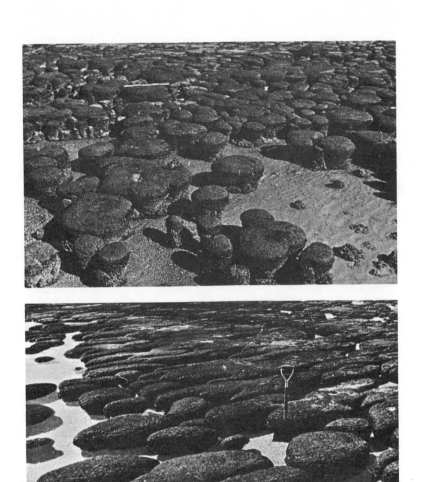

Fig. 25. Two similar types of modern stromatolites on the coast of Shark Bay, in western Australia. These are being gradually built up by the growth of thin layers of blue-green algae. Each successive layer of algae traps a layer of calcareous sediment which washes up over it at high tide, thus forming these laminated mounds. The sizes can be estimated from the shovel which is leaning up against a large stromatolite in the lower figure. These structures have adequate resistance to wave action because the sediments of which they are composed become cemented by inorganically precipitated calcium carbonate crystals. Some of the stromatolites found in ancient beds of limestone are very similar to these. From D. M. Raup and S. M. Stanley, _Principles of Paleontology_, W. H. Freeman Co., 1971, 388 p. Figure 9-15. (By permission of the W. H. Freeman Co., and Dr. Paul Hoffman.)

could have been formed rapidly. The accumulation of the many thin layers (each usually less than one millimeter thick) obviously required time, just as it does in the growth of modern stromatolites. The primary cause of the sediment accumulation is the growth of the successive layers of mucilage-forming algae over the most recent sediment surface. The repeating of this process thus depends upon plant growth, and plant growth rates are controlled by stable natural laws.

Some Practical Uses of a Knowledge of Limestone

For the person who is interested in the natural record of past events in the earth, limestone is an invaluable source of information. It is not merely "dead, cold stone," but reveals periods of time, as well as the types of environment in which it was formed. As we have seen in this chapter, most kinds of limestone are literally loaded with biologically formed structures--sedimentary particles which have been formed by living creatures, and built together by intricate processes of ion-exchange and cementation.

We are here briefly summarizing some of the practical aspects of limestone geology which we encountered in this and the preceding chapter:

1. Wherever we find thick beds of undisturbed limestone we know that that site was once ocean bottom, or at least the bottom of a large, inland lake of high mineral content.

2. When limestone is found to be made up of a natural assemblage of several sizes of sediments, such as are produced together on the Great Bahama Bank, we will realize that it was formed on the same site where the sediments were produced. In such a case it is evident that no major disturbance interfered with the natural sedimentation process. Any thick body of such limestone will be known to represent long periods of time. This is because the rates of sediment production in all seas and all climates are slow, and because the calcium carbonate content of sea water is insufficient to support sediment production of more than a few centimeters per year, even if unusually ideal conditions existed continuously.

3. When a body of limestone contains large numbers of relatively immobile, sedentary organisms such as corals and calcareous algae, still in their natural growth position, we know that we are viewing the record of a gradual growth process, on the original shallow-marine site of development. (It should be kept in mind that neither corals nor algae can grow in the dark depths of the sea.)

4. The presence of thick beds of fossil-bearing dolostone is an indication that this rock was formed in a marine environment, and that the original calcium carbonate sediments were converted to dolostone by long periods of water circulation.

5. When thin layers of algal-mat limestone, or of limestone

and dolostone, are found intact, it is evident that the rock layers
being viewed are giving us an accurate record of the cyclic deposition of sediments in that particular location.

6. The presence of relatively pure carbonate rock zones containing large numbers of the small, rounded carbonate particles we
call oöids is significant. Such zones tell us that long periods
of moderate agitation of water which was high in calcium carbonate
content helped in the formation of the rock mass.

7. Any large mass of limestone which contains numerous sizes
of carbonate particles, and contains little or no foreign material
such as clay, quartz, or volcanic debris, can practically always
be identified as having been formed in a natural setting of relatively calm waters. The absence of appreciable amounts of foreign
matter shows that there was no bottom disturbance which would bring
in foreign particles.

8. Wherever large dissolution cavities are found dissolved
out of a covered layer of a limestone deposit in the sea, it is
evident that that layer was once exposed to weathering for a long
period of time and then re-submerged. The covering layer above
the pocketed bed was added later, allowing more recent sediments
to partially or completely fill the old cavities.

9. Any broad, separable layer in a body of limestone, found
to have on its upper surface small cavities or tunnels due to boring
by marine organisms, will be recognized as having existed for a
considerable period of time as an exposed surface, after the layer
had been lithified. Hard structures such as oyster shells and the
calcareous tubes of marine worms, fastened to these surfaces, will
give further testimony to the length of time the animals were able
to work on the rock surface before the next layer was added.

10. When limestone from well cores, or from a thick bank of
carbonate rock, is examined under magnification and found to contain delicate, uncrushed fossils, and small cavities which were
present at the time when the sediment hardened, this indicates long
periods of time. The lack of compaction shows that no appreciable
weight of additional sediments was added until long after the layer
in question was deposited. If the samples being examined show
large amounts of calcium carbonate cement crystals in an orderly
arrangement in some of the original spaces, this is further testimony of long intervals of time during which the crystals were being
precipitated from circulating pore water. If the crystals are of
dolomite rather than of calcium carbonate, this likely represents
even more time.

At this point we can illustrate the use of some of these principles by considering the famous Redwall Limestone of the Grand
Canyon. The rock formations which lie immediately above and below
it will also be considered briefly, as they relate to the Redwall
Limestone. As for the term "Redwall," this limestone is not actually
red, except on its vertical surface in the canyon, where it is colored

red by dissolved iron-containing minerals which wash down over it
from above. Thus when observed from a distance, this thick deposit
of limestone has the appearance of a red wall, instead of the natural gray color of most limestone. This deposit is over 700 feet
thick in some places along the canyon, and lies at a depth of
nearly 2,000 feet below the present surface (canyon rim) at some
points.[22] The Redwall Limestone is classified as belonging to the
Mississippian geological Period. Figure 26 shows its position in
the local stratigraphic column in the Grand Canyon.

This great formation of limestone contains several types of
typical marine carbonate rock, and gives a clear record of the way
by which many of its parts were formed. The composition and texture
of many of the Redwall strata show that biological processes were
important in their deposition, and that they were formed naturally
in relatively calm seas. The characteristics of the Redwall Formation provide us with an opportunity to note some of the practical
uses of a knowledge of limestone. Prior to the time when sedimentologists, paleontologists, and biologists had acquired an understanding
of limestone formation processes, a mass of limestone such as this
was largely a mystery. Now, what was a mystery has become highly
meaningful, and has aided greatly in understanding the history of
the Grand Canyon area, as well as of other sedimentary deposits of
the earth.

We have stated that the Redwall Limestone contains a clear
record of the processes by which it was formed. Perhaps some observers who are unfamiliar with sedimentology may not recognize
these features when casually examining the walls of the Grand Canyon,
but the identifying characteristics are nevertheless present. When
we begin to study rock samples from this formation we will soon
notice that many of them have a high proportion of readily identifiable components such as are found in the sediments of the Bahama
Banks. These include both fine and coarse skeletal particles from
animals and calcareous algae, oöids, and various kinds of pellets.
There are also fossilized algal mats, which show that they had
trapped fine particles of lime mud, as they do today.[23] This and
other features of the distribution of the very fine lime-mud particles are convincing evidence that the waters were relatively quiet
during a significant part of the time that the Redwall Formation
was being deposited. Also, the presence of a high proportion of
biologically formed components shows that the formation is not a
product of mere inorganic precipitation.

One of the most striking characteristics of this formation of
limestone is its high degree of purity, coupled with the great
thickness and broad geographic extent of the deposit. (The Redwall
Formation extends for over 175 miles from north to south, and for
more than 275 miles from east to west.) In some of the parts which
lie to the south of the Grand Canyon region, appreciable amounts
of quartz sand are present; but in most other places this formation
is almost pure calcium carbonate and calcium-magnesium carbonate.
In many parts of the Canyon the amount of foreign matter present
is much less than one percent.[24] Here then is abundant testimony

141

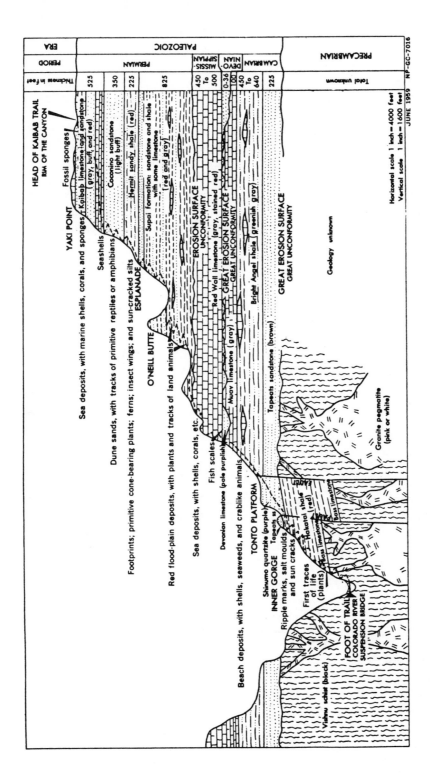

Fig. 26. Vertical section through the sedimentary layers seen on the sides of the Grand Canyon (also of the non-sedimentary layers at the bottom of the Canyon). Note the position of the Redwall Limestone Formation, and of the weathered erosion surfaces which appear just above and beneath it. See text for explanation of these erosion surfaces, and of some of the contrasting layers in the Formation. From "Kaibab Trail Trip Guide Leaflet," U. S. Department of the Interior, 1963.

that this gigantic mass of limestone was formed by natural processes
of carbonate sediment production. Any process of transporting that
much accumulation of carbonate sediments from other places where
it might have been produced would have mixed large amounts of land-
derived sediments with it (unless the entire area and adjoining
regions were already sealed over with thick beds of pure limestone).

Of significance also, with regard to the calcium carbonate and
calcium-magnesium carbonate (dolomite) content, is the fact that
the Redwall Limestone has many abrupt changes from the former to
the latter, as one proceeds up the stratigraphic column. Beds of
true limestone rest directly upon thick beds of fossiliferous dolostone, indicating that there were distinct changes of environment
as sediment deposition proceeded. Thus there were times when a
recently produced limestone layer had no opportunity to be converted
to dolostone, but at other times there were extended periods when
conditions were favorable for the slow process of dolomitization.[25]

A knowledge of some of the characteristics of limestone deposits can also be used for understanding physiographic characteristics of the Redwall Formation. These include various kinds of
unconformities, the effects of erosion, the dissolving of large
cavities in the limestone, and the refilling of those cavities.

As described earlier, an unconformity is a boundary surface
between rock layers, which shows that there was a definite time
break between the times of deposition of the two types of rock.
When the zone of contact between the Redwall Limestone and the underlying Temple Butte Limestone is closely examined, a very irregular surface caused by erosion of the underlying rock is evident.
Then farther up, about one-half way to the top of the Redwall,
there are even more definite marks of ancient erosion and chemical
changes due to weathering than are found at the base. These of
course are a record of the passage of considerable amounts of time
before more strata were added to the formation. Thus there were
different stages in the development of the Redwall Limestone.

Near the top, and also precisely at the top of this formation,
there are two other such zones of extreme weathering and erosion.[26]
It should be realized that we are not here referring to any recent
erosion, or to the downcutting of the Canyon; but that these are
ancient erosion surfaces, which extended far back into the land
mass on each side of the Canyon. In fact, these surfaces were eroded and then covered over long before the Grand Canyon was cut out.
Present erosion on the sides of the canyon merely uncovers additional
cavities, worn rock surfaces, sediment pockets, and other features
of the ancient unconformities.

The uppermost of the Redwall unconformities is of special interest to the student of limestone formations, and has some characteristics similar to those previously noted in the Great Bahama
Bank. We here refer to the highly eroded and dissolution-marked
upper surface of the Redwall Formation, where it makes contact with
the (much different) Supai Formation which lies upon it. The upper

surface of the Redwall Limestone contains many ancient caves, water-carved gullies, blocky knolls, and small mesas up to 40 feet high. There are also ancient sinkholes with down-dipping strata surrounding them. All these are marks of erosion, weathering, and dissolution which normally take place in a limestone formation which is exposed to the atmosphere and rains for long periods of time. In fact, most of these same features are present in large areas of southern Indiana and Kentucky at the present time. They are due to the continuous dissolving and eroding of the limestone beds for thousands of years, as they are exposed to the weather, resulting in what is called "karst" topography. The upper surface of the Redwall Limestone is a typical karst surface. After these severe erosion and dissolution features were produced, the area was resubmerged and covered with the contrasting sediments of the Supai Formation.

The trail of movement of these contrasting sediments can now be traced down through the ancient channels where they settled and became lithified. Figure 27 shows some of these eroded cavities and channels which were later filled with contrasting sediments which became rock. Thus in many places streaks and pockets of mudstone, siltstone, and unsorted cave breccia are now found permeating the upper 100 or more feet of the Redwall Limestone. This is especially true in the eastern canyon region. In this area the eroded surface and the rock-filled caverns were later sealed over by at least 1,800 feet of additional sedimentary rock layers. These constitute the Supai, Hermit, Coconino, Toroweap, and Kaibab Formations.

One could of course not legitimately postulate that the channels and caves which we have been describing were formed as, or soon after, the sediments were being laid down. This is because any such sediment mass has to have stability due to lithification processes before a cave or channel could be formed in it. Otherwise, the sediments surrounding the cavity would immediately slump into and fill the opening. It is equally impossible to suppose that the cavities were formed recently, because the top surface of the Redwall Limestone is much too deeply buried for karst topography to develop on it. Also, after deep burial, there was no way for the mudstone and other filling in the channels and caves to have been moved into them.

As a final feature for which an understanding of carbonate rock characteristics is of value, we will cite the porous nature and very evident lack of compaction which exists in various parts of the Redwall Limestone. The presence of masses of delicate, but unbroken, fossils in several parts of the formation is one of the evidences of a lack of compaction.[27] Another is the presence of numerous fossilized algal mats, forming small bridges across cavities in the sediments on which they were growing. Other algal mats are found binding together certain masses of sediment into distinctive forms which have been preserved intact in the rock.[28] Thus it is evident that the long periods of time which are required for lithification of carbonate sediments transpired before any heavy weight of additional sediment was added above. Even the weight of a 300 foot high column of carbonate sediment 1 x 1 inches square is approximately

144

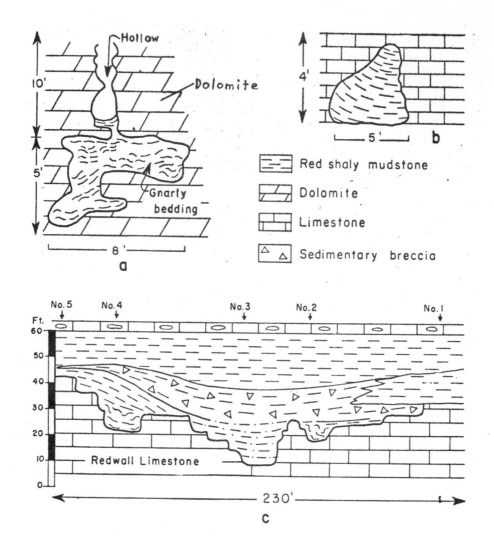

Fig. 27. Solution cavities in Redwall Limestone and contact between
Supai Formation and Redwall Limestone. Numbers refer to locations of
detailed measured sections. (a) Bridge Canyon, (b) Hance Trail, (c)
Whitmore Wash.

These solution cavities and channels were eroded and dissolved
out of the upper layers of the Redwall Formation by the downward movement of water during the long period of exposure of the limestone layers. Later the entire Formation was covered over by other deposits,
and finally the great Canyon was cut. Note that the eroded cavities
are filled with red, shaley mudstone, which washed down into them from
above, before the addition of thicker deposits above sealed them off.
From E. D. McKee, and R. C. Gutschick, History of the Redwall Limestone
of Northern Arizona, Geological Society of America Memoir 114, 1969,
726 p., Figure 33. (By permission of the Geological Society of America,
and Dr. Edwin D. McKee.)

200 lbs. So one can easily see that the compaction force exerted on the fossils in the sediment would be very great when the water level fell below that of the sediment mass, unless the sediments first became cemented. Without the required long periods of time for cementation as the sediment mass was being built up, the skeletons of most of the kinds of marine animals found in the Redwall Formation would have been completely crushed.

In summing up, we find that the nature of limestone, and of the various formations of limestone and dolostone in the earth, is extremely valuable as an indicator of long periods of time. Most of the natural processes which form such rock layers are now being observed on numerous sea coasts and sediment banks. So there is no longer any place for vague speculations as to the nature and origin of the great deposits of limestone and dolostone. God has enabled man to discover these dynamic formation processes and to use the knowledge of them in understanding the ancient bodies of these kinds of rock. The understanding of them has, in turn, enabled oil prospectors to more accurately predict the location and amounts of stored oil, thus saving the companies many needless "dry holes." Therefore, the new knowledge of the nature and origin of limestone has proven valuable both for the petroleum geologist and for the Bible student who is interested in past events.

FOOTNOTES

1. J. E. Sanders and G. M. Friedman, "Origin and Occurrence of Limestones," in Developments in Sedimentology no. 9A, Carbonate Rocks, 1967, p. 193.

2. B. B. Hanshaw, "Inorganic Geochemistry of Carbonate Shelf Rocks," American Association of Petroleum Geologists Bulletin (abstract), v. 53 (1969), p. 720.

3. This is easily determined by examining a "basement map" of the United States, such as is obtainable from the American Association of Petroleum Geologists.

4. F. J. Pettijohn, Sedimentary Rocks, 1957, p. 8.

5. Blatt, et al., Origin of Sedimentary Rocks, p. 470.

6. Bathurst, Developments in Sedimentology no. 12, p. 439-441.

7. Ibid., p. 371, 375, 395-401.

8. Ibid., p. 399-401.

9. Chilingar, et al., Developments in Sedimentology no. 9A, p. 234-236.

10. P. H. Heckel and J. M. Cocke, "Phylloid Algal-Mound Complexes

146

in Outcropping Upper Pennsylvanian Rocks of Mid-Continent," American Association of Petroleum Geologists Bulletin, v. 53 (1969), p. 1058-1064.

11. G. K. Elias, "Habitat of Pennsylvanian Algal Bioherms, Four Corners Area," in Shelf Carbonates of the Paradox Basin, Four Corners Geological Society Fourth Field Conference, 1963, p. 189-196.

12. J. L. Wray, "Archaeolithophyllum, an Abundant Calcareous Alga in Limestones of the Lansing Group (Pennsylvanian), Southeastern Kansas," Kansas Geological Survey Bulletin no. 170, Part 1, 1964, p. 1-10.

13. Heckel and Cocke, "Phylloid Algal-Mound Complexes," p. 1058-1074.

14. J. H. Johnson, Limestone Building Algae and Algal Limestone, 1961, p. 205-207.

15. R. C. G. Bathurst, Developments in Sedimentology no. 12, p. 217-230.
    A very extensive treatment of these and other stromatolites can be found in M. R. Walter, et. al., Developments in Sedimentology no. 20, Stromatolites, 1976, 790 p.

16. C. D. Gebelein, "Distribution, Morphology, and Accretion Rate of Recent Subtidal Algal Stromatolites, Bermuda," Journal of Sedimentary Petrology, v. 39 (1969), p. 49, 54-69.

17. S. Machielse, "Devonian Algae and their Contribution to the Western Canadian Sedimentary Basin," Bulletin of Canadian Petroleum Geology, v. 20 (1972), p. 201-208.

18. Johnson, Limestone Building Algae, p. 205.

19. Ibid., p. 204-205.

20. Machielse, "Devonian Algae," p. 204.

21. Ibid., p. 204-207.

22. J. S. Shelton, Geology Illustrated, 1966, p. 274-286.

23. E. D. McKee and R. C. Gutschick, History of the Redwall Limestone of Northern Arizona, Geological Society of America Memoir 114, 1969, p. 100-104, 554-556.

24. Ibid., p. 26-30, 108, 561.

25. Ibid., p. 24, 31.

26. Ibid., p. 16-17, 49-55, 68-85, 563-564.

27. Ibid., p. 100, 102, 131, 556.

28. Ibid., p. 104, 554.

CHAPTER 9

EVIDENCES FROM THE SEA FLOOR

The present decade is an exciting time of oceanographic exploration and discovery. The ocean floors are now yielding fabulous amounts of information concerning some of the earth's past history. Speculations concerning the depths of the ocean are undoubtedly as old as the human race, but it is only within the past century that man has developed the proper equipment for making a systematic study of the sea floor.

In the 19th century British scientists made some studies of the upper surface of the ocean floor in many parts of the world. They did this during the three-year-long world cruise of the Challenger, an exploration ship equipped for dredging the ocean bottom and taking other kinds of samples and measurements. Much was learned about life on the ocean bottom, and about some of the recent deep-sea sediments, but the deeper layers of the sea floor remained a mystery.

In the present century, as was mentioned in Chapter 4, man has designed drilling equipment which can penetrate more than 3,000 feet into the sediment layers of the ocean floor. This equipment is so arranged that sections of the sedimentary column can be brought to the surface intact, as cores. Each sediment core is brought out of the drill hole already encased in a metal or plastic tube which is carefully labeled and later opened for detailed chemical and biological study.

The progressive accumulation of sediments on the ocean floors has left us an important record of the past. Near to the continents large amounts of sediment accumulate fairly rapidly, being washed off the continent by rivers and turbidity currents. But farther out in the ocean the situation is entirely different. In many parts of the open ocean we find a cumulative, sedimentary record of what goes on century after century, apart from continental disturbances. The main sources of sediments for these layers are the shells of tiny, floating marine animals and plants, minute clay particles which are derived from the land but often float in the water for many years before settling to the bottom, and volcanic debris from underwater volcanoes.

The first of these three types of open-ocean sediments is so important in some waters that it is the primary sediment source. The slow fallout of the shells and skeletal fragments of these minute organisms has in some places produced as much as 2,000 feet of thickness of almost pure skeletal matter on the ocean floor.[1] Thus the study of time records in the ocean floor is not a mere measuring of the amounts of sediments which have washed off the continents, but is largely an analysis of what the sea itself has produced and laid down on the floor.

Unseen Shell-Producing Organisms

The realization that the water of the open seas contains great quantities of microscopic-sized, floating animals and plants is rather new to man.[2] Only during the last few decades have we discovered that a large proportion of these minute organisms live in hard, mineral shells which can contribute to the accumulation of sediments on the sea floor. (See Figure 28 for a magnified photograph of one of the most common types of these.) Even though the shells (usually called "skeletons") are more dense than water, they are kept afloat by tiny bubbles of gas which the animal or plant keeps producing in its protoplasm. These unicellular organisms grow and reproduce rapidly, and the old shells slowly sink to the bottom. Thus, throughout the years, there is a slow, steady "rain" or fallout of the shells, sinking down through the thousands of feet of water, to take their place on the bottom.

In the warmer parts of the oceans, most of these shell-producing organisms use calcium carbonate as the principal component of their skeletons, and the resulting deposit on the bottom is what we call "chalk." In fact, when we microscopically examine the natural chalk deposits which are now on land we find that they still contain multitudes of well-preserved skeletons of these creatures.

For the Bible student, as well as the oceanographic scientist, these deposits are of great interest. The chalk deposits on the ocean floor are many feet thick, over vast areas, and the constant production and deposition of the tiny shells provides us with a means of estimating amounts of time which have passed. This way of estimating amounts of time is particularly reliable on the higher parts of the sea floor, such as on the broad tops of what are called "rises." On these surfaces which are above the general level of the sea floor, the accumulations of the minute skeletons which sink down through the water can go on relatively undisturbed for long periods of time. And at these sites the deposition process is not disturbed by rapid turbidity currents, such as those which flow off the sides of continents and islands.

It is true that the use of the thicknesses of chalk deposits on the ocean floor as a measure of time can not be absolutely precise; but, since the ocean water is already teeming with the organisms which produce the chalk material, one could not postulate that the growth and abundance of such organisms was many times greater than it is today. (Of course we can not estimate how much more sparse their populations were in the past, so we admit that deposition could have been much slower at certain times in the past than it is now.) One reason that we can not postulate vastly greater abundance of these populations than exists at present is the universal law that in any over-populated area--whether on land or in water-- the organisms crowd each other out, as they compete for food, oxygen, and minerals.[3]

Types of Chalk-Producing Organisms

Before we take up the topography of the ocean floor, and the

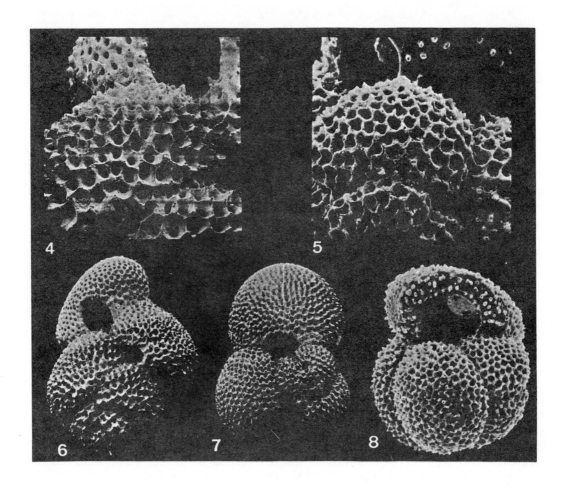

Fig. 28. The shells of three species of microscopic, floating marine animals of the Genus Globigerinoides. Numbers 4 and 5 are shown at 260 diameters magnification with only a part of the shell in view. Numbers 6, 7, and 8 are entire shells shown at 100, 70, and 150 diameters respectively. Note that all have many minute pores for water circulation. All are from the western Pacific ocean, from sediment cores taken out of the ocean floor. Numbers 4 and 6 are from approximately 150 feet beneath the ocean floor, and number 8 is from approximately 220 feet. E. L. Winterer, et al., Initial Reports of the Deep Sea Drilling Project, v. 7, 1971, p. 1351, Plate 12.

thicknesses of some of the chalk layers on it, we should briefly consider a few of the more common types of shell material which are produced in the water of the open seas. There are numerous kinds of organisms which produce what are called "non-calcareous" skeletons, composed mainly of silicon dioxide; but we will here put the greater emphasis on the chalk-forming organisms. (The skeletons of the latter are often spoken of as carbonate or calcareous in composition.)

The first (and most voluminous) of these calcareous types which we will consider here are those of the great group known as the Foraminifera. Figure 28 shows four species of these, of the genus Globigerinoides, taken from the western Pacific floor. There are 18,000 species of these organisms known, and approximately one-third of all ocean bottom is covered with calcareous "ooze" which contains a high percentage of Foraminifera shells. When a great amount of this ooze accumulates, a deposit of chalk is often formed.

The Foraminifera have usually been classified as animals, though they possess only one living cell. In animal classification systems they are closely related to the amoeba, and they obtain their food in the same manner as the amoeba. Tiny food particles are brought into the shell from the sea water through very small openings in the walls of the shell, and are then digested in food vacuoles, as in the amoeba. The many species of these organisms which float in the open sea are buoyed up by bubbles of gas which are present in their protoplasm. The Foraminifera are very abundant in the upper layers of water in nearly all parts of both tropical and temperate oceanic regions. As these organisms die their shells begin to slowly sink toward the bottom, to take their place as a part of the sediments. Since the size of most of these shells is very small, the process of sinking to the bottom is an extremely slow one, because smaller particles sink through the water more slowly than larger ones. Many of the Foraminifera are of a size which requires from several days to a few weeks to sink through 3,000 feet of nonturbulant water.

The other of the two most abundant chalk-forming organisms of the open sea is the group which produces what are called "nannofossils" (Greek nannos, dwarf, + fossil) when they sink to the bottom. Many of the test holes drilled during the recent Deep Sea Drilling Project explorations have passed through thick beds of nannofossil chalk. The most important of the organisms which contribute to this nannofossil chalk are the type of unicellular algae which are called "coccolithophores." (The prefix cocco is from the Greek word kokkos, referring to round objects. Thus the name coccolithophore literally means "the round stone bearer," or the organisms which produce tiny round calcareous plates.) Each of these microscopic-sized, unicellular plants has a cell wall or shell which has several very small, disc or button-like, calcium carbonate plates on it. These plates are known as "coccoliths," and make up more than 50% of some chalk sediments. Two types of these coccoliths from the western Pacific floor are shown in Figure 29a and Figure 29b. Notice particularly the very small size of these plates, as indicated by the high magnification. In fact, the smaller of these

152

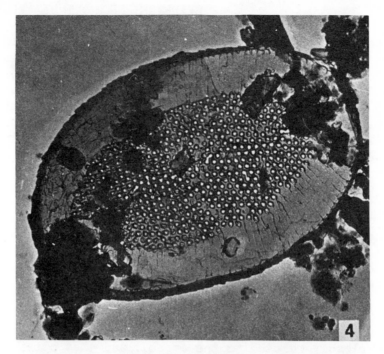

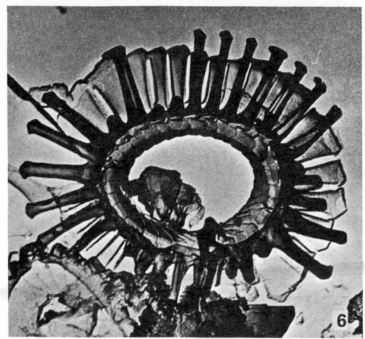

Fig. 29a. Calcium carbonate plates (coccoliths) from microscopic,
floating marine plants of the western Pacific ocean. Number 4 is
shown at 10,000 diameters magnification, and number 6 at 22,500
diameters. Both of these are from a sediment core removed from 16
feet beneath the ocean floor. A high proportion of equatorial marine sediments are composed of these plates. The several kinds of
organisms which produce them are collectively known as "coccolithophores." A. G. Fischer, et al., Initial Reports of the Deep Sea
Drilling Project, v. 6, 1971, p. 989, Plate 1.

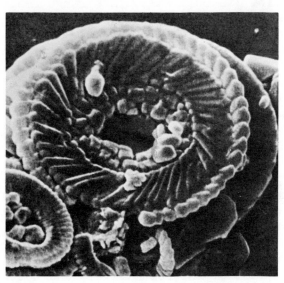

11   12

Fig. 29b. Two coccoliths (skeletal plates) from a microscopic, floating marine plant of Genus <u>Coccolith-us</u>, shown at 4,270 diameters magnification. In number 11 a smaller coccolith, and some broken parts of others, can be seen at the lower left. All are from a sediment core taken from a depth of approximately 1,080 feet in the ocean floor at Site 317 in the central Pacific. S. O. Schlanger, E. D. Jackson, et. al., <u>Initial Reports of the Deep Sea Drilling Project</u>, v. 33, 1976, p. 405, Plate 4.

can not be seen even as a tiny speck without a microscopic magnification of at least 400 diameters. Most coccoliths are less than 20 microns in diameter. (A micron is one one-thousandth of a millimeter.) Each plant has the ability to swim about by means of tiny "flagella" which whip back-and-forth in the water. During the organism's life it is protected by the coccoliths (plates) which it has secreted as a covering for its cell wall. A strange feature of their existence is the fact that they keep shedding the coccoliths from their surface and producing new ones.[4]

With respect to numbers, the coccolith-producing organisms are usually even more abundant in ocean waters than are the Foraminifera. Extensive tests have found 1,800 individual organisms per liter to be the average population density for the entire upper 650 feet (200 meters) of water in some temperate latitudes south of the equator.[5] At some water levels they are far more abundant than this. The very small size of the coccoliths prevents rapid settling, so there is no possibility of a rapid buildup of any layer of these particles. (Many of them remain suspended in even tranquil ocean water for a few years before sinking to the ocean floor.)[6] In fact, the amount of deposit of these and the Foraminifera combined is usually less than one centimeter per thousand years in the main parts of the oceans.[7] So, over 25,000 years are usually required for the production of even one foot of the Foraminifera and coccolith ooze which forms such a thick sedimentary covering over much of the ocean floor.

A few recent, popular authors have attempted to speculate that marine organisms might have been spurred into a fantastically rapid growth rate by events of the Biblical Flood. However, this would have been entirely contrary to the principles and laws of biological growth. Whenever the environmental conditions of the ocean are greatly changed by the suspension of large amounts of mud, silt, or volcanic ash, the environment is thus made unsuitable for rapid growth. This is especially true in the case of photosynthetic organisms, such as the coccolithophores and other types of algae. Furthermore, these organisms are wholly dependent upon the meager supply of ionic calcium and carbonate in the water for the building of their skeletal parts. So again we must never make the mistake of supposing that the organisms in a given habitat can go racing on beyond the limitations of their environment to accomplish some spectacular feat of growth or reproduction.

Deposits of Chalk-Producing Organisms on Land

The shells of the Foraminifera and coccolithophores not only form thick deposits on the present ocean floor, but are the major components of several large chalk deposits which are now exposed on land in Europe and the Americas. In northwestern Europe there are deposits of chalk from the Cretaceous Period which are from 330 to 450 meters (1,080 to 1,480 feet) in thickness. Much of this chalk is more than 98% pure calcium carbonate, being composed primarily of the fossilized shells of Foraminifera and coccoliths. An abundance of these shells and coccoliths are in good condition

and readily identifiable.[8] Since the deposits of chalk are made
up almost entirely of the skeletal remains of microscopic marine
organisms, and possess very little other matter, it is evident that
these beds were formed in a relatively quiet sea where the water
was not seriously disturbed by any currents which could bring in
foreign, land-derived sediments. When we remember that the chalk-
producing organisms can form only a few millimeters of carbonate
ooze per hundred years (at the most), we can see that at least
several millions of years were required for the formation of these
European chalk deposits. Then some time after the deposition was
complete the land arose--or else the sea level became lower--leaving
the chalk as a part of the continent.[9]

Methods of Sea-Floor Exploration

We mentioned earlier in this chapter that research cruises
have revealed much about the sediments of the ocean by dredging the
bottom, and by the taking of cores of sediments. The taking of
cores is a more effective method of investigating the sea floor than
is dredging, since each core is brought up as a relatively undisturbed
column of the sediment layers, in their natural order.

It was shortly after the Second World War that ocean research
vessels began to make real progress in developing better coring
methods which could bring up long cores from the sea floor, even
where the water was 2 or more miles deep. During this time, the
Woods Hole Oceanographic Institution and the Lamont Geological Ob-
servatory--both located on the east coast of the United States--were
very active in investigating marine life, sediments, and the sea
floor. The Lamont Geological Observatory had been founded in 1949
by Dr. Maurice Ewing, a professor at Columbia University. Ewing
was enthusiastic and tireless in developing a research team for investigating the sea floor, and during the next 20 years obtained a
colossal amount of data from the many voyages made with the research
vessels used by the team. The three primary types of research equipment used at sea were: (a) the echo sounder, which constantly records the exact water depth between the ship and the sea floor as
the voyage progresses, (b) the seismic survey apparatus, and (c)
the piston corer. The seismic survey equipment measures the thickness of the various deep layers of which the floor is composed,
enabling the scientists to determine with a fair degree of accuracy
the total thickness of sediments which lie on top of the deeper,
igneous (non-sedimentary) foundation. In order to obtain a recording of the seismic waves which make this analysis of the floor possible, it is necessary to produce strong, artificial shock waves
in the water by such means as detonating a charge of approximately
one-half pound of TNT explosive out in the water at frequent intervals. The shock waves produced by the explosion travel through
the water, pass into the ocean floor, and bounce back from the
harder layers beneath.

In the early days of the Lamont Geological Observatory's explorations, Ewing greatly improved the piston coring device, so that
cores of as much as 20 meters length could be brought up intact in

the coring tube. This made it possible for the scientists to study
layer-by-layer, the upper 65 feet of sediments in the natural order
in which they were laid down. Ewing's improved corer used boiler
tubing of two-and-one-half inches diameter as the main tube to be
driven into the sediments and then withdrawn with its load.[10] This
was a more effective and more economical coring device than the
original Swedish model had been.

A great many research voyages have been made by the Lamont
Geological Observatory (now the Lamont-Doherty Geological Observatory) since its beginning in 1949. During the first decade these
voyages concentrated on the Atlantic Ocean. Some important achieve-
ments of the investigations, under the direction of Ewing, were:
(a) a detailed mapping of large areas of the mid-Atlantic Ridge,
which is now known to be far larger and more extensive than the
greatest mountain ranges on the continents, (b) the discovery that
the bottom of the Atlantic Ocean has great expanses of abyssal
plain which are almost perfectly flat--much flatter than any plain
or desert on the continents, (c) the mapping and analysis of the
work of turbidity currents in helping to form the great submarine
canyons which have been cut into the continental shelf off the
eastern coast of the United States, (d) the discovery that most of
the ocean floor which is not near to the continents has a covering
of less than 3,500 feet of sediments--considerably thinner than was
expected, and (e) the observation that the earth's crust beneath
the sedimentary covering of the ocean floor is much thinner than
the crust beneath the continents. The latter two of these discoveries led to the realization that the floors of most of the oceans
are relatively young as compared with the age of the continents,
and prepared the way for the present knowledge of sea-floor spreading, continental drift, and plate tectonics.[11]

Within the past decade the Deep Sea Drilling Project, a united
research project of several marine and geological institutions, has
carried out by far the most extensive investigation of the sea floor
ever to be attempted. This project has been largely financed by
the National Science Foundation, and has concentrated on the taking
of intact cores of sediments from deep in the drill holes which
they have been able to sink into the floor. The deep cores are obtained by a rotary drilling process, rather than by the long-used
piston core process which can sample only the upper sediments of
the floor. The depth to which rotary drilling can penetrate depends
to some extent on the depth of the water at the particular drilling
site, but at one place in the Atlantic the crew was able to recover
cores from 1,412 meters (4,600 feet) in the sea floor.[12] Such an a-
chievement was practically undreamed of 20 years ago, but the
sophisticated equipment of the research vessel, the Glomar Challenger,
has made this great advantage possible. (See Chapter 4 concerning
some other details of these drilling explorations and the reports
of them which have been published.) In the succeeding parts of the
present chapter we will be referring numerous times to data published by the scientists of the Deep Sea Drilling Project.[13]

The Under-Water "Landscape"

Modern sea-floor research has given us a fairly complete picture of the topography and larger features of the ocean floors. Excellent color maps, such as those produced by the National Geographic Society, show the many abyssal plains and abyssal hills, the great ridge systems, the gentle rises, and the volcanic seamounts, as well as deep troughs, and intricately carved continental shelves.

Of interest is the fact that the basin floors of both the Atlantic and Pacific are dotted with a multitude of relatively low, broad abyssal hills. In the Pacific these are from 50 to 1,000 meters in height, with the average being approximately 300 meters (980 feet) high and 6 kilometers in diameter.[14] In most cases this is a much lower height than seamounts. Some of the abyssal hills were produced by slow intrusions of molten rock that pushed up from the underlying floor, while others seem to have had a more rapid volcanic origin similar to that of the seamounts. Most of them are now covered with fine-grained sediments which have a high proportion of pelagic, biogenic components.[15] It is now known that some parts of the ocean floor are changing with relative rapidity, whereas other parts have been exceedingly stable for long periods of time.

Some of the areas of rapid change are the great ridge systems, where fluid magma is welling up from underneath, causing a slow process of sea-floor spreading; chains of under-water volcanos, such as those which lie to the west of the Hawaiian Islands; and unstable areas around the continents. In the latter areas strong turbidity currents sweep land-derived sediments off into the deeper water to settle as thick deposits.

But many parts of the sea floor know no such change. They show by their intricately layered deposits of sediment that tranquility has been their lot during hundreds of thousands of years and more. Occasionally their sedimentary "calendar" shows the record of a period of disturbing volcanic eruptions in the distance, sending their fine particles of ash to cover the normal marine ooze; and afterward another long period of tranquility with the slow "rain" of biologically produced particles being the major sedimentary component.

Thicknesses of Sediments on the Ocean Floor

We have already referred to the Lamont Geological Observatory's discovery that the floors of most parts of the open oceans are covered with less sediment than had been expected. Now that we have the records of many more seismic surveys of sediment thicknesses, plus the measurements made by deep drillings in all the major ocean areas of the world, we are able to give a meaningful statement of several aspects of the deep-sea deposits.

The thicknesses of sediments found off-shore on the continental shelves and at the bases of the continental slopes are in many places astounding. Along the United States coast of the Gulf of Mexico, under the outer shelf, the sediments are approximately 20,000 feet thick; and many other sections of the continental shelf have from 10,000 to 30,000 feet.[16] These are the sediment masses which contain our off-shore oil reserves.

Just what these thicknesses near the continents represent in terms of time is usually difficult to say with confidence, since we do not know how much variation there has been in the rate at which moving water has carried sediments off the continents into the sea. The present rate of deposition on continental shelves is usually 15 to 40 centimeters (6 to 16 inches) per 1,000 years, though it is much greater near the mouths of rivers. The rates in the deep parts of the Gulf of Mexico and of the Gulf of California are 10 centimeters and 100 centimeters per 1,000 years respectively.[17] During the most recent period of glaciation, deposition rates near the continents were of course much higher than these. How many periods of rapid erosion and deposition there have been, due to ice-age influence and major floods, we do not know. Dating methods which are of value in a study of the great beds of sediments around the continents are available, but because of the large variation in sedimentation rates in these areas we are devoting our attention primarily to the sediments of the open oceans.

In the vast stretches of deep-sea floor where sediment deposition rates are _not_ directly affected in a major way by rates of erosion off the land masses, we can find a dependable source of information concerning some of the more recent periods of geologic history. It is true that certain major disturbances on land--especially on volcanic islands--have resulted in the rapid formation of sediment layers at considerable distances out on the ocean floor. However, layers formed in this way are so different in substance from the usual pelagic ooze which accumulates on the floor that they are immediately recognizable in the drilling cores which have penetrated the strata. When such layers are found by a research team, the measurements are duly recorded, but are kept separate from the measurements of the normal pelagic sediments.

Most parts of the deep floor of the Atlantic Ocean have a sediment covering which is from 1,200 to 3,000 feet in thickness.[18] This is the amount of deposit which lies on top of the igneous-rock "basement" of the ocean floor. (In most cases this igneous-rock foundation is basalt.) Some of the major kinds of sediments in the covering of the deep Atlantic floor are calcareous (chalk) ooze, radiolarian and diatom (siliceous) ooze, carbonate marl, pelagic clays (various kinds of clay which come from the continents), lithified chalk, limestone, dolomite, chert, and volcanic ash (volcanic mud). More than 10 cruises of the Deep Sea Drilling Project in the Atlantic have taken extensive sediment cores from numerous sites in the main floor of this ocean, as well as making many drillings on the Mid-Atlantic Ridge. Detailed descriptions of the sedimentary columns studied through these drillings are published in the series, Initial Reports of the Deep Sea Drilling Project.[19]

The sediments of the Pacific floor are of types similar to those found in the Atlantic, but the thicknesses and arrangement of the layers often differ from those of the Atlantic. Seismic surveys, confirmed by numerous drillings of the Deep Sea Drilling Project, show that a broad belt of sediments extending from east to west along the equator is often about 500 meters (1,600 feet) thick in the eastern and central Pacific,[20] and up to 1,000 meters in the open ocean in the western part.[21] (These amounts are of course much less than the thicknesses found in the deep-sea trenches adjacent to land masses.) The sedimentary covering on the sides of the above mentioned east-west equatorial belt thins out both north and south of the equatorial region, becoming as little as 100 meters or less at some of the higher latitudes.[22]

We have previously referred to the thick layers of calcium carbonate ooze which accumulate on the ocean floors due to the slow fallout of the microscopic shells and discs of the Foraminifera, the coccolithophores, and other carbonate-producing organisms living in the water. Exposed carbonate sediments (sometimes called "chalk oozes" or "foraminiferal muds") are found mainly in, and north and south of, the equatorial region of the oceans. In the Pacific and Indian Oceans these are from approximately 12° north latitude to 50° south latitude. In the Atlantic the carbonate sediment covering of the sea floor extends over a similar range, except that due to the warm Gulf Stream current it extends much farther north than in the other oceans. There are also major areas of the oceans, both north and south of the latitudes we have here named, where no appreciable amount of carbonate sediment is exposed on the ocean floor, but where lithified and partially lithified chalks are found as the drill penetrates to the deeper layers.[23] These chalk layers were formed in earlier times when the water conditions and (or) depths were more favorable for the growth and preservation of the carbonate-producing organisms. Since that time layers of very fine pelagic clay particles and siliceous shells from diatoms, radiolarians, and silicoflagellates have accumulated in varying thicknesses (often several tens of meters) over the chalk.

Growth Rates and Deposition Rates

The growth of the carbonate-producing organisms which inhabit the equatorial waters is much more rapid than at higher latitudes (except along the western shores of continents). It has been learned during the last two decades that the main reason for this more rapid growth in the equatorial oceans is the strong and continuous upwelling of nutrient-bearing water, due to the meeting of ocean currents from the northern and southern hemispheres.[24] The carbonate-producing organisms live mainly in the upper 200 feet of ocean water, so they stand to benefit greatly from nutrients being brought up from the deeper waters. In fact, this benefit is so great that it, plus the warmer temperatures which encourage growth, result in a deposition rate of from 10 to 20 millimeters of chalk ooze per 1,000 years. In contrast, in latitudes away from the equator the carbonate deposition rate drops to as low as 1 millimeter per 1,000 years.[25]

On the parts of the deep-ocean floor which do not accumulate carbonate oozes, the primary sediments formed are siliceous oozes

(composed of radiolarian, silicoflagellate, and diatom shells) and
red and brown pelagic clays. However, neither of these types accumulates nearly as fast as does carbonate ooze near the equator.

There are of course localized areas where layers of volcanic
ash, or of land-derived (terrigenous) sediments brought in by temporary ocean currents, accumulate much faster than the rates to
which we have been referring. For example, many cores from the
Deep Sea Drilling Project show rather thick layers of terrigenous
sediments in the deposits of Pleistocene age. These are usually
interpreted as being due to heavy erosion from the continents during periods of glaciation.[26] Some of these layers may represent
the period of the Biblical Flood. One must remember, though, that
the exceedingly fine nature of the carbonate and siliceous oozes,
and of the marine clays eliminates all possibility of these having
been deposited in anything like the short length of time required
for coarse erosion sediments.

Chalk-Layer Records From Deep-Sea Drillings

One of the most useful parts of the deep-sea sedimentary record,
for demonstrating the lengths of time represented by oceanic deposits, is that of the carbonate oozes and the hardened layers of
chalk formed from them. The carbonate oozes (sometimes called chalk
oozes) have been a subject of scientific investigation for nearly
a century. However, the rates of deposition of these (cited above),
and the thicknesses of ooze and chalk at various geographic locations, have been learned only during the last three decades. (The
presence of the harder chalk layers beneath the softer oozes was
practically unknown until the Deep Sea Drilling Project was begun
in 1968.) We will now consider the nature and extent of some chalk-
containing columns taken from the floor of the Pacific ocean by the
scientists of the Deep Sea Drilling Project.

Several of the cruises of the Project were devoted to a study
of the ocean floor in the Pacific along and near the equator. Lack
of space prevents us from presenting detailed data from all of these
cruises, but some of the more important ones will be considered.
The seventh cruise, known as "Leg no. 7 of the Deep Sea Drilling
Project," included deep drillings at three important sites (numbers
62, 63, and 64) north of the island of New Guinea. (See Figure 30
for a map of the area.) These cored test holes were made during
the late summer of 1969 and are described in detail in Volume 7 of
Initial Reports of the Deep Sea Drilling Project.[27]

The drillings at Site 62 penetrated to a depth of 1,905 feet
into the ocean floor, beneath a covering of 8,530 feet of water.
The site was located on a relatively low, broad ridge in the ocean
floor (the Eauripik Ridge), with water depths being considerably
greater on each side of the ridge. The water depth of 8,530 feet
on the ridge is shallow enough that the multitude of calcareous
shells continuously falling on to the floor does not suffer serious
dissolution or decomposition. Another important characteristic of
this location is that it is high enough above the level of the

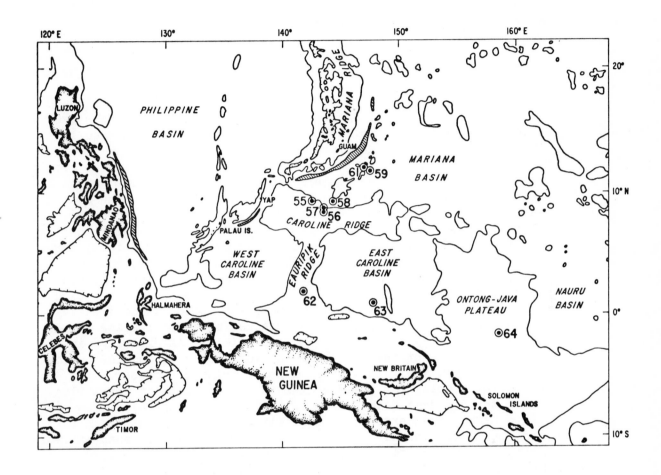

Fig. 30. Map of the western Pacific Ocean, with the drilling
sites of the seventh cruise of the Deep Sea Drilling Project
numbered. See text for descriptions of Sites 62, 63, and 64.
Winterer, Initial Reports, v. 7, 1971, p. 50.

162

surrounding basins that no appreciable quantity of contrasting sediments from them, or from elsewhere, are brought up on to the ridge by ocean currents.[28] Thus Eauripik Ridge is, and has long been, an ideal place for the slow accumulation of the shells of pelagic Foraminifera, coccolithophores, and similar organisms. This forms an excellent time-indicating record of the past.

If one is accustomed to thinking of the growth of marine life in terms of only thousands of years, the stratigraphic record here at Site 62--and also at most other sites drilled--will be little short of staggering. At Site 62 the actual sedimentary column was approximately 1,880 feet in depth, and nearly all of it shows every evidence of having accumulated by the slow, natural processes by which biologically produced deep-sea sediments are forming today. The sediment thickness at this site is more than that of some similar columns found in the eastern equatorial Pacific, but not as deep as several others drilled in the western Pacific. The sedimentary column at Site 62 was very thoroughly sampled and cored, especially the upper 1,200 feet (364 meters) of it. (See Figure 31 for a summary diagram of the column.) Of this 1,200 feet, very few sections contained less than 70% calcium carbonate, and most parts possessed from 80 to 94% of this compound.[29] When one considers that nearly all of this carbonate is from the accumulation of shells from the minute animals and plants which lived floating in the upper layers of water above, he is forced to realize that some millions of years are represented here.[30] As explained in the earlier part of this chapter, the Foraminifera, and the coccolithophores and their relatives, are the primary producers of carbonate material for these sediments.[31] The rate of deposition due to the constant "slow rain" of their shells and calcareous plates hardly ever exceeds 20 millimeters (slightly less than 1 inch) per 1,000 years. So, even if one were to assume such extraordinary growth conditions in the ancient seas as to allow for a growth rate 10 times as fast as at present--which is probably biologically impossible--over one million years would be required for producing the upper 1,200 feet of this sedimentary column.

When we examine the stratigraphic column found at Site 64 we find a composition and structure similar to that of Site 62. The drillings, like those at Site 62, were made on a low, broad ridge of the ocean floor (the Ontong-Java Plateau) and penetrated to an even greater depth than those at Site 62. This plateau (sometimes referred to as the Solomon Rise) is a large, nearly level area, over 300 miles in width. Because of its raised position, above the surrounding ocean floor, it has been protected from invasion by foreign sediments, and has accumulated an unusually reliable and uniform pattern of pelagic oozes and chalks from the shell-producing organisms which have lived in the water above the plateau. We will not give the details of this column, but they can be obtained from the same source to which we have been referring.[32] We should, however, mention that at this site, just below the 1,300 foot level, the drill began to penetrate several layers of lithified chalk ooze (which is called chalk). Farther on down, even some layers of hard limestone were encountered.[33] This presence of layers of differing

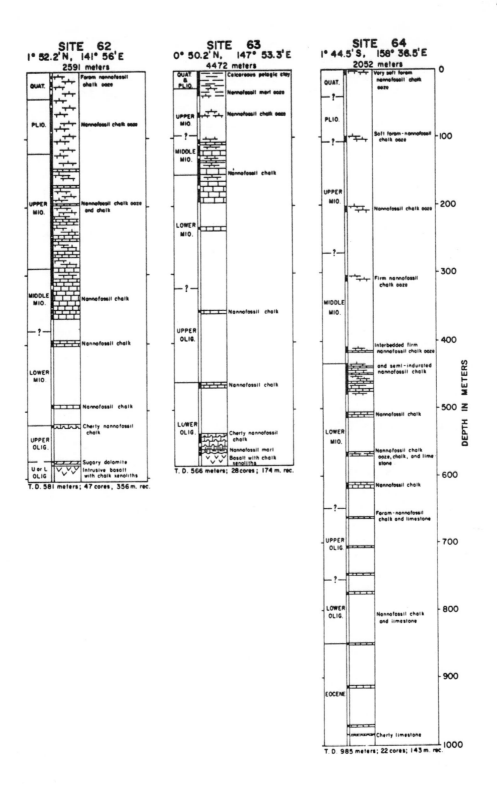

Fig. 31. Summaries of the local stratigraphic columns found
at Drilling Sites 62, 63, and 64 in the western Pacific Ocean.
Note the great depths of pelagic sediments at these sites.
Winterer, Initial Reports, v. 7, 1971, p. 6.

degrees of hardness shows that these beds of sediment which accumulated during the earlier epochs of the Tertiary Period have existed practically undisturbed for the long periods necessary for cementation of the ooze particles, to form the hard layers. Also, the fact that there are alternating layers, with contrasting degrees of hardness, strongly suggests that there were periods of time when the oceanic environment varied from what it was at other times.[34]

The rates at which the sediments originally accumulated undoubtedly differed somewhat from the present rate of near 20 millimeters per 1,000 years, and likely fluctuated appreciably at certain times. Nevertheless, the principle of the stability of the natural laws of biological growth, which we explained in Chapter 3 and in the earlier part of this Chapter 9, prevents anyone from speculating that the formation rate of these sediments was vastly greater than at present. Also, the texture, arrangement, and very fine-grained nature of the deposit prevents our postulating that the sediments were brought in from elsewhere. (The team of scientists on board the drilling vessel were alert to watch for evidences of the action of ancient turbidity currents and other swift currents, but found practically none at the sites we have been considering.)[35]

Before terminating the discussion of drillings made during the seventh cruise, we should briefly note a few facts about Site 63, which can be contrasted somewhat with the two sites we have just discussed (numbers 62 and 64). By glancing at the map (Figure 30) one can see that Site 63 lies between the other two, and that it is in a basin, rather than on a ridge or plateau. Thus we are not surprised to find that the water depth at Site 63 is 14,700 feet, a depth too great to allow deposition of any appreciable amount of carbonate sediments. One would therefore expect to find the sedimentary column at this site to be considerably different from that of the other two--and so it is. This column was approximately 1,800 feet in thickness. The upper 65 feet was found to be made up mainly of layers of various types of pelagic clay, with some siliceous microfossils. (Both the clay and the microfossils have particle sizes which allow only very slow settling in the ocean waters.) At the surface of the sea floor here the carbonate content is only 4%. Deeper, the carbonate content rises to high percentages, undoubtedly indicating that during the earlier parts of its history the basin floor was higher, with less water depth covering it than at present. However, the composition of the chalk ooze, chalk, and limestone layers which appear in the deeper parts of the column at Site 63 is very significantly different from that of the columns at Sites 62 and 64. For example, the amounts and vertical distribution of certain minerals, and of various kinds of fossilized animal skeletons (especially the Radiolaria) vary greatly from one site to another--even though the sites are relatively close to each other. The total thickness of sediment which was able to accumulate at Site 63 was much less than at Site 64.[36] So, we must recognize that each of these three sites received its sediment covering independently of the others, without appreciable exchange or transport of sediment particles.[37] (This is another of the many facts which prohibit any hypothesis that the sediments of this area were laid down by a flood or other cataclysm.)

Thus, we have a great "library" of information concerning the past, on the ocean floor. The wealth of knowledge stored there reminds us of the exclamations of the Psalmist in Psalm 104:24-25:

O Lord, how many are Thy works!
In wisdom Thou hast made them all;
The earth is full of Thy possessions.
There is the sea, great and broad,
In which are swarms without number,
Animals both small and great.

We today have the means for learning far more from the sea than even the Psalmist realized was there. We now have the privilege of observing and "reading" the ocean bottom, most of which is covered with pelagic sediments. These are a marvelous record of the slow, natural buildup of the remains of minute, floating organisms, and of very fine clay particles which remain suspended in the water for years before finally coming to rest on the bottom. Therefore it is evident that most of the deep ocean bottom provides us with the records of long periods of sedimentary activity--a sedimentary activity which has taken place apart from any significant accumulation of land-derived materials.

As stated earlier, approximately one-third of all ocean bottom has a covering of chalk ooze; and much of this is thick enough to include an extensive time record. This is not necessarily superior to the time record in the non-carbonate parts of the ocean floor, but since the great carbonate areas--such as the broad equatorial belt--are more accessible and less complex for study, we are emphasizing these.

The sites drilled on the seventh cruise of the Deep Sea Drilling Project are only illustrative of the great number of excellent carbonate stratigraphic columns which have now been revealed by this Project. There were other very old columns of this same type located on rises and plateaus of the Pacific floor, and cored during the sixth, seventeenth, twenty-first, and twenty-ninth cruises. Some of these carbonate columns, including those at Sites 47, 55, 167, 207, 208, 209, 277, 279, and 281 were found to possess from 390 to 2,800 feet of chalk sediment. This is mainly Foraminifera and coccolith ooze, but includes some layers of lithified chalk and limestone at some of the locations.

During Cruise seventeen, the scientists on board decided to make as complete a coring as possible of the sediments on the Magellan Rise. The results illustrate what an enormous amount of pelagic carbonate sediment can accumulate where the water depth has been shallow enough that the minute carbonate shells settling down on the sea floor do not dissolve to an appreciable extent. The Magellan Rise is a submarine plateau, some 1,400 miles southwest of the Hawaiian Islands, named in honor of the great Portuguese explorer who first crossed the Pacific. The path of Magellan's famous voyage is believed to have passed close to this plateau, though it is very unlikely that any of Magellan's soundings detected it. The drilling operations at this site (no. 167) revealed 3,800 feet of practically undisturbed sediments. The upper 2,000 feet of this column proved to be almost pure Foraminifera and coccolith chalk ooze and chalk, with most cores testing over 90% calcium carbonate. And a large proportion of the cores from the lower parts of this test hole were similar in composition to the upper 2,000 feet.[38]

While making any study of the carbonate columns from rises and plateaus we should also remember to contrast the sedimentary columns from nearby drillings in deeper waters, off the rises. Some of these, drilled during the cruises we have just listed, are at Sites 51, 53, 166, 206, 210, 278, and 283. In all cases these are within a 600 mile radius (usually much less) of at least one of the carbonate columns numbered above. These contrasting columns have, in most of their sections, a substantially different composition from the nearby carbonate columns, thus showing that the two types were accumulated independently of each other without interchange of sediments. The contrasting columns are in most cases composed of sequences of marine clay, Radiolaria and diatom ooze, chert, and fine volcanic ash, with occasional layers of chalk or chalk ooze. The greater water depth at these sites is the main reason that chalk oozes were less likely to accumulate, as was explained earlier. These columns which contain extensive sections without appreciable amounts of carbonate sometimes give an even more detailed record of the environmental history at the site of deposition than do the great carbonate columns. The latter usually do not lack well fossilized Foraminifera shells and coccoliths for identification throughout the column, but the shells (or spicules) of the Radiolaria and diatoms are even more durable, and therefore show excellent preservation. In cases where the radiolarian and diatom skeletons did finally partially dissolve, they frequently formed layers of chert (flint is a variety of chert). This provides us with additional information concerning the history of the stratigraphic column.[39] So, here again, the sediments of the ocean floors tell a very complete and reliable story of the past.

Quantities of Equatorial Chalk

We can better visualize the broad expanse and thickness of one basic kind of sediment (the chalk-oozes and chalks) in the ocean floor if we briefly review some of the data from the Deep Sea Drilling cruises which concentrated on the central part of the Pacific. Actually, similar amounts of these same sediments were found in extensive areas of the Atlantic and Indian Oceans, but we can not attempt to summarize so many cruises in a work of this type.

West of South America begins a broad equatorial belt of very thick carbonate ooze and chalk deposit which extends from approximately 10° north latitude to 20° south latitude, and westward for several thousand miles. During the seventh, eighth, ninth, seventeenth, and thirty-third cruises of the Deep Sea Drilling Project,

numerous test holes were drilled in this area. We have already described or at least mentioned 8 of the sites drilled in the western
part of this carbonate belt. Most of the test holes of Cruises eight
and nine were drilled in the broad plain of the ocean floor, far
from islands or other sharp topographic features which would appreciably affect the accumulation of sediments. (See Figures 32 and
33 for the locations of these sites.) When the stratigraphic columns at these sites are considered we find a thick sediment cover
made up primarily of the skeletal remains of the microscopic,
mineral-secreting plants and animals which live in the open sea.
The greater proportion of these organisms were the chalk-producing
types which we have been considering, but where the water depth is
greater than 15,000 feet the radiolarians and other organisms which
have shells of silicon dioxide predominate. (In water of this depth
the carbonate shells rapidly dissolve, leaving the more durable
siliceous shells as the dominating component of the ooze.) At
these greater water depths the surface of the sea floor is covered
with siliceous ooze, often to a depth of 60 feet, and sometimes
much deeper. Beneath the siliceous ooze practically all drill holes
revealed thick sections of chalk ooze, chalk, or limestone. Most
of these carbonate layers are from a time when the ocean floor at
that site was higher, with a correspondingly decreased water depth.

When taken together, all the stratigraphic columns revealed
by the drillings in the equatorial belt form an important body of
information concerning the past. The average thickness of highly
fossiliferous ooze, plus the hardened chalk and limestone, found
in these columns was approximately 370 meters (1,210 feet). We
should remember that all of this is practically pure, biologically-
produced ("biogenic") sediment, and that most of it is chalk ooze
and chalk.[40]

So, the Deep Sea Drilling Project has provided abundant verification of the data collected by earlier scientific explorations,
concerning the extent and nature of the sediments in the open ocean.
There is no longer any doubt that the thick covering over major
parts of the ocean floor is composed primarily of biologically-
produced components which accumulated as a slow, natural buildup
of pelagic organisms.

Total Quantities of Biologically-Produced Sediments in the Deep Sea

We will not attempt to state the total quantities of these sediments in tons, cubic miles, or similar units; but we do wish to
ponder the significance of the great quantity of biogenic sediments
which cover most ocean bottom. In the open ocean, any covering of
even a few feet of Foraminifera shells or the skeletal parts of
coccolithophores, Radiolaria, diatoms, or silicoflagellates means
that the waters above had to be teeming with these creatures for
over one hundred thousand years. The accumulation of their skeletal
structures has produced a natural buildup of almost inconceivably
great breadth and volume.

It may be that some persons will be tempted to postulate that

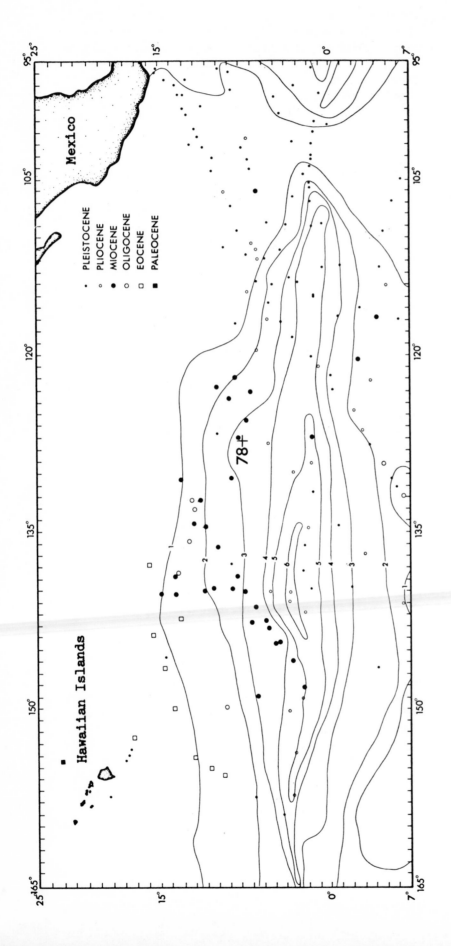

Fig. 32. Map of the area investigated during the eighth and ninth cruises of the Deep Sea Drilling Project, in the eastern Pacific. The small numbers give the thicknesses of sediments, in hundreds of meters, outlined by the enclosing isopach lines. Note that the buildup of these (carbonate) sediments is thickest near to the equator, where floating, sediment-producing organisms grow the most rapidly. J. D. Hays, et al., Initial Reports of the Deep Sea Drilling Project, v. 9, 1972, p. 210.

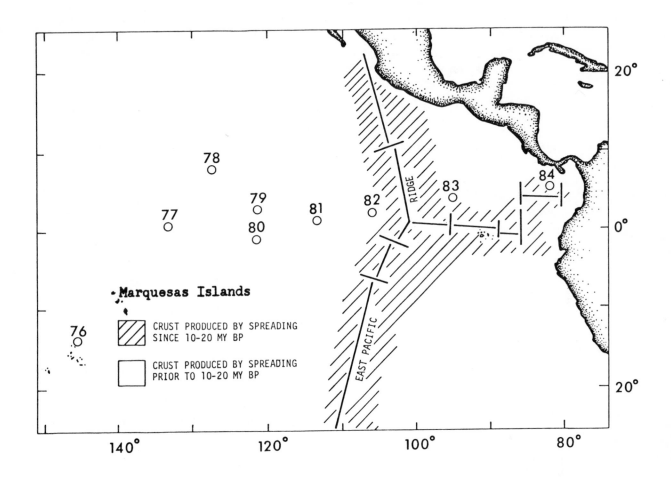

Fig. 33. Map showing the location of drilling sites of the ninth cruise of the Deep Sea Drilling Project. See Footnote no. 21 for explanation related to the East Pacific Ridge. Hays, Initial Reports, v. 9, 1972, p. 917.

this great expanse of biogenic ooze came from huge, concentrated
centers of origin, and was spread over the ocean bottom by unusually
strong water currents. But there are numerous reasons why this
could not have been. Some of these reasons are: (a) The natural
habitat of these sediment-producing creatures is the open sea, so
they could not congregate together and rapidly produce huge reservoirs of sediment; (b) The breadth and length of the areas of
ocean bottom covered with a fairly uniform thickness of one basic
kind of sediment is often thousands of miles;[41] (c) Any process of
rapidly transporting fine-grained, microfossil sediment from considerable distances would result in a heterogeneous mixture of such
components as volcanic ash, volcanic glass, and land-derived sand
and silt along with the microscopic-size shells; (d) Even if there
were some way for large quantities of these shells to be transported
rapidly, they are so small that they could not settle out of the
water rapidly, as was pointed out earlier; (e) The quantity of sediments which are composed primarily of the skeletons of microorganisms is so vast that there are no conceivable areas of water elsewhere
where they could have grown and been stored; (f) The upper set of
layers of these biogenic sediments, representing deposition from
the present, back at least several hundred thousand years, is
typical of present-day biological production at the various latitudes represented. For example, diatoms are more prevalent at the
higher latitudes, in colder waters, whereas many of the species of
Foraminifera thrive (and have thrived) only in the warmer waters
closer to the equator.

It should be explained here that, in some locations which are
from 500 to 1,500 miles from the North American continent, an occasional layer of land-derived, silty sediment is found in the upper
part of the column of biologically-produced oozes. These layers
are identified as belonging to the glaciation periods, when large
amounts of terrigenous matter were swept out to sea. Nevertheless
these layers are found to be only temporary interruptions in the
normal deposition of biogenic sediments which we have been describing. That is, very much the same type of ooze usually continues
below the terrigenous layer, showing that the microorganisms of that
part of the ocean were much the same before the glaciation as afterwards.

This arrangement of the strata, plus the many previously cited
facts concerning the sediments, can only lead us to the conclusion
that there is no possibility that the deposits on the ocean floor
were produced in only a few thousand years, as some theologians
have unwittingly postulated. Even with the sediment-producing
organisms growing at the fastest possible rate, only a very small
fraction of the oozes and chalks of the sedimentary columns we have
been considering could have been produced in so short a time.

The Mediterranean Sea

The Mediterranean Sea--the "Great Sea" of the Bible--was an
awesome mystery to the mariners of Bible times. It was then an
abyss poorly known and greatly feared. It has now been well charted

for several hundred years, but its real past has begun to come to light only very recently.

In August of 1970 the scientists of the Deep Sea Drilling Project moved into the Mediterranean with their drilling equipment to begin the investigations of their thirteenth cruise. It was a time of keen anticipation, as preliminary samplings of the bottom sediments had for several years given hints that there was something special and different about this sea. As we now know, the team was to find some very different sediment layers in the sea floor here from what they had found out in the Atlantic and other oceans. Of course some of the layers were of the usual oceanic types, but the drillings also revealed many thick layers of evaporite minerals buried deep in the Mediterranean floor and extending to practically all areas of this sea. This condition was more like what one would expect to find in modern shallow seas where rapid evaporation produces layers of salts and other evaporite minerals.

The Mediterranean is by no means a shallow sea, being over a mile deep in most places. But the evidences brought to light by the deep drillings show that there was a long period of time when this entire body of water was essentially a great evaporative basin which was receiving and storing thick layers of salts all across its floor. Some of the chief scientists of Cruise 13 even went so far as to conclude that this sea was once a dried up basin with only small salty lakes here and there--something like California's Death Valley, only much larger.[42] Much evidence for this condition was found, and many oceanographers have adopted the dried-up basin view. On the other hand, some prefer to see the evaporative period as a time when the water was of only moderately shallow depth, with evaporative loss high enough to provide for precipitation of calcium carbonate, gypsum, and occasionally halite (common salt). The physical laws according to which these minerals are precipitated are well known, and several aspects of them are described in Chapters 5 and 6 above.

In any event, the presence of thick and sea-wide layers of these evaporitic minerals deep in the Mediterranean floor leaves absolutely no doubt that there were at least a few hundred thousand years of evaporative deposition, after which greater quantities of water became available to return this sea to a salinity level similar to that of the oceans. Because of the presence of a few to several hundreds of feet of normal oceanic sediments now covering the evaporite layers, most oceanographers believe that the time of evaporite deposition ended about 5.5 million years ago, near the close of the Miocene Epoch.[43] We will consider the nature of both these and the evaporitic layers in succeeding paragraphs.

One question which may be asked is, "Does the Bible say anything about a time when the Mediterranean Sea was drying up, or was more salty than usual?" It is not likely that we can find any direct reference to these events which occurred so long before the creation of man, but there are a few interesting statements in the Old Testament concerning God as having power to dry up the seas (Isaiah 44:27;

50:2; Nahum 1:4). These references show us that the drying up of seas is at least a possible or likely event in the mind of God.

The More Recent Sediments Above the Evaporite Beds

During the thirteenth cruise, test holes were drilled at 14 different sites in the Mediterranean Sea, as shown in Figure 34. In those test holes which were drilled in the parts well out to sea, away from land masses, the thickness of the sediments above the evaporite layers ranged from approximately 250 to 1,100 feet. At the sites where the greater thicknesses lay, there were often rather thick layers which contained considerable amounts of land-derived sands and silt, in between layers of finer, ocean-formed oozes. The layers of land-derived materials show that there were periods when moderately strong water currents brought sediments out to sea. However, the presence of layers of pure ocean-formed oozes at some sites demonstrates that there were very long periods when tranquil seas prevailed, with no appreciable water currents to interfere with the settling out of very minute pelagic particles.[44]

At some of the drilling sites there were layers of these pelagic oozes which were made up of 70 to 80% Foraminifera shells and coccoliths (chalk-forming microfossils), with a correspondingly high content of calcium carbonate. The sedimentary column found at Site 125, in the Ionian basin, southwest of Crete, is of particular significance in this respect. At this location, the ocean floor has a gentle rise in it, and is far enough from land masses so that the sediments which accumulated above the evaporite beds are almost purely pelagic in nature, being composed mainly of the skeletons of minute carbonate-producing organisms. The thickness of this deposit of oceanic sediment was found to be approximately 250 feet, and its fossil Foraminifera and coccolith plates are very abundant and well preserved. The upper 105 feet of this column is of the Recent and Pleistocene Epochs, and the lower 145 feet (down to the evaporite beds) is Pliocene.[45]

The nature of the pelagic oozes at Site 125 also provides a useful source of information concerning the changes of climate and local environment during the long period of sediment accumulation. Climatic cycles reflecting important temperature changes, and changes in the degree of stagnation at the bottom in deep water, can be readily detected by observing the kinds of organisms which thrived, or did not thrive, at various levels in the column. The periods of stagnation to which we refer here are not those characterized by rapid increase of salinity due to excessive evaporation, but were long intervals of time during which the water in the deep sea bottom accumulated excessive amounts of organic matter, due to a lack of mixing and a consequent lack of oxygen. The layers which show this characteristic serve to assure us even further that the oozes at this site accumulated in exceedingly calm and tranquil water.[46]

One can gain some idea of the minimum time required for accumulating the 250 feet of pelagic oozes at this site by using the

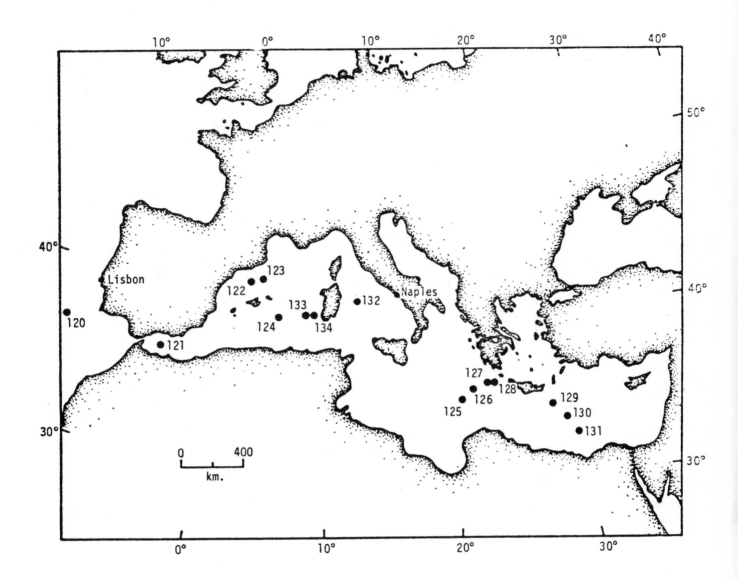

Fig. 34. Locations of sites drilled in the Mediterranean
Sea during Cruise 13 of the Deep Sea Drilling Project.
W. B. F. Ryan, K. J. Hsü, et al., Initial Reports of the
Deep Sea Drilling Project, v. 13, 1973, p. 818.

174

growth and accumulation rate of the shell-producing organisms which
are found in the oozes--just as we did in the case of Pacific Ocean
sediments. The _minimum_ time is the number of years required for
deposition, when we assume that the highest growth and accumulation
rate of the ooze-producing organisms was maintained continuously
for the entire 250 feet, with no interruptions due to unfavorable
climatic conditions. (Actually, it is extremely unlikely that such
favorable environmental conditions were maintained continuously.)
The highest accumulation rate for pelagic oozes of this type in the
Mediterranean Sea has been found to be 3.5 centimeters (35 millimeters) per 1,000 years.[47] When we divide the 250 feet (76 meters)
of Pleistocene and Pliocene oozes of Site 125 by this amount, we
arrive at 2,170 as the number of _thousands_ of years minimum time
required for the accumulation of this deposit. We accept this as
an accurate minimum time because there is no way by which fine particles such as make up these sediments could be deposited rapidly
by turbulent waters. As we pointed out in discussing the sediments
of the Pacific, long settling times and quiet water are absolutely
necessary for particles of such small size to be able to sink down
to the ocean floor.

The Evaporite Beds

    A record of additional periods of time is provided by the lay-
ers of evaporite minerals (salts) which lie beneath the oozes we
have just considered. In the Mediterranean, these minerals consist
of layers of anhydrite, gypsum, and halite (common salt), with
frequent layers of dolomitic marl between them. (Marls are unlithi-
fied sediments which contain a considerable proportion of calcium
carbonate or dolomite mixed with fine clay particles.) As stated
above, these minerals are a testimony to long periods of evaporation
which concentrated the sea water sufficiently for the salts to
begin to precipitate out of the water.

    The existence of these periods of evaporation is not difficult
to understand when we consider the fact that the entire supply of
sea water to the Mediterranean has to flow through the narrow Strait
of Gibraltar. The several tectonic changes which are known to have
occurred in this area in the past brought about restrictions in the
flow of water through this strait, during certain periods. It is
easy to see that any cutting off of the supply of water from the
Atlantic Ocean would soon result in an evaporative concentration
of the water in the Mediterranean Sea. At present this sea is dependent upon the Atlantic for nine-tenths of its water supply.
(Rainfall and the inflow of water from rivers supply only one-tenth
of the water which is lost by evaporation each year.)[48]

    The sediment cores from the Mediterranean drillings show us
the _great_ _contrast_ between the relatively pure oceanic carbonate
oozes above the evaporite layers, and the evaporite deposits themselves. The abundance of open-ocean type microfossils in the oozes
which overlie the evaporites shows that there has been a normal,
well-oxygenated, marine environment during most of the time since
the laying down of the evaporite beds.[49] But no such environment

characterized this sea while the evaporite layers were being formed. The water had a low oxygen content and was of high salinity. (See Table 1 in Chapter 5 for the concentrations necessary for the precipitation of the three main kinds of salts from sea water.)

The results of this warm, highly saline aquatic environment are best seen in the lower strata penetrated at drilling Sites 124, 125, 132, and 134.[50] At Site 124 approximately 190 feet of these layers were drilled and intensely studied. The upper half of this evaporitic series consisted of layers of dolomitic marl ooze. This type of marl is characteristic of stagnant, somewhat hypersaline water, and contains only minor numbers of fossilized Foraminifera and other microfossils. At some levels in the upper half of this 190 foot series a considerable amount of gypsum was found, showing that the water had reached the high level of salinity necessary for precipitating this form of calcium sulfate.[51]

The lower half of the evaporitic series was much more highly varied, consisting of approximately 95 feet of alternating layers (beds) of solid anhydrite and laminated (thinly layered) dolomitic marls. Some of the layers of anhydrite also are finely laminated.[52] Fine laminations in both the marls and the anhydrite layers show that the deposition of these layers was a slow, particle-by-particle accumulation, in a very tranquil aquatic environment. (A tranquil environment is always necessary for the deposition of such fine particles as these.) At this Site 124 some of the anhydrite layers penetrated measured over 5 feet in thickness, while others were only a few inches. The total amount of anhydrite which was drilled was approximately 75 feet.[53] Some of the thicker layers contained an abundance of mosaic-arranged anhydrite nodules. Nodular anhydrite of this type (also called "chicken-wire textured anhydrite") is strongly indicative of its having been formed in a hot, very highly saline, shallow-water environment.[54] (Such nodular anhydrite is being formed at the present time along the Trucial Coast, as described in Chapter 5.)

The evaporitic layers encountered at the other sites mentioned above are similar to those just described for Site 124. However, at Site 134 there was the significant difference that some beds of halite (common salt) were found between layers of anhydrite. This shows that in this part of the Mediterranean Sea (nearer the edge than Site 124) the sea water was concentrated to an even stronger brine than at some of the other sites. (As shown in Table 1 of Chapter 5, the water must be reduced to approximately 10% of its original volume in order to begin to precipitate halite.)

At Sites 124, 132, and 134 there were some layers of fossiliferous, dolomitic marl <u>interbedded</u> <u>with</u> the layers of evaporitic salts (see Figure 35). Several kinds of marine, shallow-water fossils were found in these marl layers. One should not overlook the significance of this fossiliferous marl, for it indicates that there were periods of inflow of major amounts of less-saline water which diluted the brine enough that neither calcium sulfate nor halite could precipitate--and apparently enough that some of the more

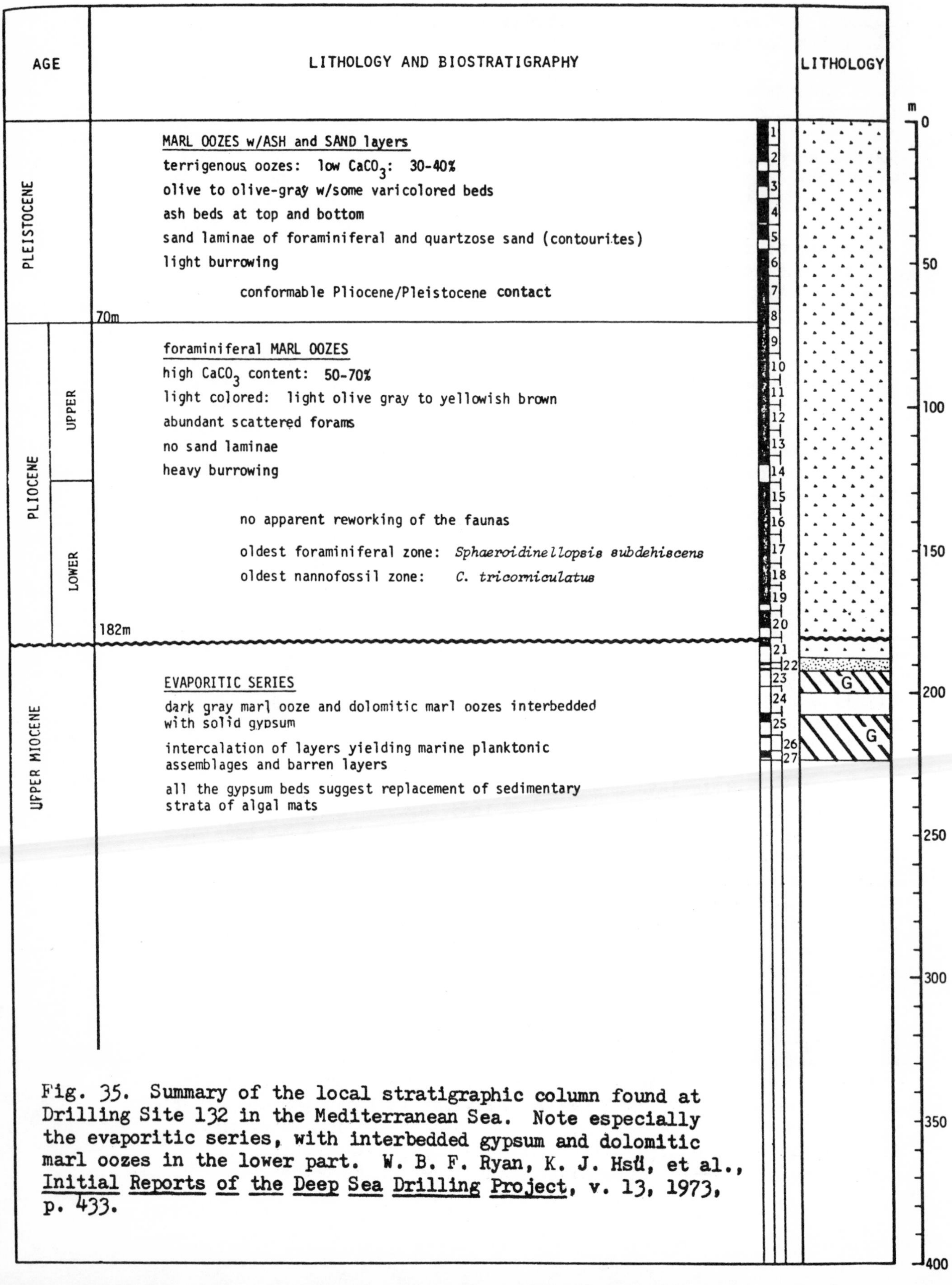
AGE
LITHOLOGY AND BIOSTRATIGRAPHY
LITHOLOGY
m
PLEISTOCENE
MARL OOZES w/ASH and SAND layers
terrigenous oozes: low $CaCO_3$: 30-40%
olive to olive-gray w/some varicolored beds
ash beds at top and bottom
sand laminae of foraminiferal and quartzose sand (contourites)
light burrowing
conformable Pliocene/Pleistocene contact
70m
PLIOCENE
UPPER
LOWER
foraminiferal MARL OOZES
high $CaCO_3$ content: 50-70%
light colored: light olive gray to yellowish brown
abundant scattered forams
no sand laminae
heavy burrowing
no apparent reworking of the faunas
oldest foraminiferal zone: *Sphaeroidinellopsis subdehiscens*
oldest nannofossil zone: *C. tricorniculatus*
182m
UPPER MIOCENE
EVAPORITIC SERIES
dark gray marl ooze and dolomitic marl oozes interbedded with solid gypsum
intercalation of layers yielding marine planktonic assemblages and barren layers
all the gypsum beds suggest replacement of sedimentary strata of algal mats
1
2
3
4
5
6
7
8
9
10
11
12
13
14
15
16
17
18
19
20
21
22
23
24
25
26
27
G
G
0
50
100
150
200
250
300
350
400

Fig. 35. Summary of the local stratigraphic column found at Drilling Site 132 in the Mediterranean Sea. Note especially the evaporitic series, with interbedded gypsum and dolomitic marl oozes in the lower part. W. B. F. Ryan, K. J. Hsü, et al., Initial Reports of the Deep Sea Drilling Project, v. 13, 1973, p. 433.

saline-resistant microorganisms could survive, leaving their shells
behind in the marl ooze.[55]

With respect to the fossils contained within the evaporite
series penetrated in these drillings, we must note first that the
layers of anhydrite, gypsum, and halite are barren of animal-type
fossils (except for a few which lodged in dessication cracks which
formed after the layers of salts had hardened). However, many of
the cores of hard anhydrite which were brought up contained almost
unmistakable stromatolite-type bulges in the laminations.[56] (See
Chapter 8 for an explanation of the nature of stromatolites.) All
stromatolites are formed by the growth of one or more types of algae.
Since present-day stromatolite growth is regularly observed on saline flats of the Trucial Coast and elsewhere, we thus have further
strong evidence that the water was of very shallow depth during the
deposition of the anhydrite in the Mediterranean floor. (The algal
cells of course have to have light; so, they can grow and form the
stromatolites only at shallow depths where the sunlight can penetrate.)[57]

Thus, the presence of the evaporitic series of deposits deep
in the Mediterranean floor provides a number of kinds of very strong
evidence that this sea was a shallow evaporative basin for a long
period of time prior to the deposition of the oceanic oozes which
are above the evaporite beds.[58] The exact length of this period
of evaporative deposition is difficult to determine, but the following facts and principles can help us gain some idea of the
minimum length of time.

The process of depositing anhydrite and gypsum from sea water
is necessarily slow, because of the small amount of calcium sulfate
in the water. (Both anhydrite and gypsum are composed of calcium
sulfate, except that gypsum molecules contain added water.) In
Chapters 5 and 6 we referred to the fact that the amount of water
which evaporates from an ocean or lagoon surface annually in even
the most arid and hot parts of the world rarely exceeds 5 meters
(16 feet) depth, and that this amount of normal sea water contains
only enough calcium sulfate to deposit a 2.2 millimeter layer of
anhydrite. When we apply this deposition rate to the 23 meters
(75 feet) of anhydrite drilled at Site 124 we arrive at 10,400
years as the absolute minimum time for depositing this portion of
the stratigraphic column at Site 124. Since the column at this
site also contained several hundred feet of other slowly deposited
sediments, it is obvious that the 10,400 years mentioned here is
only a small fraction of the total deposition time for the anhydrite
and the sediments above it.

At this point we should also recognize the fact that the evaporite deposits of the Mediterranean (such as the anhydrite just
noted) are not the lower-most sedimentary strata of this sea floor.
During Cruise 13 the crew of the Deep Sea Drilling Project was
unable to drill beyond the evaporite layers, due to the difficulty
of penetrating the hardened anhydrite with the drill bits they had
at that time. However, some of the additional drillings made in

the Mediterranean in 1975 (Cruise 42A) penetrated on down beyond the evaporite series. For example, at Site 372 in the Balearic basin, east of the Balearic Islands, approximately 300 meters (980 feet) of pelagic ooze, marl, and marlstone were found beneath the evaporite deposits. These are normal, open-ocean sediments with a high proportion of Foraminifera shells and coccoliths.[59] We recognize these as having been deposited in the same way as the similar sediments which were laid down on top of the evaporitic series (discussed in the previous subsection).

When we apply the same accumulation rate to these deposits as we recognized in the similar ones lying above the evaporites, we will add a minimum of 8.5 million years to the age of the sedimentary column here and at other related sites drilled. On the basis of data recorded from the many Mediterranean drillings, and known accumulation rates, we are thus able to determine that the deposition of sediments in this famous sea has been going on for a good many millions of years. The deepest sediments drilled were recognized as belonging to the Early Miocene Epoch of geologic time. (Most geologists date the beginning of the Miocene as approximately 25 million years ago.)

In summary, we can therefore say that in the central parts of the Mediterranean, away from land, the sea floor has thick layers of very fine-grained, biologically-produced sediments, just as has been found in the central parts of the great oceans of the world. In addition, layers of evaporitic minerals in the Mediterranean reveal that this sea underwent long periods of extensive evaporation with a deficiency of fresh water. Both of these basic groups of sediments are of types which require long periods of quiet water for the particles to settle to the sea floor.

FOOTNOTES

1. E. L. Winterer, J. I. Ewing, et al., Initial Reports of the Deep Sea Drilling Project, v. 17, 1973, p. 145-234.

2. Animals and plants which float in the open water (rather than living on the bottom) are known as "pelagic" organisms. This term is widely used in oceanographic literature, but for the sake of simplicity we have used it only occasionally in this chapter.

3. See Chapter 3 for a discussion of the laws of biological growth, and the stability of these laws.

4. G. W. Prescott, The Algae: A Review, 1968, p. 170.

5. R. S. Wimpenny, The Plankton of the Sea, 1966, p. 224. Compare Prescott, The Algae, p. 171 and 318.

6. M. G. Gross, Oceanography: A View of the Earth, 1972, p. 112, 119.

7. Ibid., p. 127.

8. Chilingar, et al., Developments in Sedimentology no. 9A, p. 235-236.

9. P. A. Scholle, "Diagenesis of Upper Cretaceous Chalks from England, Northern Ireland, and the North Sea," in Pelagic Sediments on Land and Under the Sea, International Association of Sedimentologists, Special Publication no. 1, 1974, p. 177-210.

10. Wm. Wertenbaker, The Floor of the Sea, 1974, p. 103-104.

11. Ibid., p. 66-127.

12. A. Kaneps, "Deep Sea Drilling Project," Geotimes, v. 21, January 1976, p. 16.

13. For a convenient, popular description of the research vessel, equipment, and work of this project, see S. W. Matthews, "This Changing Earth," National Geographic, v. 143, January 1973, p. 1-36.

14. H. W. Menard, Marine Geology of the Pacific, 1964, p. 34.

15. Gross, Oceanography, p. 61, 127.

16. F. P. Shepard, The Earth Beneath the Sea, 1967, p. 177.

17. Gross, Oceanography, p. 127.

18. Shepard, The Earth Beneath, p. 176.
Initial Reports of the Deep Sea Drilling Project, volumes 2, 3, 4, 12, and 14.
Geotimes, v. 19 (1974), November, p. 16-18; v. 20 (1975), March, p. 26-28, June, p. 22-24, July, p. 18-21, December, p. 18-21; v. 21 (1976), February, p. 23-26.

19. Volumes 2, 3, 4, 12, and 14 (reporting on the deeper Atlantic drillings) have been published as of December 1976, and future volumes no. 36, 37, 39, 40, 41, 43, and 44 will deal with other parts of the Atlantic.

20. Harry E. Cook, "North American Stratigraphic Principles as Applied to Deep-Sea Sediments," American Association of Petroleum Geologists Bulletin, v. 59 (1975), p. 824.

21. B. C. Heezen and I. D. MacGregor, "The Evolution of the Pacific," Scientific American, v. 229, November 1973, p. 105.
It now seems evident that the primary reason for the greater thicknesses of sediments in the western Pacific, as compared with the eastern, is that the spreading center at which new ocean floor is formed is on the eastern side (along the East Pacific Ridge). As new floor is formed it moves westward. Thus the older floor is in the west, and has had more time to receive sediments than that of the east or central Pacific floor.

22. The reasons for the thinner sediment covering at higher latitudes are mainly two: slower production of carbonate skeletal matter in the colder waters, and rapid dissolution of calcium carbonate (by carbonic acid) at ocean depths greater than 4,000 meters.

23. Initial Reports of the Deep Sea Drilling Project, v. 19, Sites 183 and 192; v. 20, Sites 195, 196, and 199; v. 28, Sites 265 and 267; v. 29, Site 278.
   Geotimes, v. 19 (1974), November, p. 16-17; v. 21 (1976), March, p. 21-22.
   Also see Winterer, Ewing, et al., Initial Reports, v. 17, 1973, p. 412-427; and R. L. Larson, et al., Initial Reports, v. 32, 1975, p. 891-907, for discussions on lithification of chalk oozes in the deeper ocean floor.

24. Heezen and MacGregor, "The Evolution of the Pacific," p. 102.

25. Cook, "North American," p. 824.

26. T. A. Davies, "Oceanic Sediments and Their Diagenesis: Some Examples From Deep-Sea Drilling," Journal of Sedimentary Petrology, v. 43 (1973), p. 382.

27. E. L. Winterer, et al., Initial Reports, v. 7, 1971.

28. Ibid., p. 3, 49, 50, and 1,009.

29. Ibid., p. 54-55 and 847-853.

30. The 1,200 foot level in this column is classified by the authors as belonging to the Miocene Epoch, and the 1,800 foot level as Oligocene. Ibid., p. 49, 80, and 847.

31. In the "Lithology and biostratigraphy" columns of the Initial Reports, volume 7, the types of fossilized organisms found are shown almost meter-by-meter for the entire columns of the two holes drilled at Site 62 (p. 82-320). In these columns the terms "Foram nannofossil chalk ooze," "Nannofossil chalk ooze," and "Nannofossil chalk" are frequently found. The word "foram" is an abbreviation for Foraminifera, and the term "nannofossil" refers mainly to the very small (usually less than 25 microns) calcareous plates and other skeletal parts from unicellular plants, such as the coccolithophores.

32. Ibid., p. 473, 855-858, and 978.

33. Ibid., p. 478-500.

34. For an excellent, brief discussion of the cementation and hardening of deep-sea chalks, see J. M. Hancock and P. A. Scholle, "Chalk of the North Sea," in Petroleum and the Continental Shelf of Europe, A. W. Woodland, ed., 1975, v. 1, p. 413-425.

35. Winterer, et al., Initial Reports, v. 7, p. 1009.

36. Ibid., p. 6, 324-352, 847, and 853-855.

37. An exceptionally clear example of extensive carbonate sediment deposition on a rise in the ocean floor, with contrasting sediment columns off to the side in deeper water, was found in the Indian Ocean, southeast of the island of Ceylon. Sites 214 and 216 were drilled on the crest of Ninetyeast Ridge, where the water depth is sufficiently shallow for the accumulation and preservation of carbonate sediments. There is good evidence that this ridge has had a high degree of stability since Eocene times, so it is not surprising that it was found to be covered by a 1,000 foot buildup of calcareous, highly fossiliferous, planktonic ooze. Off the Ridge, in water over 3 miles deep, contrasting, non-carbonate, pelagic columns were found at Sites 213 and 215. (C. C. von der Borch, J. G. Sclater, et al., Initial Reports of the Deep Sea Drilling Project, v. 22, 1974, p. 85-266.)

38. Winterer, Ewing, et al., Initial Reports, v. 17, 1973, p. 145-234 and 927-930.

39. G. M. Friedman, "International Congress of Sedimentology," Geotimes, v. 21, February 1976, p. 18.

40. J. I. Tracey, Jr., et al., Initial Reports of the Deep Sea Drilling Project, v. 8, 1971, p. 17-23, 38-39, and 61-709.
        J. D. Hays, et al., Initial Reports, v. 9, 1972, p. 43-496.
        Winterer, Ewing, et al., Initial Reports, v. 17, 1973, p. 145-234.

41. It is true that there are local irregularities in the sediment cover, due to slumping on abyssal hills of broad plains, but this is very understandable, and does not alter the fact of one basic kind of sediment over a large area.

42. K. J. Hsü, "When the Mediterranean Dried Up," Scientific American, v. 227 (1972), December, p. 26-36.

43. W. B. F. Ryan, K. J. Hsü, et al., Initial Reports of the Deep Sea Drilling Project, v. 13, 1973, p. 142, 413, 1057, 1259.

44. Ibid., p. 133-169, 175-210, 403-445, 465-508.

45. Ibid., p. 182, 185, 194-195, 204-210, 1266-1267.

46. Ibid., p. 194-195, 198, 203, 1398.

47. Ibid., p. 198, 1039, 1057.

48. Hsü, When the Mediterranean, p. 29.

49. Ryan, Initial Reports, v. 13, p. 157, 412-413.

50. Ibid., p. 673-693.

51. *Ibid.*, p. 150-152, 168-169, 674-677.

52. *Ibid.*, p. 153-155, 165, 675-676.

53. *Ibid.*, p. 155, 168-169.

54. *Ibid.*, p. 154-155, 676.

55. *Ibid.*, p. 196, 413, 425, 488, 508, 690, 1036-1037, 1205.

56. *Ibid.*, p. 425, 689-690, 705, 1046. Also Hsü, *When the Mediterranean*, p. 19-31.

57. For further evidence that the evaporites were formed in very shallow water, see *Ibid.*, 465-466, 488, 490, 689-690, 704-706, 1037, 1203-1205, and 1210-1214.

58. Many oceanographers and geologists find evidence that the floor of the Mediterranean was some thousands of feet below sea level during this time, and nearly all agree that the water depth was shallow. It is true that R. F. Schmalz has set forth a hypothesis that major deposition of evaporites could be made at the bottom of a deep body of water, by the sinking of brines (and later salt crystals) from the surface of the body of water as normal evaporation proceeds. However, no case of appreciable deposition by such a process is known to exist at present, and it may well be that such deposition has never occurred anywhere. (*Initial Reports*, v. 13, p. 1208, 1211; and P. Sonnenfeld, "The Significance of Upper Miocene (Messinian) Evaporites in the Mediterranean Sea," *Journal of Geology*, v. 83 (1975), p. 302-303, 310.) Furthermore the fossiliferous marl layers, the nodular and stromatolitic nature of the anhydrite, and several other characteristics of these deposits provide outstanding evidence that they could have been formed only in a shallow, saline body of water. Even if the deep-water deposition hypothesis were true, all who propose such a process admit the necessity of extensive periods of evaporation in order to produce the concentrated brines from which the salts precipitate.

59. "Glomar Challenger Returns to the Mediterranean Sea," *Geotimes*, v. 20 (1975), August, p. 16-19. (This and other sources report that the sedimentary column found at Site 375, southwest of Cyprus, was very similar to that of Site 372.)

CHAPTER 10

EARLY CHRISTIAN RESPONSES TO GEOLOGIC DISCOVERIES

What has been, and what should be the Christian's response to the scientific evidence for a long earth history? The past two centuries have been characterized by a wide variety of responses among Christian groups, but for the most part there has been an increasing trend toward acceptance of the scientific evidences. Yet islands of traditionalists in Christian circles of the western world have produced some interesting and often bitter conflicts. In this and the following chapter our purpose is to deal with the progress and failures, together with the strengths and weaknesses of the Christian response during the past two hundred years.

One of the most basic causes of conflict concerning the evidences for a long history of the earth has been a lack of knowledge both of the methods and of the results of scientific research. The clergy, as well as most of the lay members of the Christian community have nearly always had very little training or experience in science. Thus the Christian community usually has had no way to properly evaluate scientific data. Also, it usually has lacked effective means of protecting itself from theological antagonists who promote the view that the Bible and the discoveries of science can not be reconciled. As a result, pockets of heated resistance against scientific research have arisen among evangelicals. Sometimes this resistance centers on a rejection of medical science, with exclusive emphases on faith and "natural foods." At other times the emphasis is on a condemnation of geologic research, or on condemning practically all science as being evolutionary and atheistic.

All too often theological students have taken only the bare, required minimum of science during their years of training, and have--along with most of their parishioners--considered science to be largely unrelated to the facts of history and to the great principles of human thought. This seems to be the case particularly among the more conservative evangelicals. At least among the latter, there has been a frequent failure to recognize the great principle that science can and should be used as a legitimate means of discovering many of the details of God's creative work, which could not be given in the brief Biblical account.

Similarly, another side of the problem is that most students in training for scientific careers have avoided courses in theology and religion. These students seem to consider theology and religion to be far removed from the principles of science, and thus irrelevant for the scientist. So, here again there has been little concern or expectation for reconciling theological truth with the discoveries of science. Most scientists, like many theologians, have been willing to allow the two disciplines to exist side by side in their minds as unreconciled bodies of knowledge.

The Late Eighteenth and Early Nineteenth Centuries

The response of churchmen to geological discoveries was largely negative from the 16th to the first of the 19th century. For that day, this was perhaps understandable, for the early reformers, including Luther, held to the view that the earth is only about 6,000 years old. The gap of misunderstanding between the men who were doing scientific research and the theologians was tremendous. Even after a serious and systematic geologic research was begun (in the late 18th century), geological training was by no means as easy to obtain as it is now. This meant that the clergy had little opportunity to learn the methods by which scientific observations were made, or the specific results of those observations. The scientists could--and often did--sit in the pew and gain a fair degree of understanding and appreciation of the work of the theologian; but the reverse almost never took place. As a result, many leading clergymen of the day--both Protestant and Catholic--took to attacking geological science from the pulpit. This resistance to the discoveries of science was strongest in England, though it also existed on the Continent and in America.[1] On the other hand, strong opposition to religion from research scientists was not evident at that time. However, such opposition did develop later, after the publication of numerous evolutionary biological and paleontological works.

In the late 18th century we find theologians strongly upholding the idea which Luther had championed, that the fossils of the earth were formed during the Biblical Flood.[2] It is perhaps understandable that Luther and the other early reformers would have adopted this position, since they had no way of learning about the types and methods of formation of the rocks in which the fossils were found, or the depth and extent of the fossil-bearing strata. Even the scientists who were at that time attempting to study the strata of the earth did not have the benefit of deep well drilling records or of cores taken from the sea floor. They could only go to the cliffs, canyons, and coal mines, and study the strata which are near to the surface. It is true that the early geologists learned a great deal about the history and nature of the earth in this way, but what they learned by these surface observations was not easy for the theologians to understand.

Leonardo da Vinci, near the beginning of the 16th century, pointed out that many of the fossils of marine animals have the same skeletal structure in minute detail as their living counterparts.[3] This caused some of the more alert theologians to admit that here was a problem for any belief that the earth was only a few thousand years old. But since these men lacked scientific training, having only the tools of philosophy and theology, they too usually attempted to explain the fossils as relics of the Biblical Flood. Their analyses did not take them far enough to see that, since the Bible does not mention fossils as having been produced by the Flood, no amount of deduction from that sacred Book could establish their hypothesis. Such a hypothesis could be tested only by direct field observations, such as scientists have carried out within the past two centuries.

So, from the time of Martin Luther (16th century) until the 19th

century few churchmen questioned the claim that the fossils were
relics of the Biblical Flood.[4] One of the strongest influences which
prepared the way for the great polemical conflicts of the late 18th
and early 19th centuries was the publication and wide circulation
of the book Sacred Theory of the Earth. This was an eloquent four-
volume work published in England, in the late 17th century, by the
theologian Thomas Burnet. Burnet was highly respected as a royal
chaplain and as a cabinet officer, and his work remained popular for
at least a century. It was even translated into some other languages.
Burnet put great emphasis on the Biblical Flood as the force, or
series of forces, responsible for practically all geologic features
observed upon the earth today. Taking II Peter 3:5-6 as his premise,
he developed a highly imaginative and detailed description of the
work of the Flood in producing the present, observable form and characteristics of the earth. He held that "before sin brought on the
Deluge, the earth was of perfect mathematical form, smooth and beautiful, 'like an egg,' with neither seas nor islands nor valleys nor
rocks, 'with not a wrinkle, scar or fracture'...."[5] He greatly
stressed the "breaking up of the fountains of the great deep," spoken
of in the Old Testament, asserting that this cataclysm released the
water from the interior of the earth, to fracture and erode the
earth's surface into its present rugged form, and to deposit the
fossiliferous strata which are now so abundant.[6]

Georges Buffon

In the late 18th century the work of geological science began
to take on a more organized form. During this period the French
scholar Georges Buffon attempted what were perhaps the first scientific, numerical estimates of the various phases of the earth's past
history. His work was soon stopped by the theological faculty of
the University of Paris, which forced him to make a public recantation.
However, he later regained courage and in 1778 published his work
entitled Epochs of Nature. The opening paragraph of this book summarizes the method of his work:

> Just as in civil history we consult warrants, study medallions,
> and decipher ancient inscriptions, in order to determine the
> epochs of the human revolutions and fix the dates of moral events,
> so in natural history one must dig through the archives of the
> world, extract ancient relics from the bowels of the earth,
> gather together their fragments, and assemble again in a single
> body of proofs all those indications of the physical changes
> which can carry us back to the different Ages of Nature. This
> is the only way of fixing certain points in the immensity of
> space, and of placing a number of milestones on the eternal path
> of time.[7]

Buffon did not reject the Biblical account of creation, but
rather attempted to keep his work within the bounds of the Scrip-
tural framework. He considered each "day" of the creation to be an
"epoch," estimating the length of each epoch by mathematical calculations based on the length of time required for the cooling of
certain types and amounts of matter. (He considered the earth to

have been a hot, molten mass.) This was of course an oversimplifi-
cation of the problem, but his work did have wide influence, and
encouraged others to make further investigations based on the lengths
of time required for various physical processes. Thus Buffon set
the stage for some of the more realistic estimates of the age of the
earth which would be made during the next century; but in so doing
he retained a profound respect for the Biblical record of creation.[8]

In spite of Buffon's recognition of the authority of the Bible,
most theologians rejected his work. Very few churchmen were yet
willing to admit that one might invoke the laws governing the rates
of familiar natural processes as a means of estimating the antiquity
of the earth. In England, during the late 18th century, opposition
to geological science arose to an extreme peak under the influence
of John Wesley, Adam Clark, Richard Watson, and other clergymen.[9]
These men seemed unable to tolerate the idea that God has allowed
man a degree of freedom to investigate the past history of His work
of creation. They largely followed the then-current opinion that
all knowledge of the earth's past history should come from the Bible
itself. The fact that the Biblical authors do not purport to give
anything like a complete summary of scientific information, or to
state the age of the earth, apparently did not affect the views of
these ministers.

Thomas Chalmers

In contrast, there were a few leading clergymen at the beginning
of the 19th century who took the discoveries of geology seriously,
and attempted to point out the agreement between geologic data and
the Biblical account of creation. One of these was Thomas Chalmers,
a highly conservative preacher and leader in the Scottish Church.
Between 1804 and 1814 he published various works setting forth the
view that between the original creation of the heavens and earth,
and the first day of creation spoken of in Genesis 1:3-5, there was
a long period of time. He took the first one and one-half verses
of the chapter as referring to the original creation of the earth,
and a subsequent time when the earth became desolate and uninhabit-
able.[10] This view is often referred to as the "gap theory of creation," or the "restitution hypothesis." It takes the Scripture
account as leaving a time period before the six days of creation
began, and postulates that most of the sedimentary deposits of the
earth, with their fossils, were laid down during that period. Chalmers felt satisfied that most of the geologic record could be fitted
into that expanse of time, and thus used this view to quell the fears
of those who felt that the science of geology was posing a threat to
the teaching of the Bible.

Actually, Chalmers was not the originator of the gap view of
Genesis one. The Flemish scholar and monk Saint Victor Hugo, in the
12th century, definitely held that there was a very long time period
between the original creation of the earth and the six-day creation
described in Genesis one. He also stated that the existence of such
a period of time had "already been debated" by earlier scholars.[11]
Some other theologians who accepted the idea of this time gap were

St. Thomas Aquinas in the 13th century, the Benedictine philosopher Pererius in the 16th century, Dionysius Petavius in the 17th century, and J. G. Rosenmuller and J. A. Dathe in the 18th century.[12]

William Buckland

Following the revitalizing of the gap view of Genesis one, several other theologians and churchmen began to use this and similar methods of reconciling the geological and Biblical records. One of these men, William Buckland, soon took the lead in trying to give recognition to the objective observations of geology, and yet not to do violence to the Scriptures. Buckland was a devoted leader in the Church of England, but also was an accomplished geologist, and well known for his geologic field research. He also held the position of Professor of Geology at Oxford for more than a decade and lectured widely on the subject.[13] He, along with his contemporary, Cuvier in France, strongly upheld the evidence of a universal Biblical Flood and of the very recent creation of man, but found many difficulties in the custom of trying to fit nearly all the sedimentary deposits of the earth into the Flood period. Buckland therefore adopted the view of Cuvier, that the contrasting strata of the sedimentary records represent a series of several epochs of time and catastrophic events in the past, with the final catastrophe being the Biblical Flood.[14] Cuvier, being an accomplished vertebrate zoologist and paleontologist, had noticed the stratigraphic evidence for definite time distinctions between different levels of fossils. In his Discours sur les révolutions de la surface du globe (first published in 1812), Cuvier emphasized the fact that "in stratigraphic successions, fossils occur in the chronological order of creation: fish, amphibia, reptilia, mammalia--the older the strata, the higher the proportion of extinct species. No human fossils have turned up anywhere."[15] Thus Cuvier found strong evidence for long periods of time prior to the creation of man, at the same time strongly opposing evolutionary theory and insisting on the accuracy of the Biblical account of the recent origin of man.

As for the point in the Biblical record at which the epochs of time occurred, Cuvier held that these were either synonymous with or included in the six days of creation set forth in Genesis one. For a time, Buckland accepted this same view, but later began to favor the position of Chalmers; namely, that the earlier epochs of time, and the catastrophes between them, occurred during the long period which the first verses of Genesis at least seem to allow prior to the six-day creation period.[16]

The work of Cuvier and Buckland made possible the recognition of sufficient time for the accumulation of the vastly extensive geologic deposits, and gave a reasonable explanation for the great contrasts between the types of fossils which usually existed in the successive strata in a given locality. It also formed a rather impressive series of arguments against the pure uniformitarianism[17] which had recently been set forth by James Hutton, and was soon to be elaborated by Charles Lyell. Thus Buckland and Cuvier were hailed as heroic scholars who were willing to defend the sacred Scriptures, yet were aware of the value of geologic observations. Numerous English theologians rejoiced in this seeming solution to the problem.

However, as Buckland made further geologic studies he began to feel that the series of catastrophes which he and Cuvier had visualized could not have produced all the kinds of geologic structures and formations which he was observing in his field studies. In the fourth decade of the century Buckland participated in the writing of the famed Bridgewater Treatises, under the direction of the Church of England and the Royal Society. This was a series of eight treatises which were to be written with the purpose of "demonstrating the power, wisdom, and goodness of God, as manifested in the Creation." Buckland's contribution, the sixth of the series, entitled Geology and Mineralogy Considered with Reference to Natural Theology, was published in 1836. In it he continued to uphold the Mosaic account of creation, but repudiated his earlier emphasis on the Biblical Flood as producing many of the geologic strata. His position was now nearer to that of Charles Lyell, and he viewed Lyell's long periods of natural geologic processes as occurring prior to the six days of creation.[18] He did not reject the Biblical account of the Flood as a judgment on man, but along with Lyell and many others, adopted the belief that it was more local in its extent, and not the major world catastrophe which most theologians up to that time had thought.

Buckland's change in position with regard to the importance of the Flood caused a great uproar in theological circles, and even among the common church people. Many ministers publicly denounced him as heretical, and many unbecoming insults were hurled at him and at those who held similar views. Even the science of geology itself was frequently denounced as "not a subject of lawful inquiry," "a dark art," "a forbidden province," etc.[19] Nevertheless, Buckland continued to show himself loyal to the Scriptures and, during the next several years, lectured widely on the agreement of geology and the Biblical record. In his Bridgewater Treatise he had stated that natural phenomena "abound with proofs of some of the highest attributes of the Deity," and that the science of geology "when fully understood will be found a potent and consistent auxiliary to (revealed religion), exalting our conviction of the Power, Wisdom, and Goodness of the Creator."[20] Buckland's public lectures continued to emphasize these themes to the middle of the century.

Adam Sedgwick

Likewise, some of Buckland's best known colleagues were defending the trustworthiness of the Bible and reiterating the fact that there is true harmony between the findings of geology and the Mosaic account of creation. One of the most noted of these was Adam Sedgwick, whose position and career was similar to that of Buckland. Sedgwick, like the latter, was an ordained minister and church leader, and also a capable field geologist. He occupied the chair of Geology at Cambridge during most of the time Buckland was at Oxford. Though Sedgwick abandoned his former defense of the Biblical Flood as a major factor in forming the geologic strata, he maintained a long and effective witness of his faith in divine creation. This was especially evident during the 1840's when he publicly opposed the irresponsible evolutionary ideas which had been set forth recently by Robert Chambers in the popular book Vestiges of the Natural History of Creation. In a review of this book in the Edinburgh Review, Sedgwick wrote:

> I do from my soul abhor the sentiments...false, shallow, worthless, and with the garb of philosophy, starting from principles which are at variance with all sober inductive truth. The sober facts of geology shuffled, so as to play a rogue's game; phrenology (that sink-hole of human folly and prating coxcombry); spontaneous generation; transmutation of species; and I know not what; all to be swallowed, without tasting or trying.... If the book be true, the labours of sober induction are in vain; religion is a lie; human law is a mass of folly, and a base injustice; morality is moonshine; our labours for the black people of Africa were works of madmen; and man and woman are only better beasts.[21]

Sedgwick, during this controversy, presented strong arguments, derived mainly from the works of Cuvier and Agassiz, for the existence of "unbridgeable gaps between species and organic orders which correspond with similar gaps between geologic periods."[22] Sedgwick's confidence in Biblical truth is seen in the following quotation from his works:

> Thus we rise to a conception both of Divine power and Divine goodness; and we are constrained to believe, not merely that all material law is subordinate to His will, but that He has also (in the way He allows us to see His works) so exhibited the attributes of His will as to show himself to the mind of a man as a personal and superintending God, concentrating his will on every atom of the universe.[23]

The works of Sedgwick and Buckland thus serve as examples of the capable and responsible continuance of Christian orthodoxy meaningfully aligned with advancing geologic knowledge.

During the 25 years following the publication of Buckland's Bridgewater Treatise, the wider dissemination of geologic evidence in favor of a more complex and extensive history of the earth brought about the writing of a large number of books attempting to harmonize the facts of geology with the Genesis account of creation.[24] Some of these were little more than denials of the nature of fossils and of sedimentary deposits; others made genuine attempts to reconcile the two bodies of evidence. The series of catastrophes proposed by the French naturalist Cuvier continued to be used by numerous authors as an explanation which would allow the necessary time for growth and depositing of all the fossilized animals and plants. However, some other methods of reconciliation were attempted. For example, an English naturalist, Philip Gosse, published an extensive work setting forth the doctrine of creation "with appearance of age." In this he asserted that all things had been created in six literal days,

and that "the glacial furrows and scratches on rocks,...the tilted
and twisted strata, the piles of lava from extinct volcanoes, the
fossils of every sort in every part of the earth, the foot-tracks
of birds and reptiles, the half-digested remains of weaker animals
in the fossilized bodies of the stronger," etc., were all created
ready-made by God.[25] The attitude of Gosse was a very pious one,
and he freely stated that his only desire in setting forth this hypothesis was to glorify God and to uphold what he thought the Scriptures taught. However, the work of Gosse was taken seriously by
very few, since it represented God as producing an enormous body
of deception.

A Calm After the Storm--The Latter Half of the 19th Century

By 1850 most of the leading churchmen in the British Isles had
come to realize that the geologic evidence for long periods of time
was real, and that it was inappropriate to contradict it. It is
true that a great controversy between science and theology was yet
to be carried out, namely, the controversy concerning Darwinian evolution. But that was a conflict against a theory which in some of
its representatives took almost the form of a religion--not against
the value of many complex series of fossiliferous rock layers. Theories of evolution were set in array against the direct statements
of the Biblical account concerning the creation of life, but the
actual geologic evidence for time did not oppose direct Biblical
statements. The influence of Hutton, Buckland, and Lyell had been
effective in showing the value and acceptability of systematic geologic observations. Not only the observations of geologic evidence
by these men, but also their personal views were generally accepted.
Along with this the Biblical Flood came to be regarded as a local,
rather than global, judgment. Theologians as a rule were sincere
and emphatic in their belief in the Genesis account of creation, but
conceded that the history of the earth has been more elaborate and
extensive than the brief summary in Genesis sets forth.

It was indeed fortunate for Christendom that the early geologists
who discovered the evidences which brought about this change of attitude were not anti-biblical in their purpose or in their tone of
writing. In the latter part of the century a pronounced anti-biblical tone did arise among some scientists who were promoting theories
of evolution, but this was not the case with those who had founded
the science of geology.

In order to understand the problem of the 19th century opposition to geology, and the solution which finally came to be generally
accepted, we will here consider the works of four outstanding mid-
19th century evangelical writers, Hitchcock, Miller, McCaul, and
Birks.

Edward Hitchcock

Edward Hitchcock was a well-known president of Amherst College,
in Massachusetts. A large collection of his public lectures was
published in 1851, under the title The Religion of Geology and its
Connected Sciences.[26] These lectures did a great deal to alleviate

misunderstandings concerning the subject of geology. Dr. Hitchcock
was well educated both in Biblical studies and in geology; and, in
addition to his duties as president of the College, served as Professor of Natural Theology and Geology and did a large amount of
geological research in New England. The above mentioned publication
represented the work of over 25 years of comparing Biblical, theological, and scientific materials. The author had long felt a special
burden to help the public understand that the Bible and the science
of geology are really complementary to each other, rather than being
contradictory.

In the first lecture of the series Dr. Hitchcock clearly states
his uncompromising belief in the "divine inspiration" and "paramount
authority" of the Bible. He states that whenever science comes for-
ward with "probable deductions" which are contrary to the teachings
of the Bible, "science, I say, must yield to the Scripture." (p. 2)
Throughout the book he refers many times to the great truths of the
Bible, which he gladly accepts. These include the physical resurrection of the body, all the miracles of the Bible, heaven as a real
place, the recent creation of man in the Garden of Eden as described
by Moses, the temptation and fall of man, and salvation by grace
through the substitutionary death of Christ.

Hitchcock begins by laying down some of the basic principles
necessary for a proper understanding of the Bible in its relation
to science. One of the most important of these is given in the following quotation:

> ...we ought not to expect to find the terms used by the sacred
> writers employed in their strict scientific sense, but in their
> popular acceptation....Revelation may describe phenomena ac-
> cording to apparent truth, as when it speaks of the rising and
> setting of the sun, and the immobility of the earth; but science
> describes the same according to actual truth.... Had the lan-
> guage of revelation been scientifically accurate, it would have
> defeated the object for which the Scriptures were given; for it
> must have anticipated scientific discovery, and therefore have
> been unintelligible to those ignorant of such discoveries. Or
> if these had been explained by inspiration, the Bible would have
> become a text-book in natural science, rather than a guide to
> eternal life. (p. 3-4)

A failure to realize that the sacred writers were conforming
to the general usage of the day, rather than speaking in accurate
scientific terms, can only lead to such absurd and unfortunate con-
troversies as that of the Church's opposition to the discovery that
the earth travels around the sun. Hitchcock says concerning this:

> Until the time of Copernicus, no opinion respecting natural
> phenomena was thought more firmly established, than that the
> earth is fixed immovably in the centre of the universe, and
> that the heavenly bodies move diurnally around it. To sustain
> this view, the most decided language of Scripture could be quoted.
> God is there said to have established the foundations of the

earth, <u>so</u> <u>that</u> <u>they</u> <u>could</u> <u>not</u> <u>be</u> <u>removed</u> <u>forever</u>; and the sacred
writers expressly declare that the sun and other heavenly bodies
<u>arise</u> <u>and</u> <u>set</u>, and nowhere allude to any proper motion in the
earth. And those statements corresponded exactly to the testimony
of the senses. (p. 10)

Anything which contradicted this <u>apparent</u> teaching of the Bible was
denounced as heresy, "throwing discredit upon the Bible" and upon
"the unanimous opinion of the wise and good,--of all mankind indeed--
through all past centuries." A great many very convincing Scripture
references were formerly quoted to show that any person who contradicted this "plain teaching" of the Scriptures was in rebellion a-
gainst God. What could be clearer than the teaching of Psalms 104:19
concerning the sun's movement across the sky, or of Psalms 93:1;
104:5; and 119:90-91, that the earth does not move? Is it not strictly the rebellion of man which would contradict such definite teaching
given by the Spirit of God who understands the universe far better
than we? And yet, after many decades of firm and bitter resistance,
the Christian world finally had to admit that they had interpreted
the Scriptures wrongly, and that "the whole difficulty lay in (their)
assuming that the sacred writers intended to teach scientific instead
of popular truth." (p. 11-13)

So it turned out that science, instead of harming the sacred
writings or men's comprehension of them, had been an aid to understanding God's revelation. This leads Hitchcock to ask,"If the
principle (of using the discoveries of science to aid in the interpretation of Scripture) has been found of service in chemistry,
meteorology, and astronomy, why should it be neglected in the case
of geology?" (p. 14) His desire to see this intelligent use of the
discoveries of geology become universal in Christian circles appears
numerous times in the lectures contained in the book. In most of
these lectures he emphasizes that the science of geology illustrates,
rather than opposes, divine revelation, and that "the varied principles of science are but so many expressions of the perfections of
Jehovah" (p. 498). He also has much to say against those scientists
who fail to see that God is the author of nature, and that He reveals
himself therein (p. 499-508).

Hitchcock, in his efforts to show the harmony between geology
and the Bible, naturally finds it appropriate to deal with the subject of creation, and to state a summary of numerous geologic discoveries which indicate that the earth has a great age. In fact,
one might say that this group of lectures contains a summary of most
of the main evidences for geologic time which were recognized by
Bible-believing geologists up to that date. Below are a few of these
evidences, as given in the lectures:

1. We are, in this present era, able to observe the actual
formation processes of many kinds of sedimentary rocks. As we do
this we find that the rocks being formed by these known processes
today are very similar to the rocks found in the deeper strata of
the earth. It is therefore logical to assume that the thick and
extensive series of sedimentary rocks which exist were formed in

the same way, and thus at similar, slow rates. (p. 51-52)

2. A high percentage of the sedimentary rock layers of the earth contain a large proportion of well-worn fragments which show evidence of having been modified by the action of moving water over long periods of time. This includes huge quantities of extensively worn pebbles composed of earlier sandstone, and fragments of hard igneous rock which, after having been eroded from their parent rock, have been ground smooth by many years of river action. These fragments have then accumulated downstream from the source, and have formed layered deposits (often with strata of fine sandstone and shale in between). (p. 52-53)

3. The amount of sedimentary rocks and other sediments which have accumulated on the surface of the earth during the past 5,000 or 6,000 years almost nowhere exceeds 200 feet of thickness. This is but a minute fraction of the total thickness of fossiliferous sedimentary strata--which in some places exceeds six miles in thickness. The layers of even these thickest deposits are composed mainly of familiar types of sediments, which originate by slow processes of erosion supplemented by organic growth. Thus the processes of sediment formation upon the earth are much too slow to have accumulated anything like the total existing deposit in the short time that man has been upon the earth. And, since the climates on the earth between Adam and the Flood were not greatly different from those existing since, sediment production rates were surely not greatly different from the rates since the Flood. (We might add, if the climates of the earth were more tranquil between Adam and the Flood than now, as many believe, very few feet of sediments could have been produced upon the earth during one or two thousands of years.)

Added to the fact of the existence of such thick deposits of sediments over a large percent of the globe, is the fact that "neither the works nor the remains of man have been found any deeper in the earth than in the upper part of that superficial deposit called alluvium." (This is true even in the Near East, which is usually regarded as the area where man first lived.) Thus, since the works and remains of man are found only in the upper fraction-of-one-percent of the sedimentary strata, Hitchcock offers this as further evidence that the great majority of sediments were laid down long before God placed man upon the earth. (p. 54-55)

4. The arrangement of the groups of extinct fossils in the series of sedimentary layers, in many places gives testimony to long lapses of time. Hitchcock states that, at the time of his lectures, some 30,000 fossil species of animals and plants had been identified, and that only those from the uppermost rocks "correspond to those now living on the globe." Furthermore, paleontologists had by that time identified five--and in some places more--zones of earlier life, showing that "entire races have passed away, and (were) succeeded by recent ones; so that the globe has actually changed all its inhabitants half a dozen times. Yet each of the successive groups occupied it long enough to leave immense quantities of their remains...."
(p. 55-56) In another lecture he states that these extinct fossil

races are found to be "entirely distinct," and "so unlike that they could not have been contemporaneous" (p. 121).27

5. The great depth and size of numerous canyons and gorges in the world are a record of periods of erosional activity many times longer than the history of man on the earth. This evidence is made all the more convincing when we take note of the fact that many of these canyons were eroded by rivers into hard, igneous (non-sedimentary) rock. Three of the examples Hitchcock cites are: (a) "Near the source of the Missouri River are what are called the Gates of the Rocky Mountains, where there is a gorge six miles long and twelve hundred feet deep." (b) "Similar cuts occur on the Columbia River, hundreds of feet deep, through the hard trap rock, for hundreds of miles...." (c) "On the Potomac, ten miles west of Washington, the Great Falls have worn back a passage sixty to sixty-five feet deep, four miles continuously--a greater work, considering the nature of the rock, than has been done at Niagara." (p. 57) In all these cases the erosion has been accomplished by rivers, and the rocks which were cut away were hard varieties of non-sedimentary, igneous formations.28

In presenting his list of geologic reasons for accepting a great antiquity of the earth, Hitchcock does not evade the question of how these facts can be reconciled with the Bible. He recognizes mainly two workable methods, and points out that there is no necessity for us to decide which of the two is right, or to take a firm stand for either the one or the other, since neither does violence to the Scriptures. These two methods are essentially the "gap theory" of Thomas Chalmers, and the "day-age theory." He very fairly presents a list of advantages for each, though he does state his personal preference for the view of Chalmers (p. 63-67).

One of the lectures is entitled "The Noachian Deluge Compared with the Geological Deluges." In this the Biblical Flood is definitely accepted as a historical event, but the audience is reminded that the frequently stated idea of the complete breaking up or dissolving of the earth's surface during the Flood is incorrect. As evidence that this view is in error, the following is cited: "(the Scriptures) distinctly describe the waters of the deluge, as first rising over the land (including mountains) and then sinking back to their original position, with the same land...again emerging. Indeed, a part of the rivers proceeding out of the garden of Eden are the same as those now existing on the globe." (p. 116-120)

Hitchcock then gives numerous geologic evidences to show that most of the sedimentary deposits of the earth were, of necessity, deposited long before the Noachian Deluge. Included are references to several of the types of existing sedimentary deposits and other geologic formations which could not have been produced by flood waters, or as a result of a flood. Also, he cites the fact that no scientific observations have positively identified strata which were produced by the Flood of the Bible. (p. 122-126)

As a final observation on Hitchcock's lectures, we find it significant that he not only defended geology as in agreement with the Bible, but actually used geologic truth to increase his hearers' appreciation for God. In several of his lectures he shows how both the wisdom and benevolence of God are seen in the "vast series of operations" of which we have the record in the strata of the earth. He sees the active power of God, rather than evolutionary processes, creating and sustaining the countless thousands of generations of animals and plants which have lived upon the earth (p. 179-263). In the final lecture of the collection (p. 476-510) he strongly upholds Biblical truth, deplores any "perversion of science" which dares to oppose true religion, and declares that "scientific truth, rightly understood, is religious truth." He defends the latter statement as being valid because scientific truth very naturally and logically contributes to our understanding of the nature of God, and because a revealing of God's marvelous wisdom and benevolence in the natural world has a tendency "to produce right affections toward God."

Hugh Miller

One of the best known geologists of the early 1850's, influential in molding Christian opinion toward a favorable view of geology, was Hugh Miller. Miller was one of those rare geniuses who came out of an impoverished Scottish background, learned about geology while laboring as a stone mason, and eventually was recognized as an able geologist and man of letters. His extensive studies in the geology of the British Isles gained national recognition for him, so that he was made president of the Royal Physical Society of Edinburgh in 1852. Miller was a devout and active member of the Presbyterian Free Church of Scotland, and was known for his warm, evangelical witness and thorough belief in the full inspiration of the Scriptures to the end of his life.[29]

One of Miller's greatest concerns was to show the agreement and harmony between geologic science and the Biblical account of creation. His lectures and writings probably did more to heal the breach between geology and theology than the works of any other layman or scientist. The Testimony of the Rocks (1857), the last of his published works, was devoted primarily to this task. It was one of the most widely circulated books of its kind during the latter half of the 19th century, and served as an encouragement to many conservative Bible students and scholars during that period. The total number sold was approximately 42,000, which was an unusual circulation for this type of book in those days.[30] The importance of using both Biblical exegesis and the observations of science was emphasized in this work. The use of exegesis and Biblical philology alone was viewed as inadequate, because it tends to "commit the Scriptures to a science that cannot be true." That is, he who would restrict his studies to exegesis and philology is apt to interpret the Scriptures as teaching pseudoscientific ideas.[31]

Miller rejected the gap view of creation which was then held by numerous theologians, and took the days of creation to be long periods of time. His main reason for rejecting the gap view was his

196

observation of a continuity between the most recent (upper) fossil
deposits and the living animal and plant populations on the earth.
In other words, the fossil record is continuous on into the present
time, with many of the more recent fossils being very similar to
species which are still living.[32] And when the entire paleontologic
record was compared to the Mosaic account, Miller saw a satisfactory
resemblance between the two. The vast quantities of fossilized plant
life of the Carboniferous Period, he took to represent the climax
of the third day of creation. The Cretaceous Period with its great
number of large reptiles seemed to him to be the climax of the fifth
creative day. The first strata containing mammals, and all the succeeding strata deposited, up to the creation of man, he viewed as
belonging to the sixth day.[33] Miller reminds his readers that the
Mosaic account does not mention nearly all the types of plants and
animals which we find on the earth, so there seems to be no reason
for great concern over some apparent discrepancies between the Biblical and fossil records. His explanation of this is as follows:

> I have referred in my brief survey to extended periods.
> It is probable, however, that the prophetic vision of creation,
> if such was its character, consisted of only single representa-
> tive scenes, embracing each but a point of time; it was, let
> us suppose, a diorama, over whose shifting pictures the curtain
> rose and fell six times in succession,--once during the Azoic
> period, once during the earlier or middle Paleozoic period,
> once during the Carboniferous period, once during the Permian
> or Triassic period, once during the Oölitic or Cretaceous per-
> iod, and finally once during the Tertiary period.[34]

Miller found abundant evidence demanding that each of the great
eras of life on the earth be recognized as far older than the human
race. This evidence was seen especially in the fact that many kinds
of animals and plants have a distinct beginning in the fossil record,
show an extended duration, and finally come to a distinct end, with
no more of them appearing above that level in the strata. There are
many specific examples of marine shell animals which, in the paleontologic record, appeared, flourished, and then became extinct, after
which they were replaced by other types.[35]

The idea of an evolutionary origin of the various lines of animal
and plant life was, in Miller's eyes, particularly objectionable and
without real scientific support. A great deal of his time and effort
were spent in combating the hypotheses of "development" (evolution)
which had been set forth by Lamarck and popularized by Chambers.[36]
Miller visualized the numerous lines of organisms as having come into
existence directly by "the creative fiat" during the successive days
of creation, climaxed by the creation of man by means of a further
creative fiat on the sixth day.[37]

A. McCaul

The Rev. A. McCaul, Professor of Hebrew and Old Testament exegesis at King's College in London, was the author of an essay entitled
"The Mosaic Record of Creation." This was the fifth of nine conservative theological essays prepared by mid-19th century clergymen of

the Church of England as an "aid to those whose faith may have been shaken by recent assaults."[38] The editor of this series of essays, William Thomson, was at the time serving as Lord Bishop of Glouchester and Bristol. The series thus represented the response of a large segment of the English clergy to the recent advances of theological liberalism. The other essays of the series defended the reality of miracles, the divine inspiration of the Bible, the genuineness and authenticity of the Pentateuch, etc.

In his essay McCaul first gives a defense of the historical character and unity of the Genesis account of creation.[39] He then proceeds to show that all claims that this account is in disagreement with the discoveries of science are in error. In this he strongly affirms his belief in the fact of creation, and deals with the antiquity of the events of the first chapter of Genesis.[40] By means of Hebrew exegesis he finds strong evidence that the Hebrew expression translated "In the beginning" does not cite a specific time or point in eternity when God created. Quotations are given from several other Bible scholars who held that "'In the beginning' includes the idea of pre-mundane existence...and answers to 'Before the world was' (John xvii. 5)." McCaul says of these, "All are agreed that 'beginning' refers to _duration_ or _time_, not to _order_, and that it is indefinite in its signification, and may mean previous eternity, or previous time, according to the subject spoken of." Thus he translates the first statement of Genesis as, "Of old, in former duration, God created the heavens and the earth," and states that the Hebrew here allows at least as many millions of years as the discoveries of geology indicate.[41]

McCaul finds convincing evidence in the Scripture for taking the days of creation as periods of indefinite length, most of them being long. Among these evidences he cites the figurative use of the word "day" in numerous places throughout the Bible, and notes the peculiar extent of the first day of creation (Genesis 1:3-5). In this passage we should note that the first day is described as consisting, not merely of an evening and a morning, but of a period of light (following the creation of light) _plus_ "an evening and a morning." Therefore the first day is represented as indefinitely longer than the second, and represents a "mode of reckoning unique in the Bible, and peculiar to this first chapter of Genesis."[42]

McCaul sums up his position with regard to geology and the Scriptures as follows:

Thus a comparison of the actual statements of Moses with the discoveries and conclusions of modern science is so far from shaking, that it confirms our faith in the accuracy of the sacred narrative. We are astonished to see how the Hebrew Prophet, in his brief and rapid outline sketched 3,000 years ago, has anticipated some of the most wonderful of recent discoveries, and can ascribe the accuracy of his statements and language to nothing but inspiration. Moses relates how God created the heavens and the earth at an indefinitely remote period before the earth was the habitation of man--geology has lately discovered the existence of a long prehuman period.... Moses describes the process of creation as gradual, and mentions the order in which living things appeared, plants, fishes, fowls, land-animals, man. By the study of nature geology has arrived independently at the same conclusion. Where did Moses get all this knowledge? How was it that he worded his rapid sketch with such scientific accuracy? If he in his day possessed the knowledge which genius and science have attained only recently, that knowledge is superhuman. If he did not possess the knowledge, then his pen must have been guided by superhuman wisdom. Faith has, therefore, nothing to fear from science....[43]

T. R. Birks

In 1862 the Religious Tract Society of London published the book The Bible and Modern Thought, by the Rev. T. R. Birks, rector of Kelshall, in Hertfordshire. The Preface states that the book was written "in order to supply some antidote, in a popular form, to that dangerous school of thought which denies the miracles of the Bible, explains away its prophecies, and sets aside its Divine authority."[44] This volume contains 19 chapters and 5 appendices, dealing with such topics as, "The Supernatural Claims of Christianity," "The Reasonableness of Miracles," "The Historical Truth of the Old Testament," "The Historical Unity of the Bible," and "The Inspiration of the Old Testament." Chapter 14 is entitled "The Bible and Modern Science." In it Birks takes a position very similar to that of Hitchcock, whom we discussed above--though without the breadth of scientific knowledge shown by the latter. Birks, like Hitchcock, emphasizes that the purposes of the Bible are religious and moral, rather than scientific. He astutely observes at this point that, if its purpose were scientific, it would have to contain a great deal more of scientific detail than it does, in order to be of much value as a scientific work.[45]

Birks accepts the scientific observations of astronomers and geologists as valuable and as descriptive of real events and real periods of time. In this chapter we are reminded that any seeming disagreements between the Mosaic account of creation and the observations of science easily disappear when we realize that the Biblical account is "optically given, or describes changes as they would appear to a terrestrial observer." The "optical" nature of the account is seen as a recording of events according to the way they would appear to a human observer. The reality of such a method of revelation is said to be supported by the fact that such a style "is the constant usage of all historians, without exception, ancient and modern," and "is the idiom of the Bible itself in every other part of the sacred narrative." The record of the 4th day of creation is one of the places where we most clearly see that Moses was writing in an "optical" style, since the celestial bodies were very evidently created prior to the 4th day.[46]

As for the location of the greater part of the geologic ages in time, Birks places them just after "the absolute creation in the first verse," and before "the six days of creation that follow."[47] He summarizes his view of creation in relation to geology as follows:

The relation, then, between the latest conclusions of modern science, and the Bible history of creation, is one of independent truth, but of perfect harmony. Science reveals a long series of changes, once unsuspected, by which the strata of our planet were formed, and a succession of nearly thirty vegetable and animal creations, which were suited, no doubt, to the state of the earth in which they appeared....[48]

The works of Hitchcock, Miller, McCaul, and Birks, which we have cited above, give us an accurate picture of the sound integration of theological truth and geological data which had been worked out by about the middle of the 19th century. It is true that some points of the geologic theory of uniformitarianism, as outlined by Hutton and Lyell, had been extreme in failing to recognize catastrophic activities during the history of the earth, but the conservative writings to which we have referred show that these did not mislead conservative theologians. After all, Hutton and Lyell had never set their geologic theories up in opposition to the Biblical record.[49]

A Period of Progress for Evangelical Faith

A very influential part of Christianity in both the British Isles and the United States was still theologically conservative, and now great numbers of theologians and other clergymen realized that they could profit from the research of earth scientists without relinquishing their faith in the divinely inspired record of creation. The latter half of the 19th century was an era of great progress in the Protestant faith in Great Britain, with a large number of outstanding evangelical Bible-study and theological books being written during that time. In fact, a high proportion of the conservative resource material used at the present time in our Bible institutes, Bible colleges, and conservative seminaries is derived from this era. We can even safely say that a major part of the great body of Christian literature which is the heritage of present-day evangelicals (including fundamentalists) was produced during this latter half of the 19th century. And it seems very evident that the achievement of basic agreement in theological circles concerning the value of geologic evidences contributed greatly to the spirit and opportunity which brought forth these renowned theological and Biblical works. Some of the outstanding conservative authors of this era are listed in Appendix III. Nearly all of these men recognized the natural evidence for long periods of time, and had integrated this into their own theology.

We wish here to quote at some length from one of the better known of these works, as a typical illustration of the wholesome attitude which existed at that time among a great number of churchmen and theologians. It is refreshing to find here an uncompromising belief in the Bible as fully inspired by God, coupled with an appreciation for what science was revealing concerning the past history of the earth. The quotations are from the "Introduction to the Mosaic Account of Creation," by Rev. Robert Jamieson, in the well known Commentary on the Old and New Testaments, by R. Jamieson, A. R. Fausset, and David Brown.[50] Jamieson served as pastor of St. Paul's Presbyterian

200

Church of Glasgow from 1844 to 1880. In the quotations which follow, it will be noted that Jamieson was not accepting the full uniformitarian view which was popular in scientific circles at that time. On the other hand, we do not find him condemning science as a detriment to religion merely because some scientists were going farther in theoretical speculations than one might wish. (Numerous earlier theologians had categorically condemned geological science as entirely detrimental.)

It is of indispensable importance, however, to keep in mind the end which, in giving his account of Creation, the inspired historian had in view. It was no part of his business to tell of the powers and properties imparted to matter,--to enumerate the successive changes which...took place in the earlier stages of the world's progress, or to describe the order and arrangement established in its several departments, and to which we give the name of the laws of nature. He did not propose to expound a system of natural science.... He aimed at an object infinitely more important--that of communicating the principles of pure and undefiled religion by proclaiming the grand and fundamental truth, that there was a God before and above all things, who brought the universe into being, and on whom all creatures are continually dependent. In prosecuting that object he was, of necessity, led to speak of Creation--the origin of all things; but he adverts to the facts and processes of that creative work only in so far as they seemed to bear on the province of religious instruction.

Then after referring to what he regards as abundant geologic evidence "that animal and vegetable life had flourished on the pre-adamite earth, in numerous forms," he says of the science of geology:

Her province is to deal with facts drawn exclusively from the volume of nature: and these facts--of which she has accumulated a vast store--the more closely and thoroughly they are investigated, will be found to prove the truth, and give strong confirmation to the statements contained in the Mosaic account of Creation. With regard to those facts which are not mentioned in the inspired Record, she has supplied the light of a new commentary, disinterred from the earth, where for ages it lay unseen and unread--a commentary which we should hail as a powerful auxiliary to the truth, inasmuch as the Bible being a Divine Revelation, which cannot contain anything implying a misapprehension of the laws of nature, the works and the word of God, when properly understood, will always be found to agree. It is so in the instance under notice, and the same thing holds true in regard to other branches of science--Astronomy, Zoology, Physiology, Botany, and Ethnology--which embrace other classes of objects mentioned in the Mosaic narrative of the Creation. "Science and religion," it has been well said, "were married by God when he placed man in paradise, and what God hath joined together, let not man put asunder." Alas! man has already done the sinful deed, and the union between them cannot be fully effected again till we walk within the precincts of another Eden.

But let us beware of arraying them the one against the other, or making Geology, for instance, in the present immature state of that science, appear antagonistic to Scripture on the ground of some alleged discoveries affecting the antiquity of man. Essentially they love each other, and long to be united....

Thus, when the thoroughly established principles of Geological Science are viewed in connection with the Mosaic account of the Creation, we find that not only do they not impugn a single doctrine or statement of the sacred historian, but are in perfect unison with the whole of his narrative. With regard, for instance, to the assertion of geologists, that the earth has been in existence through the duration of countless ages, the language of Moses, far from invalidating, admits in the largest extent the truth and justness of this claim to a high antiquity....Moses, writing under the influence of Divine inspiration, seems to have been led, perhaps unconsciously to himself, to employ language which contains a latent expansive meaning, the full import of which time only can evolve, and which, when rightly interpreted, would be capable of adjustment with all the researches and discoveries which the progress of scientific light might shed on the works of God in all future time.[51]

Near the end of this introductory article Jamieson sets forth the reasonableness of a series of "physical revolutions, at different eras and on a vast scale, having successively changed and renewed the face of the globe," much as Cuvier held, and then states: "...if the world has, by this long and regulated series of revolutions, been brought to its present state of arrangement, when it was adapted to be the residence of intelligent creatures,--does not this progressive and careful development of a mighty plan exhibit a new and beautiful evidence of the power, wisdom, and goodness of the Creator?"[52]

It is obvious from these quotations that Jamieson, like most of his colleagues, was opposed to any careless condemnation of science, but was also cautious so as not to accept scientific theories as a substitute for Scripture. He was simply making use of the evidence from geology to enhance his understanding and appreciation of the Biblical record. We are glad to observe that this attitude was fairly typical of the era we have considered here.

During the last four decades of the 19th century many evangelicals made heroic efforts to stop the advance of Darwinian evolution as a force which was opposing evangelical Christianity. The acceptance of the data of geology as valid and useful, by such a high percentage of evangelical Christian leaders, put this group in a much better position to intelligently and effectively oppose evolutionary theory. Those who may be interested in studying the work of one of the most renowned of these evangelicals should consider the published works of Sir William Dawson, who lived from 1820 to 1899.[53]

Dawson was a native of Nova Scotia who, after receiving a thorough education in Scotland, eventually accepted the principalship of McGill University where he served for many years. He was highly respected in scientific circles, both in Great Britain and in the United States, and the geologic research which he carried out in Nova Scotia and other parts of eastern North America was widely used. Dawson was trained in theology and the original Biblical languages, as well as in geology and paleontology. Throughout his life he remained a staunch conservative and a defender of the full inspiration of the Scriptures. Like Hugh Miller, he recognized the Biblical account of creation as being easily understood when the days of creation are taken as long periods of time. A major part of Dawson's life work was directed toward a defense of the unity and divine origin of the human race, and the nonacceptability of evolutionary theories.[54] He lectured widely and published many articles and books setting forth the weaknesses and objectionable features of Darwinian evolution. Conservative evangelicals, both during his lifetime and for several decades thereafter, considered Dawson to be one of their strongest bulwarks against evolutionary theory. It is significant that in all his work for the cause of Biblical creation Dawson accepted the geologic evidence for a very old earth, and made good use of the data of geology and paleontology in upholding the Biblical doctrines.

FOOTNOTES

1. A. D. White, _A History of the Warfare of Science with Theology in Christendom_, v. 1, p. 217.
        Note--This author, as well as several of the other authors used in these references, does not represent a theologically conservative position. Though we often have to disagree with the sentiment expressed by these authors as they report historical events, we nevertheless find the factual materials which they report to be highly meaningful from our conservative standpoint. This same principle also applies to a number of the sources used in the previous chapters of this book.

2. _Ibid._, p. 218-230.

3. W. B. N. Berry, _Growth of a Prehistoric Time Scale_, 1968, p. 16-17.

4. It must be remembered, as pointed out in earlier chapters of this book, that the great majority of fossils are not the bones of vertebrate animals, but are the shells and other skeletal structures of invertebrate, marine animals.

5. White, p. 219.

6. _Ibid._, p. 218-219.

7. As quoted in S. Toulmin and J. Goodfield, _The Discovery of Time_, 1965, p. 144.

8. _Ibid._, p. 146-149.

9. White, p. 220.

10. A. C. Custance, *Without Form and Void*, 1970, p. 25-26.

11. *Ibid.*, p. 21.

12. *Ibid.*, p. 21-24. Custance also cites references from early Jewish literature, and from the Christian scholar Origen of the third century A. D., showing that belief in an early period of indefinite length seemed to be fairly common in Jewish and Christian circles (p. 11-18 and 120-121).

13. J. R. Moore, "Charles Lyell and the Noachian Deluge," *Journal of the American Scientific Affiliation*, v. 22 (1970), p. 108-109.

14. Buckland's best known work setting forth this position is his *Reliquiae Diluvianae*, published in 1823.

15. C. C. Gillespie, *Genesis and Geology*, 1951, p. 101.

16. F. C. Haber, *The Age of the World: Moses to Darwin*, 1959, p. 221-222.

17. The uniformitarian view, as set forth by Hutton and Lyell, held that all of the geologic features now present upon the earth were formed by physical forces of the same type, and essentially the same intensity, as those now in operation upon the earth. This view was somewhat modified in later years by geologists, as they began to recognize evidence of certain events in the past which at least approached catastrophic proportions. For example, it is readily recognized by sedimentary geologists that the rate of deposition of sediment, and the rate of erosion, in a given locality are increased manyfold during severe storms, earthquakes, and floods.

See Kenneth L. Currie's treatment of the development of the science of geology, and the place of uniformitarian views in it, on pages 46-51 of the book *Rock Strata and the Bible Record*, by Paul A. Zimmerman, editor, Concordia Publishing House, 1970.

18. Haber, p. 220-222.

19. White, p. 223 and 232. Compare Haber, p. 246.

20. William Buckland, *Geology and Mineralogy Considered with Reference to Natural Theology*, London, 1836, I, p. 8-9. (as cited in Haber, p. 221.)

21. As cited in Gillispie, p. 165.

22. Gillispie, p. 166.

23. As cited in Gillispie, p. 167.

24. Haber, p. 219-225 and 237-257.

25. White, p. 241-242.

26. Edward Hitchcock, The Religion of Geology and its Connected Sciences, 1851.

    We are treating this book at considerable length because it is perhaps the most complete and well organized work of its kind produced in the mid-19th century.

27. More recent research has yielded much evidence that, though the fossils of very old strata are not at all comparable to those of recently formed layers, they and the others which immediately succeed them in any comprehensive stratigraphic column show many similarities and relationships. In other words, the fossils of the Cambrian and other early periods contrast greatly with those of recent geologic periods; but in between, the change or progression from one fossil group to another was less abrupt than earlier geologists believed. This evidence has accumulated mainly as paleontologists have studied and compared fossil assemblages of the same age or level throughout the world. Many of the large gaps in the geologic record in western Europe (where most of the pioneer work in geology was done) are more or less closed by sedimentary deposits in other areas which can be readily correlated into the European type sections.

28. See Appendix II for recent measurements of the downcutting rate of the Nile River through hard, igneous rock.

29. Peter Bayne, Life and Letters of Hugh Miller, 1871, v. I.

30. Gillispie, p. 172.

31. Hugh Miller, The Testimony of the Rocks, p. 158.

32. Ibid., p. 146-147, 154-156.

33. Ibid., p. 160-174, 195-196.

34. Ibid., p. 204.

35. Ibid., p. 214-217.

36. Gillispie, p. 174-176.

37. Miller, p. 177, 220-222. Compare 228-232.

38. William Thomson, editor, Aids to Faith, A Series of Theological essays, 1861. p. iii.

39. Ibid., p. 188-198.

40. Ibid., p. 199-234.

41. Ibid., p. 199-203.

42. Ibid., p. 213-215.

43. Ibid., p. 232-233.

44. T. R. Birks, The Bible and Modern Thought, 1862, p. iii.

45. Ibid., p. 308.

46. Ibid., p. 319, 330-331.

47. Ibid., p. 322.

48. Ibid., p. 334.

49. Haber, p. 219.

50. Wm. B. Eerdmans Publishing Co., 6 vols., 1945. (The original was published in 1871.)

51. Jamieson, Fausset, & Brown, v. 1, p. xlvi-xlviii.

52. Ibid., p. xlix.

53. Charles F. O'Brien's Sir William Dawson, A Life in Science and Religion, 1971, lists 22 books and 34 journal and other periodical articles published by Dawson. A great many of these deal with the subject of the agreement between the Bible and science.

54. Ibid., p. 16-144.

CHAPTER 11

CHRISTIAN RESPONSES OF THE TWENTIETH CENTURY

The 20th century did not begin with widespread and intense controversy on the subjects of the age of the earth and the Biblical Flood, as did the 19th. In the present century there have been numerous varieties of response to the observations of geology, just as there were earlier. However, the issue of the age of the earth has not reached the proportions among the clergy that it did in the days of Buckland and Lyell. Because both conservative and liberal theologians had finally come to accept the basic evidences for age, the early part of the 20th century did not see many serious debates on the subject. Due to the publications of Darwin's Origin of Species, in 1859, evolutionary theory now held more of the attention of the conservatives than did the matter of age.[1]

Following the dissemination of Darwin's writings many conservative theologians adopted a theistic evolution position, whereas others rejected evolutionary theory but at the same time acknowledged the validity of geologic evidences for an older earth. Liberal theologians usually rejected the historicity of the Genesis account of creation, and substituted naturalistic explanations of both the earth and life upon it. The Biblical account was regarded as mythical, and in a similar category to that of the creation myths of Babylonia and Egypt. Another (less prominent) group was that of traditionalists who continued to reject practically all scientific research as incompatible with the Bible, and to hold to the idea of an earth only a few thousand years old.

The main stream of conservative, evangelical Christianity during the early 20th century recognized the validity of a large part of geological and paleontological research, but continued to hold strongly to the doctrine of the divine inspiration of the Scriptures. Consequently, as the century progressed, evangelical Bible scholars continued to make various attempts to reconcile the Biblical account of creation with the data of science. It will be remembered that during the latter 18th and in the 19th centuries there were numerous attempts at such reconciliation, though several of these efforts eventually came to be recognized as premature and unsupportable.

One of the early 19th century attempts at reconciliation which had continued to be used was the gap theory of Thomas Chalmers and others, which was mentioned in the previous chapter. This view received new momentum during the latter part of the 19th century as a result of wide circulation of the book Earth's Earliest Ages, by G. H. Pember.[2] Pember's primary interest, as expressed in this book, was in the activities of Satan and the demonic forces which he believed were responsible for the catastrophic ruin of the pre-adamic earth. Nevertheless, the book exercised a considerable influence among evangelical Christians in promoting belief in a very old original earth. This publication by Pember seems to have been a primary factor in popularizing the gap theory among the creationists[3] of the

206

first half of the 20th century.[4]

Early Fundamentalism in America

The term "fundamentalism" did not come into use until about 1920, but millenarian dispensationalism (out of which fundamentalism developed) became strongly established in America during the late 19th century. This form of doctrine took shape in England in the mid-19th century under the leadership of the Plymouth Brethren minister J. N. Darby. Darby's influence was very strong in both England and the United States. The type of millenarian doctrine which he taught was dominant at the well-known Bible conferences which were held at Niagara-on-the-Lake, Ontario, from 1883 to 1897. Many very capable Bible scholars were speakers at these conferences, and mutual cooperation was good. In addition to the various phases of dispensationalism and prophecy which were discussed, there was great concern over the then-current, rapid spread of theological liberalism in the major denominations.[5] This trend toward liberalism was such a threat to evangelicalism at that time that numerous outstanding conservative theologians who were not millenarians joined forces with the latter in an effort to stop the spread of liberalism. Among these conservative theologians were the faculty of Princeton Theological Seminary, and many other leading members of the Presbyterian denomination.[6]

The most prominent issues being emphasized by this "millenarian-conservative alliance" were the inspiration and authority of Scripture, the deity of Christ and his virgin birth, supernatural miracles, the atoning death of Christ, and the physical resurrection and personal return of Jesus Christ.[7] In 1910 the General Assembly of the Northern Presbyterian denomination adopted a five-point statement of essentially these same five doctrines, and reaffirmed the same in 1916 and in 1923.[8] From 1910 to 1915 the millenarian-conservative alliance published a well known 12-volume series of small books entitled The Fundamentals, with A. C. Dixon as general editor. There were 64 authors in all. The above named doctrines, plus several others, were discussed at length in this work.[9]

Practically all of the millenarians completely rejected the doctrine of evolution, but for a time did not press this issue. The magnitude of the liberal opposition to what were recognized as "the fundamentals" of Scripture brought about such a concentration on the defense of these that the evolution problem did not really enter the foreground until late in the second decade of the century.[10] At no time in these decades of fundamentalist activity did the question of the age of the earth become a prominent issue. Even when the great evolution controversy of the 1920's was raging, the fundamentalist leaders did not consider age to be the important issue. The recognition of the validity of geologic observations which Christian leaders had gained during the 19th century was still an effective leveling influence among them during the early 20th century.[11]

One of the most important influences in maintaining order among fundamentalists, with respect to recognition of geologic data, was the publication of the Scofield Reference Bible, in 1909, with a second edition in 1917. This Bible used the King James Version, but the nine conservative editors provided a large number of explanatory notes to supplement the text. As already mentioned in Chapter 4 above, the notes which were provided to accompany the first chapter of Genesis favored the idea of a very old earth, with a long time gap between verses 1 and 2, as Chalmers, Pember, and others had taught. The notes also allowed for the possibility of creation days much longer than 24 hours, pointing out that the word "day" is used in several different senses in the Bible.[12] The majority of fundamentalist leaders, during the period up to 1950, held to one or the other of these two views. Usually these leaders were not in serious conflict with each other concerning which of the two views was held, since both allowed for the full inspiration of the Bible and recognized the first chapter of Genesis as historical rather than mythical.[13] It is also significant to note that the acceptance of the great antiquity of creation, which these men readily admitted, did not lead them to accept evolutionary theories. On the contrary, their interest and efforts in opposing evolution increased greatly, until in the 1920's fundamentalists carried on an intensive campaign against this doctrine.

During the early 20th century there was of course a large part of the Christian world which did not consider the details of the first chapter of Genesis to be of great significance. As stated earlier, the liberals considered the entire account to be mythical. Also, a great many of the moderate conservatives held that it is an inspired, but basically nonhistorical account, having little or no relation to the discovered scientific facts. Along with the nonhistorical views, a theistic version of biological evolution usually was accepted.[14] Nonhistorical views are still very popular among moderate conservatives today, and have been diversified into several forms. Such conservatives usually hold that the Genesis account of creation is a part of inspired revelation, but that it tells us nothing about the order God used in creation. They maintain that the purpose of the account is almost entirely a spiritual one.

During the first half of the 20th century there was no sizeable segment of the Christian community attempting to promote the Flood explanation of the fossil record. However, there was one prominent Seventh-Day-Adventist author, George M. Price, who wrote several works attempting to minimize the geologic evidence for great age, and to account for the fossil record by appealing to the Biblical Flood. His published works date from 1913 to 1935.[15] A few fundamentalists made considerable use of these books. This they did, failing to realize that what was being called a "new" geology was little more than a restatement of views which were formed in previous centuries before anyone had ever recorded observations of the deeper sedimentary strata of the earth.

From 1950 to the Present

At the midpoint of the present century all of the views which were prominent during the earlier decades were still being held by at least minor groups within the Christian community. Nonhistorical views were gaining adherents, but a sizeable percentage of evangelicals still accepted either the gap theory or the day-age theory of creation--or a combination of the two. However, a considerable number of evangelicals felt that a precise interpretation of the Biblical account of creation was unnecessary, and that it would be better for Christians to let such matters be handled by professionals of the scientific world. It was felt that perhaps the first chapter of Genesis gives us only the bare information that God was the author of creation, together with spiritual lessons which might be drawn from this fact. The number which hold this view has continued to increase up to the present time.

Soon after the midpoint of the century the seeds of a sizeable revival of the old "flood geology" view began to germinate. Many of the basic problems which we mentioned at the beginning of Chapter 10 began to be in evidence, even as they were in the 18th and 19th centuries. Lack of acquaintance with the methods and results of scientific research, among the clergy and among theological students; and the tendency to avoid the task of integrating the discoveries of science into one's own theological system, were two of the more prominent contributing factors in this revival of "flood geology." At the start of this resurgence of the old view, a few fundamentalists began to intensively use George M. Price's books on the Flood view of geology,[16] and to study older theological writers concerning the effects of the Biblical Flood. As a result of this trend, we now have several rather vocal groups of fundamentalists who are giving much the same negative response to the geologic evidence for age as the theologians of the early 19th century did. They are unfamiliar with the evidence, and usually feel that it would be improper for them to make a serious study of it. Most of them seem to be honest in their contention that the Bible is the only source-book needed when it comes to studying the past history of the earth.

The willingness of these fundamentalists to take an anti-science stance with regard to the past undoubtedly has been enhanced by the fact that several segments of the scientific community have, during the past decade, come under heavy fire from the general public. (This has been seen in the frequent condemnation of scientists for doing work which has led to the production of destructive weapons, and to pollution of our environment.) Another factor contributing to their lack of confidence in science is that many scientists frequently have promoted their theories and hypotheses too boldly, and have failed to properly communicate their data to the public. A third enhancing factor has been the (mistaken) feeling that somehow the evidence for great age in the earth is inseparably tied to the theories of evolution. And, since the theories of evolution have so many obvious weaknesses, it is felt that the evidence for time should be disregarded along with evolutionary theories. With reference to this position, there is a failure to realize that even though many geologists do make the facts regarding age a part of their own evolutionary system, their use of the facts in this way does not invalidate or "contaminate" the evidences for age. No human being can invalidate any part of God's natural record by misusing it.

There are many shades of belief, and a large variety of emphases, among those who accept and propagate the doctrine of a very young earth. Some of the most prominent and commonly held points of belief found among these people are listed below.

1. The doctrine of creation, including the age of the earth, is believed to be of major importance in any statement of Christian faith.

2. The word "day" in the Genesis account of creation is taken to refer only to literal 24-hour days, and must be understood in the light of a completely literal interpretation of Exodus 20:11. Any figurative interpretation of the word "day" constitutes a rejection of the principle of the verbal inspiration of the Scriptures.[17]

3. The earth was somehow provided with sufficient light to maintain order during the first three days of the "creation week," and then on the fourth day the sun, moon, and stars were created.[18]

4. No death, except that of plant cells, plant embryos, and certain kinds of invertebrates which are supposedly less alive than other animals, could have occurred before the Fall of man.[19]

5. The evidences for natural events and processes of the past are always in error if they point to an age greater than 15,000 to 20,000 years.[20]

6. As a means of compensating for the lack of time for natural sedimentary processes, the Biblical Flood can be taken as sufficiently versatile to have produced nearly all the series of fossil-bearing sediments wherever they occur on the earth.[21] Furthermore, it is proper for Christians to formulate many hypotheses for explaining how the Flood formed these sediments, even though the hypotheses may border on the imaginative and not be comparable to observed natural phenomena.

7. The order of fossils in the strata of the earth has no systematic arrangement as to earlier species versus more recent species, and no fossils are being formed today.[22] The separation of certain forms of fossils from others, which is observed in some series of strata may be partially due to the fact that the lower ones were living farther down; for example, on the sea bottom, at the time of the "mass burials" which are attributed to the Flood. This condition has been called "ecological stratification" by some proponents of the Flood view of geology.[23]

8. The earth was created with all of its parts and contents possessing an "appearance of age." Therefore, scientists have no way of determining whether or not observed ages of minerals, rocks, strata, etc. are real or only apparent. However, many young-earth creationists recognize the difficulties of applying the "appearance of age" idea to the fossils of the earth, and hold that they are true relics of organisms which were once alive.[24]

9. Scientific observations and studies of the strata of the earth can reveal little or nothing about the prehistoric past. Or, as Emmett Williams and George Mulfinger state it, "Whatever happened before man was created cannot be subjected to scientific investigation."[25]

10. A recognition of any large amounts of time by a Christian is automatically a compromise with evolutionary doctrine, because evolutionary theories require large amounts of time. The easiest way to combat evolution is to try to show that long periods of time never existed.[26]

11. Both the gap and day-age theories of creation are inherently evolutionary.

12. All forms of radiometric dating are invalid, being based on assumptions which never can be proven.[27]

13. The matter of the age of the earth already has been settled by a fully literal interpretation of the Scripture. Therefore there can be no valid evidence for great age.

14. It is not proper for Christians to propagate or publish evidences for great age, even though they might at the same time clearly reject evolutionary theory in the statements they make.[28]

15. Christians should continue to believe the views of the 17th and 18th century theologians until sufficient evidence is produced to show those views to be wrong.[29]

In addition to definite beliefs of the young-earth school of thought, we will here point out some of the methods of reasoning or techniques of study which are prevalent among authors who embrace this doctrine. We are not looking upon these methods as divisive schemes used for persuading the public, but merely noting that their use is a prominent characteristic of the modern young-earth movement. It is probable that most of those authors who employ these methods are unaware of their misleading nature.

1. The practice of dealing mainly with surface features of earth structure, rather than with entire stratigraphic columns. The difficulties of this have been discussed in Chapter 4. Therefore, we will pause here only to give an illustration of the use of this technique of study.

Near the town of Glen Rose, Texas, are a number of fossilized dinosaur footprints, along with large man-like footprints. These impressions are in beds of rock along the Paluxy River. A number of fundamentalists who hold the young-earth view have taken an interest in the footprints and have made some studies of them. Dealing with this subject is a film entitled "Footprints in Stone," which is now well known in the United States and Canada.[30] However, a very real difficulty with the entire series of studies represented in this film is that they consider only the fossil-bearing layers which are near the surface. Those who made the studies used a bulldozer to go down a few feet at the side of the river bed, but no deep drillings were made; and practically no reference is made to the results of drillings which were made earlier in that area for oil exploration.[31] It turns out that the rock beds in which the footprints are located are underlain by over 5,000 feet of sedimentary layers which contain innumerable invertebrate fossils.[32] Thus the studies which were made for the film included much less than one percent of the fossil record in that area. Yet the film represents the study as giving conclusive information that the Glen Rose area contains no evidence for great age.

We do not know what factors were responsible for this failure to consider the major parts of the stratigraphic column in that area, but the fact that this kind of oversight is very common in studies which are made by those who hold to the young-earth view is some cause for alarm. Perhaps a major factor which has contributed to this fault is the lack of financial resources among these creationist groups. It is true that few if any such Christian organizations have the tremendous sums of money which are required for deep drillings and thorough laboratory studies of the many rock layers and fossil types encountered in drilling. Nevertheless, this lack of finances should not prevent them from using the many extensive studies which have been published in detail, and which are available in the libraries of our nation. At any rate, this is a point on which we certainly hope we will see improvement in the future "Christian response" to geologic data.

2. The practice of rejecting an entire geologic principle, because of one or a few flaws or variations found in the geologic record on which the principle is based. For example, because a certain group of rock layers in a two-mile-thick stratigraphic column is found to be wrongly or questionably identified, it is assumed that the entire stratigraphic column is wrongly classified and wrongly understood. Or again, because some of the details of dolomite formation in the past are not well understood, all of the many principles which are known concerning this process are rejected. Instead, an over-simplified hypothesis which ignores the chemical and structural differences between dolomite and limestone is proposed.[33]

3. The practice of classifying all works having to do with geological observation, either as "representing the uniformitarian position," or "representing the creationist position." Any work which points out geological processes which require long periods of time is almost invariably classified as "uniformitarian," and is usually avoided, even though other parts of the same work may recognize numerous catastrophic processes, and a global Flood. The categorizing of written resource material in this manner has regularly caused large numbers of Bible students to completely ignore works which actually contain materials that are very important to creation studies.

4. The study technique of taking individual examples of fossil

deposition as necessarily representative of practically all deposition. This is very commonly done in young-earth creationist circles. Various deposits of rapidly covered animal shells, plant remains, and vertebrate skeletons are considered to be sufficient evidence that all, or practically all, sedimentary deposits formed in the past were formed rapidly by the Flood.[34] But since rapid burial of many such organisms occurs regularly today during under-water landslides, hurricanes, and other natural disturbances, it is reasonable to assume that such burials also occurred in pre-Flood times.

One of the most commonly cited examples of relatively rapid burial of fossil materials is that of partially upright tree trunks in certain coal beds in the European area. Some of the trunks lie at a sharp slope, and penetrate up through several layers of coal, indicating that the entire mass was buried before the wood had opportunity to decay. It is therefore reasonable to believe that this is a true example of relatively rapid deposition, with perhaps not more than one hundred years being required for producing the series of layers with their "polystrate" fossil tree trunks. However, the existence of the few coal beds which have this characteristic is taken to mean that there are no slowly formed coal deposits, and that the many careful descriptions of slowly formed coal layers in various parts of the world are erroneous. The fact that there are numerous kinds of coal, and a variety of circumstances under which it can be formed is practically disregarded.

Other examples of rapidly buried materials which are mistakenly taken as representative of nearly all sedimentary processes are the fossilized skeletons of fishes, preserved with fins extended, and the fresh-frozen carcasses of mammoths in Siberia. Some of these could well be genuine examples of the action of the Biblical Flood; but the existence of a few such cases, in strata near the surface, is not an indication that the entire, vast array of fossiliferous strata of the earth was formed rapidly. Also, in the case of fossilized marine animals, it must be remembered that under-water landslides, caused by earthquakes, very often bring about sudden smothering and burial of large numbers of organisms.

5. The practice of setting aside certain geologic observations by proposing a new, untested hypothesis as a substitute for the generally accepted explanations. We of course recognize that there is nothing wrong with suggesting an alternate explanation for a particular structure or process, so long as the new hypothesis has been backed by a considerable amount of serious research on the topic. But it has become customary in several of the young-earth groups to quickly propose the hypothesis, and then hope that research can be begun later. However, in nearly all instances the fundamentalist Christian community immediately accepts the hypothesis as a valid substitute for the classic explanation which was based upon elaborate research. This has happened in many, many cases having to do with rock layers and with radiometric dating.

One of the best known examples of such an acceptance of a hastily formulated hypothesis is the young-earth view of the formation of the

Grand Canyon. Most of the young-earth creationists accept the following widely disseminated hypothesis: The Canyon is said to have been formed by "relatively rapid deposition out of the sediment-laden water of the Flood. Following the Flood, while the rocks were still comparatively soft and unconsolidated, the great canyons were rapidly scoured out as the waters rushed down from the newly uplifted peneplains to the newly enlarged ocean basins."35 This idea has continued to gain popularity during the past decade, in spite of the fact that most of the rock layers of the Grand Canyon are of types which could not have been formed rapidly. This fact concerning their types is easily demonstrated by even routine studies of the microscopic texture and chemical nature of samples from the layers.36 One must remember that strata of shales, and of various types of limestones and dolostones, are not so simple in their make-up that they can be rapidly spread down like concrete and asphalt road pavings, or like peanut butter and jelly on a piece of bread.

In order to avoid such misunderstandings as these, we should discipline ourselves to put forth new hypotheses only with great caution. In the use of the scientific method of research, the hypothesis is not formed as a wild, initial guess, but is based upon a sizeable amount of previous investigation of the topic or problem. Even after the hypothesis has been formulated, and circulated among other scientists, it is well understood that more research is to be done before it is to be regarded as a true answer.

6. The expectation that some new chemical test, a magnetic or astronomical calculation, or a newly discovered deficiency of some mineral in the oceans, can suddenly nullify practically all the facts and principles which are known concerning the sedimentary deposits of the earth. (The reports of such tests and calculations are constantly causing excitement among fundamentalists.)37 To believe that the painstaking and systematic geologic studies of the past 200 years could suddenly be brought to naught by some laboratory test or mathematical calculation is to entirely misunderstand the methods and content of those studies.

A belief that the facts and principles of sedimentary geology could be refuted so easily is comparable to the claim of a quack doctor who might suddenly begin to announce that he has proved carbohydrates to have no food value. He may support his claim with isolated examples of "evidence," but the fact that the people of the earth have been deriving most of their energy from carbohydrates for thousands of years remains in spite of the isolated examples. The quack doctor needs to go back and learn the real background which lies behind his pieces of evidence, before he tries to overthrow well-known principles. It is also important to remember that laboratory tests are not infallible. The tests that are made with the aid of complex instruments are especially subject to error. And arguments based on deficiencies of certain minerals in the oceans are of no more value than an "argument from silence" in human relations or in archaeology. So, one should never expect firmly established principles to be suddenly invalidated by one or a few pieces of seemingly contrasting evidence.

7. The practice of adopting and publicizing unusual styles of Biblical interpretation for use on Scripture passages having to do with creation. It is of course always possible that some valid new method will be discovered; but, in view of the great amount of literature on Biblical interpretation which has been accumulating ever since the first century A. D., great caution in this should be exercised. One must remember that the Holy Spirit has been at work in the Church down through the centuries, and has already guided Bible scholars in discovering a great many exegetical principles. These must not be regarded lightly, nor should substitutes for them be accepted uncritically. Any proposed, unusual method of interpretation will have to be tested thoroughly, and found consistent, in order to be worthy of confidence.

While those theologians who hold to the young-earth view usually try to use the grammatico-historical method of interpretation, they have also branched out into the use of accessory, questionable methods. For example, the passage in Exodus 20:11 is used as a proof-text to assert that the creation days were of the same length as the days in the time of Moses. In using this Scripture in this way they are no doubt using a "grammatical" method, but are not using a true "historical" method. They are in reality forcing one kind of passage to be a commentary on an entirely different type of Scripture. The reference in Exodus to the days of creation was not being used in a lesson or teaching unit on the subject of creation, but was being used merely to illustrate the principle that one time unit out of seven was to be used as the sabbath. Verses 9 and 10 of the same chapter show that the purpose of verse 11 is to teach the Israelites the value of the sabbath, and their responsibility to keep it. Thus when this verse is used for teaching the length of creative days, two very dissimilar parts of the Divine revelation are being called upon to comment upon each other.[38]

A second very widely used example of a questionable type of interpretation is the so-called "numerical adjective" or "ordinal number" argument for 24-hour days of creation. This argument has proven to be of no value, since there is actually no place in Scripture to test it, as is explained in Appendix I.

A third type of faulty interpretation used by young-earth creationists is the belief that, because some part of the created world is not mentioned in the Creation account, it did not yet exist. A well-known example of this pictures Genesis 1:11-12 as teaching that the very first kinds of plants created were the higher plants; namely, grass and fruit trees. It is true that these are the first plants mentioned, but there is no statement that these were the first plants. Many other kinds of plants which are not mentioned at all in the Creation account may have been created prior to the grass and fruit trees. For example, the most abundant of all plants, the many kinds of algae, are not mentioned anywhere in the Book of Genesis. It is right to assume that God did create both marine and fresh-water algae; but, just because the Biblical account of creation makes no reference to them, we are not justified in saying that the grass and fruit trees were created first. The fossil record indicates that many kinds of algae lived long before seed-bearing plants. So, here is another place where the use of poorly established methods of interpretation is bringing embarrassment to Christians.

Thus a prominent segment of evangelical Christianity has now developed a series of awkward and misleading methods of reasoning and techniques of interpretation. These already have become a real hindrance to the Christian work which is being attempted by this type of fundamentalist, and frequently casts a harmful shadow across the work of all evangelicals.

Among the fundamentalist groups which emphasize the young-earth view, we find high ideals, but their position is too restricted to be of use in understanding the scientific evidence or in properly relating it to the Bible. The view is similar to the narrow field of a telescope. Even though there may be a clear object or idea out beyond the end of the telescope, the viewer is missing out on the great mass of beauty and meaning in the landscape.

The growth of the young-earth movement during the past decade has been close to phenomenal. The position held with regard to the great Biblical truths of God, man, sin, and salvation is very similar to that held by the other evangelicals of the Christian community. But the position taken on the age of the earth, being magnified to such proportions as it has, usually draws a sharp line of separation between the young-earth groups and other evangelicals. Let us hope that this line can be softened in the future, so that all those who believe the fundamental truths of Scripture can work together more effectively for the cause of the Gospel.

Prospects for the Future

It appears that the present trends of divergence and conflict concerning the doctrine of creation will continue, for some time at least. Theologians of the less conservative persuasions undoubtedly will continue to insist that the Biblical account of creation has religious value, but practically no historical purpose. Evangelicals probably will remain divided into the groups we have already mentioned.

Since this book is written primarily for evangelicals, we will now list some goals and principles which can be of use in our efforts to properly represent our God as we live in this world.

1. We should emphasize the historical value of the Biblical account of creation (but at the same time not become hyperliteral). The tendency to see only spiritual lessons in the first chapters of Genesis can only weaken our testimony concerning God's revelation. The two complementary facts that human language is meaningful, and that the first chapters of Genesis are not poetry, make it necessary for us to assume that God, in giving us these chapters, was attempting to reveal some of the facts concerning origins. To allegorize the entire account, as some attempt to do, is to raise the enormous problem of how much of the remainder of the Bible should be considered

as merely figurative.

2. All groups of evangelicals will want to hold firmly to the principle that faith must go beyond reason, but not against reason. We are not to make science our God; but neither are we to disregard the discoveries of science. An anti-science view usually erects barriers between ourselves and the people we want to help. Wherever it does not erect such a barrier, it at least introduces an irrelevant factor into our discussions of important, eternal truths. We need to exercise great caution so as not to damage our youth by insisting that they adopt questionable positions with regard to the Biblical teaching on creation and the age of the earth. When a student adopts an unsupportable position, thinking that it is a part of true Bible doctrine, and then later learns the actual facts as they are being observed in the earth, the resulting shock often causes him to place a much lower value on the entire Bible.

3. We should try to keep ourselves properly informed concerning modern discoveries. Dwelling on the past to the extent of reverting back to views which man developed before he possessed the technologies for investigating the deeper strata of the earth is an unfortunate and restricting way of thought wherever it occurs. If we will openly face the facts which have been discovered, and admit their validity, we will avoid the embarrassment of being found fighting a pointless war against prehistoric time as an imaginary enemy.

4. Once we have recognized the principles of the inspiration and historical nature of the Genesis account of creation, we should always be willing to reconsider and rethink our position on creation in the light of the objective observations of science. (Note here that we are recommending primarily the objective data discovered by science. We are not asking Christians to rethink their position on creation in the light of scientific theory, or even in the light of the general consensus of scientific opinion. Theories are necessary for the advancement of science, but the fact that they may fluctuate greatly is a reason for caution in their use.)

5. The future ministry of evangelicals can be improved by a stronger emphasis on scientific studies within our Christian institutions. This will provide a foundation so that the abundance of scientific data now available can be properly understood and used. The non-radiometric time indicators should be given more attention, as these are more easily understood by the general public. These can be an extremely helpful aid in illustrating the greatness and wisdom of God, in contrast to the widespread conception of God as small and time-bound. The long periods of time seen in these indicators can help us present a clear picture of the magnitude and extent of God's creative and sustaining works in the earth.

6. Future conflicts and misunderstandings can be reduced greatly by making a clear-cut distinction between the question of great age and that of evolution, just as many of the early evangelical leaders in America did. The separating of these two issues can be of untold value, both in promoting mutual understanding between Christians and

in helping to present the Biblical account of creation to the public. For example, the gaining of respect for the Creation story in public education will be largely dependent on our showing that the Biblical account is compatible with the better known principles of earth science. (Most scientists will admit that the theories of evolution are not yet established fact, but the matters of age are far more certain.) Whenever we attempt to "throw out" both evolutionary theory and the established facts concerning the age of the earth, we will find unrelenting resistance. Public school teachers and pupils should be, and can be, alerted to the transitory nature of evolutionary theory if we will not at the same time deny the geologic evidences for age.

Let us hope that during the present decade Christians will determine to emphasize the fact that, even though the Bible is not a handbook of science, it is scientifically respectable. The teachings of the Bible and God's time records in nature are fully compatible.

FOOTNOTES

1. It is not within the scope of this book to discuss the problem of the theory of evolution. Those who desire a brief scholarly treatment of the weaknesses of the theory, from the biological standpoint, should refer to the following works, and to sources included in their bibliographies:
Cora A. Reno, Evolution on Trial, Moody Press, 1970, 192 p.
Wayne Frair and P. W. Davis, The Case for Creation, Moody Press, 1972, 93 p.
There may be some who will say that it is impossible to discuss the geologic evidence for age without also discussing evolution. It is true that many of the higher forms of animals and plants are found only in the upper strata of the geologic record, and that there is an abundance of extinct lower forms only in the lower strata. However, such an arrangement does not logically demand that the higher organisms evolved from predecessors in the lower. It may mean only that no higher forms were brought into existence during the earlier days of creation, and that the most complex forms were created later. The geologic record does contain strong suggestions of evolution within groups, as in the case of the bryozoans; but the primary evidences for time are not dependent upon such relationships or progressive series. Therefore we feel no compulsion to include a treatment of evolution in this work.

2. New York: Revell, c.1876; and London: Hodder and Stoughton, 9th ed. 1901.

3. The term "creationist" properly refers to any person who believes that the events of creation were divinely instigated and miraculous in their nature, with the various forms of life having been brought into existence by special creation. Some creationists hold that these events occurred many millions of years ago (or even longer); others hold that they are recent.

4. B. Ramm, The Christian View of Science and Scripture, 1954, p. 135-137.

5. E. R. Sandeen, The Roots of Fundamentalism, British and American Millenarianism 1800-1930, 1970, p. 132-144.

6. Ibid., p. 130-131, 167-170, 198.

7. J. I. Packer, Fundamentalism and the Word of God, 1958, p. 28. Also compare Sandeen, p. xiv.

8. Sandeen p. xiv.

9. Ibid., p. 188-207. (The Fundamentals were revised by the faculty of the Bible Institute of Los Angeles, in 1957-1958, and re-published in two volumes by Kregel Publications, of Grand Rapids.)

10. Ibid., p. 206, 266-268.

11. Concerning the reputation of fundamentalists, it should be explained here that during the 1940's a significant part of the fundamentalist group began to be overly dogmatic concerning several of the smaller points of their belief. Frequently the members of this more vocal segment actually sought out opportunities for conflict with those who disagreed with them on both large and small points of doctrine. Thus the term "fundamentalism" was brought into disrepute, and now often conveys the idea of an unreasonably dogmatic, fighting type of Christian. Unfortunately, this same desire for controversy still exists among many fundamentalists, and is even increasing in some quarters.

12. Another volume which exercised a considerable influence in popularizing the gap theory of creation during this time was Dispensational Truth, or God's Plan and Purpose in the Ages, by Clarence Larkin, Philadelphia, The Rev. Clarence Larkin Est., 1920, 176 p. This was a handsome volume, with 90 large, detailed charts portraying various aspects of Biblical teaching. At several points the gap view of creation was taught, and the cause of the earth's first destruction declared to be the activity of Satan and the angels who fell with him.

13. Two prominent fundamentalists who argued effectively for long creation days were W. B. Riley, the founder of Northwestern Schools in Minneapolis; and J. O. Buswell, Dean of the Faculty of Covenant Seminary in St. Louis, Missouri. Both were strong defenders of the full inspiration of the Bible. Dr. Buswell's treatment of the days of creation is found in J. O. Buswell, A Systematic Theology of the Christian Religion, Zondervan Publishing House, 1962, v. 1, p. 134-162.

14. Two of the nonhistorical views are the "framework hypothesis," and the "revelatory days hypothesis." These and similar views are discussed in the following works:
    E. J. Young, Studies in Genesis One, Presbyterian and Reformed

Publishing Co., Philadelphia, 1964.

     B. Ramm, <u>The Christian View of Science and Scripture</u>, Eerdmans Publishing Co., Grand Rapids, 1954.

     G. G. Cohen, "Hermeneutical Principles and Creation Theories," <u>Grace Journal</u>, Grace Theological Seminary, Winona Lake, Indiana, v. 5, no. 3, 1964, p. 17-29.

15.   Two of his best known books were <u>The New Geology</u> (1923), and <u>The Modern Flood Theory of Geology</u> (1935).

16.   See Footnote no. 15 above.

17.   See Appendix I.

18.   J. C. Whitcomb, Jr., <u>The Early Earth</u>, Baker Book House Co., 1972, p. 58-59.

19.   See Appendix IV, "The Problem of Death Before the Fall of Man."

20.   See Chapter 10 for numerous evidences for greater age which were cited by conservative theologians and geology professors during the 19th century.

21.   This belief contains a subtle danger for those who wish to be true to the Scripture. Many sedimentary deposits show unmistakable evidence of having been laid down long before there were any verte-brate animals or human beings on the earth, and at least many hun-dreds of thousands of years ago. These deposits include such as the lower parts of the Eniwetok atoll, the deeper parts of the Bahama Banks, and the underground coral reefs of Canada. In each case the covering layers above show that they could not have been produced as a result of a destructive flood, and that hundreds of thousands of years were required for applying them. (See Chapters 3 to 7.) To attribute such sedimentary structures to the Biblical Flood im-plies that Noah and his family lived at a time far earlier than the Biblical account seems to indicate. There is nothing wrong with ac-cepting a worldwide flood, but to make it the means of forming all the time indicators which are described in the previous chapters of this book, is both illogical and impossible. See Chapter 4 for some further discussion of the effects of the Flood.

22.   Both of these statements have been very easily refuted many times over by field studies, and can be disproved even by an amateur paleontologist in the field. Hundreds of ancient, extinct species of brachiopods and of mollusks are found only in the lower, older strata, even though they have counterpart, more recent species of similar sizes and densities in the higher strata. Also, the lower strata show no trace of any vertebrate fossils. (See Chapter 4 for further information on this subject.) As for present-day formation of fossils, one has only to dig into a modern coral reef to find numerous kinds of marine animal and plant skeletons in various stages of fossilization.

23. When one tries to account for an ecological stratification by a violent, cataclysmic flood, numerous problems arise. For example, how can this be reconciled with the prevalent view that the "breaking up of the fountains of the great deep" (Genesis 7:11) violently disturbed the sea floors and swept heterogeneous, convulsing masses of sea life out into other localities before they were finally deposited? It is much more reasonable to account for ecological stratification by the many scientific evidences which indicate that most animals and plants which were fossilized were preserved near to their own life habitat by natural means of burial, similar to the burial forces we see at work today.

24. See Appendix II for further discussion on the "appearance of age" idea.

25. Emmett Williams and G. Mulfinger, Physical Science, Bob Jones University Press, 1974. (As quoted in Bible-Science Newsletter, Bible-Science Association, Inc., Caldwell, Idaho, v. 13, February, 1975, p. 2.)
See Chapter 2 for a discussion of the stability of natural laws, and of man's God-given ability to rationally observe and to analyze what he observes. Many Christians believe that we should gladly make use of geologic data in order to avoid our making false claims concerning the strata of the earth, the Flood, etc.--just as we make use of the facts of genetics and biochemistry in order to assure accuracy in the statements we make concerning evolutionary theory.

26. H. M. Morris, Biblical Cosmology and Modern Science, Craig Press, 1970, p. 19-24.

27. There is a strange, but widespread, misunderstanding among the people who hold this view, concerning carbon-14 dating. The present author has found that the usual student reaction (among those who have been exposed to young-earth teaching) is, "Scientists are trying to prove the earth to be millions or billions of years old by the carbon-14 method." Also, large numbers of tracts and articles specifically denouncing carbon-14 dating are currently being circulated. All this seems wholly unnecessary, in view of the fact that this dating method is used only for ages up to 50,000 years. The reason for this is that the half-life of carbon-14 is relatively short (5,700 years). This means that by the time 50,000 years have expired, following the death of the organism storing the carbon-14, there is such a small amount of the active isotope remaining that it can no longer be detected accurately. Therefore, radiation dating laboratories usually do not even attempt to make carbon-14 tests on materials older than this. Of course, some other types of radiation dating are useful for older materials. Nevertheless, it is important to keep in mind that our knowledge that the earth is very old is not really dependent upon any of the radiometric dating methods. Even if all of these were suddenly to be found invalid, we would still have the great body of primary evidences to which we have been referring in this book.

28. See Creation Research Society Quarterly, v. 9 (1972), p. 140,

for the official policy of the Quarterly in this matter.

29. This point of belief is very strange, in the light of the vast body of published, objective data which is now available. If one were to review the earth-science journals which are available in many libraries, compiling only the nonradiometric, objective, non-evolutionary evidence for great age, he would need several years for the task, and would end up with thousands of pages of material. Many Christians seem totally uninformed concerning the great "treasure" of information which has been brought forth from the depths of the earth and sea by modern methods of deep drilling. Extensive contacts with numerous members of young-earth groups in the United States have shown that, almost without exception, they are completely unaware of the existence of the non-radiometric evidences for age such as we have given in Chapters 3-9. (These include great underground algal limestone formations still intact as they grew, the 200,000 evaporite couplets in the Delaware basin, extensive, ancient erosion on some of the layers which lie deep in the walls of the Grand Canyon, and thick deposits of practically pure pelagic microfossils on even the higher parts of the ocean floors.) This lack of knowledge of the evidence is similar to that which existed among the early 19th century theologians, in spite of the fact that the data are now far more available than they were in that day. One reason for this lack of knowledge of the data is that there are practically no sedimentary geologists in the young-earth creationist groups.

30. Produced by Films for Christ, Peoria, Ill., 1973.

31. S. E. Taylor, "The Mystery Tracks in Dinosaur Valley," Bible-Science Newsletter, v. 9, April 1971, p. 1-7.

32. "Basement Rocks of Texas and Southeast New Mexico," University of Texas Bureau of Economic Geology Publication no. 5605, 1956, Plate I. Also, R. F. Solis-I, "Subsurface Geology of the Central Part of the Fort Worth Basin," The University of Texas, 1972 (unpublished Master's Thesis), Figure 19 and text.

33. W. G. Peters, "Field Evidence of Rapid Sedimentation," Creation Research Society Quarterly, v. 10 (1973), p. 92-94.

34. Ibid., p. 94-96.

35. J. C. Whitcomb, Jr., The World That Perished, 1973, p. 74.

36. See Chapter 8 above, concerning some of these rock types of the Grand Canyon.

37. For example, the mathematical calculations of some young-earth creationists concerning the apparent decay of the earth's magnetic field have caused a considerable amount of excitement. However, such calculations have led to wrong conclusions because they do not take into consideration the numerous complete reversals of the magnetic field which have been naturally recorded in many deposits of

igneous rocks.

38. See Appendix I for a discussion of the length of the creative days.

APPENDIX I

THE LENGTH OF THE DAYS OF CREATION

We wish here to offer some further comments on the creative days, which did not seem necessary in Chapter 4, but which are important to Christians today. It is true that a high percentage of the Christian community during the past millenium has accepted the days of creation as literal, 24-hour days. Nevertheless, there have also been some careful, conservative Bible scholars who have held that these days were much longer than a single, solar day. Such a view is not new in Christian circles, though it has gained much wider acceptance during the past fifty years than it formerly enjoyed.

Some of the conservative scholars of the present century have taken a special interest in setting forth the arguments for extended creative days, and the footnotes on Genesis 1:3 and 5 in the Scofield Reference Bible recognize the validity of such an interpretation. There were also several Bible scholars in the 19th century who defended essentially the same view. We wish here to state a few of the principles given in this vein, in the Introduction to A Commentary on the Holy Scriptures, Genesis, by J. P. Lange. This volume was originally published in German in 1864, but an English translation was soon produced by Philip Schaff, et al. (New York: Charles Scribner & Co., 1868). A part of the Introduction was written by Lange himself, but Professor Tayler Lewis, whom Schaff in the Preface describes as "one of the ablest and most learned classical and Biblical scholars of America," contributed most of the parts dealing with the days of creation (p. 125-159). Judging from the sections of the Introduction written by Lange, it is evident that he was in essential agreement with the principles and views given by Lewis. The Lange Commentary thus gives us one of the more extensive, conservative, exegetical and theological treatments of the days of creation.

Early in his treatment Lewis gives a grammatical exegesis of the first two verses of Genesis one, but reminds his readers that an exegesis of these verses can never answer all of the questions concerning origins (p. 129-130). After all, if a grammatical exegesis could give us the final answer concerning the amount of time which has elapsed since the creation of the earth, conservative scholars would have adopted that position long ago, and would have ceased expressing disagreements concerning it. One can never extract more information from a Biblical passage than was originally put into it by the authors.

Some of the arguments given in this Introduction, for accepting extended (rather than 24-hour) days are:

1. Reference is made to the works of St. Augustine who strongly maintained that the days of creation were "God-divided days and nights," belonging to a higher chronology than the mere solar days of our thinking. The evenings and mornings were "solemn pauses in

the divine work," and are not to be thought of as diurnal.

Lewis says of Augustine:

> He could not read the first of Genesis and think of ordinary days. It was the wondrous style of the narrative that affected him, the wondrous nature of the events and times narrated; it was the impression of strangeness, of vastness, as coming directly from the account itself, but which so escapes the notice of unthinking, ordinary readers. Wonderful things are told out of the common use of language, and therefore common terms are to be taken in their widest compass, and in their essential instead of their accidental idea. It is the same feeling that affects us when we contemplate the language of prophecy, or that which is applied to the closing period, or great day of the world's eschatology. No better term could be used for the creative _morae_, pauses, or successive _natures_, as Augustine styles them; and so no better words than evening and morning could be used for the antithetical vicissitudes through which these successions were introduced. _See_ Augustine wherever the subject comes up, in his books _De Genesi ad Literam_, _Contra Manichaeos_, and _De Civitate Dei_. (p. 131)

2. The statements in Genesis 1:2, that the earth was originally "waste and void," and that "darkness was upon the face of the deep," strongly imply that the period of emptiness and darkness was one of significant duration. (Otherwise we would have to say that the second great declaration of the creation account merely tells us that for the first few hours everything was mixed up, until God began to organize it.)

3. The use of the article "the" in the last part of verse 5, in the King James Version, to form the statement, "_the_ evening and the morning were the first day," has given a wrong impression to many. The Hebrew text does not possess the article here, so "the true rendering is, 'and there was an evening, and there was a morning, the first day'" (p. 133).

4. Since there is no mention of any solar or astronomical time keepers in the early verses of the chapter, it is unlikely that the terms "morning" and "evening" have any reference to the influence of these bodies. The terms "morning" and "evening" probably were placed here by the divine author of the text to indicate the definiteness of the different stages of creation, "without any computed duration" being indicated (p. 133).

5. The use of the Hebrew word _olam_, "from _olam_ to _olam_," in Psalm 90:2 does not mean "from everlasting to everlasting," as most English versions read, but conveys the idea of great units of divine time measurement, during which God's creative processes may have been going on. The next few verses following verse 2 support this view, and lead us to believe that the Hebrew writer was not thinking of the creative days as being mere ordinary days. Also supporting this view is the fact that the word translated "worlds" in Hebrews 11:3 is

really the Greek <u>aion</u>, rather than <u>kosmos</u>, and thus means "ages," or "worlds in time." (p. 136, 137, 140, 141)

6. Those who say that the word "days" in Exodus 20:11 has to refer to the ordinary days of man's knowledge, forget that the same passage also speaks of the works of God. (The usual English translation is, "Six days shalt thou labor and do all thy work, for in six days the Lord made heaven and earth.") "God's days of working, it is said, must be the same with man's days of working, because they are mentioned in such close connection. Then God's work and man's work must also be the same, or on the same grade, for a similar reason"--a conclusion which none of us would accept (p. 135).

The belief that the days of Genesis one were really ages of indefinite length is very much in agreement with the use of the word "day" in other parts of the Bible. As in English, so in Hebrew and Greek this word (Hebrew <u>yom</u>, Greek <u>hemera</u>) is sometimes used literally and sometimes figuratively. Even in the Creation account itself we find the word "day" referring to a period of time which included all six creative days of Genesis one (Genesis 2:4). (Compare footnote no. 20 of Chapter 4.) Another outstanding example of the figurative use of this word is seen in the expression "Day of the Lord" which is used so often in Scripture, referring to the entire future period of Christ's judgment and millenial reign of 1,000 years. Other similar expressions such as "my day" and "in the last day" are used in the New Testament in a figurative sense. We have also made reference in Chapter 4 to the outstanding examples found in II Peter 3:3-4 and 8-9, and Psalm 90:1-4.

Such expressions of long time units should not surprise us, in view of the eternity and timelessness of God. The Biblical writers seemed to be aware of this characteristic of God in relation to time in the earth. The Apostle John even told his readers, "Children it is the last hour (Greek <u>hora</u>); and just as you heard that antichrist is coming, even now many antichrists have arisen; from this we know that it is the last hour" (I John 2:18). Since this "hour" has now continued for more than 1,900 years, it should not be surprising that some days in Scripture are also of long duration. Furthermore, when we take note of the fact that, down through the milleniums, God has dealt with man by great events spaced far apart, it does not seem strange that his special creative acts should be divided by long periods of time.

It is sometimes objected that the expression "evening and morning," used in Genesis one, limits the creation to 24 hours. However, there is no necessary reason why this expression in the Hebrew language should do more than designate "the beginning and the ending." In Psalm 90:5-6 the words "morning" and "evening" are very obviously used together in a figurative sense. Here we have reference to the common experience of seeing grass grow up luxuriantly, only to be withered away when a drought comes "in the evening." We find similar figurative usages of these words in Ecclesiastes 11:6, and in Isaiah 17:11.

Another question which is sometimes raised is that of the supposed absence of the sun until the fourth day of creation. It is said that the Bible indicates that the sun was not created until the fourth day, and that this would have made a long period of plant growth prior to that impossible. Actually this is no problem at all when we realize that the Biblical text does not say that the sun, moon, and stars were created on the fourth day. It is readily admitted by all Bible scholars that the Hebrew word used here (Genesis 1:16) is asah, and that this Hebrew word is (correctly) translated in numerous ways in our English Bibles. It is very probable that here in 1:16 the word "made" (asah) is intended in the sense of "set" or "established," in reference to the sun and moon's becoming visible in the sky, after having been hidden by the earlier blanket of vapor which is referred to in verse 7. In this connection we should remember (a) that 1:1 says "the heavens," as well as the earth, were created "in the beginning," and (b) there were regular, alternating periods of light and darkness, as described in 1:4-5, prior to the latter five days of creation. It is very reasonable to believe that the sun was responsible for these alternating periods of light and darkness, just as it is today, but that the blanket of vapor did not allow the sun to be seen as such in the sky until the fourth day.

In support of this interpretation we should observe the varied uses of the Hebrew word asah in the Old Testament. Besides the 631 times it is translated in the King James Old Testament as "to make" (e.g., Genesis 3:7 and 21), it is also used 1292 times in the sense of "to do" (e.g., Exodus 22:30), 50 times as "to deal" (e.g., Exod. 21:9; Ruth 1:8; Ezek. 8:18), 5 times as "to bestow" (e.g., II Chron. 24:7), 3 times as "to bring to pass" (e.g., Gen. 50:20), 50 times as "to execute" (e.g., I Sam. 28:18), 7 times as "to maintain" (e.g., I Kings 8:59), 3 times as "to set" (e.g., II Chron. 2:18), and 2 times as "to appoint" (e.g., Job 14:5). Another excellent example of the use of the word asah in the sense of "to appoint" is found in I Kings 12:31, where it is said that Jeroboam appointed priests when he set up his new centers of worship. Even a brief examination of the passages where the word is used will show the reader that it usually does not mean anything like an original creating process, so it is unreasonable to insist that it has to be taken as an original creative process in Genesis 1:16. Thus note no. 4 on page 3 of the Scofield Reference Bible (note no. 6 on page 1 of the New Scofield Reference Bible) states that in verses 14-18 no "original creative act" is implied, and that "the sense is 'made to appear; made visible.'"

One of the most frequently encountered arguments used in recent years for literal, 24-hour creative days is the so-called "numerical adjective argument." This argument is based on the fact that in every other place in the Bible where the Hebrew or Greek word "day" is used with an ordinal number ("first day," "second day," etc.) it refers to literal, 24-hour days. This is taken to mean that the numerical adjectives in Genesis one likewise indicate literal days. In reply to this we should note that there is no other Scripture passage where ordinal numbers could be used with figurative days. The Bible uses ordinal numbers with literal days, such as in Leviticus 23:36, where the people are told that "the _eighth_ day shall be as an holy convocation." But all such cases refer to the activities of _man_ (or to God's acts in relation to man), which were according to a calendar, and thus naturally were 24-hour days.

Then when we come to the obviously figurative uses of the word "day" ("day of the Lord," "day of wrath," etc.), we find that these always refer to a single period of time which will not be repeated. Such expressions thus could not be used with a numerical adjective. For example, it would be absurd to speak of the "first day of the Lord," because there will never be but one such day. So we must conclude that there is no place in Scripture, or in other Hebrew literature, where the so-called "numerical adjective rule" can be tested or confirmed. Furthermore, no such rule appears in the Hebrew grammars. This leaves us free to accept both the days of creation, the day of the Lord, and several other "day" expressions in the Bible, as referring to long periods of time.

In a consideration of the length of the "days" of creation it is worthwhile to consider the nature of some of the statements made in Genesis concerning the sixth day. According to the first chapter this day included the formation of at least the larger land animals, and the creation of Adam and Eve, as well as an elaborate series of activities carried out by Adam. A comparison of Genesis 1:27-31 with 2:8-23 enables us to list some of the activities which were included in "the sixth day." These included God's "planting" of a garden, the "causing to grow" of various trees, the placing of Adam alone in the garden with instructions to cultivate it, the instruction concerning the tree of the knowledge of good and evil, the forming of "every beast of the field and every bird of the sky" and the bringing of them to Adam to observe and name, the realization of Adam that none of these animals could be a suitable mate for him, the putting of Adam to sleep and removal of a portion of his side, the forming of Eve, the presentation of Eve to Adam, and Adam's joyous response.

According to the text all these events occurred on the sixth day of creation, before God rested on the seventh. At least the reading of the account of these events does not sound as though they all happened in 24 hours (or 14 hours of daylight). If the doctrine of 24-hour days were so important as some would have us believe, it is indeed strange that Moses used expressions which naturally lead one to think of considerable amounts of time. The expression "planted a garden," of 2:8, does not indicate any caution on the part of the writer in emphasizing only a 24-hour period. Practically all English versions read "planted," because the word is the main Hebrew verb for the planting of vineyards, etc. (nata); for example, Genesis 9:20 where Noah planted a vineyard. If God had wanted the creation account to convey the idea of only a few hours of time in the sixth day, surely He would not have allowed Moses to use a horticultural term such as this. (The Hebrew language did not lack for words which could express rapid or instantaneous action.) The same can be said of the statement that God "caused to grow" the trees of the garden. If God had wished to convey rapidity of action, He would surely have led the writer to merely say that He "placed" them in the garden.

Adam was then put into the garden, given instructions to cultivate it, and assigned the task of naming "every beast of the field," and "every bird of the sky." How are we to suppose that this task was accomplished in a matter of a few hours? Especially in the light of the vast number of animals, the Biblical custom of care and consideration in the assigning of names, and Adam's evaluation of each to see if it might be a suitable companion for himself (2:20), Moses' readers certainly must have regarded this as an extended task.

A study of Genesis 2:20-23 definitely shows that Adam had been considering the various animals from the standpoint of his own person, had experienced a feeling of disappointment and loneliness in finding none compatible with his own personality, and had finally rejoiced upon receiving a mate who was "now bone of my bones, and flesh of my flesh." In the Hebrew text the word for "now" in this passage is really happa'am, meaning "now at last," or "now at length," (as pointed out in the Brown, Driver, and Briggs lexicon, and in numerous commentaries and versions). This same word, with its article as here, also appears in several other places in Genesis, Exodus, and Judges, with the same connotation of final realization after long waiting. For example, in Genesis 29:34 Jacob's wife Leah, after a long time of frustration in not being loved by her husband, bears her third son to Jacob and exclaims, "Now this time (happa'am) my husband will be joined to me." It is obvious that such human emotional feelings do not arise in a mere few hours of one day, or during a frantic rush of naming all the beasts of the field and birds before the darkness of one solar day should fall.*

Thus we must recognize that even the text of the first chapters of Genesis contains some strong indications that at least the sixth day of creation was much longer than 24 hours. This, together with the other factors we have been considering, leads us to believe that most, if not all, of the six creative days were long periods of time (most likely of varying length).

*I am indebted to Rev. R. John Snow of Elizabethtown, Pennsylvania, for several of the points contained in this section on the 6th Day. Another source of information on the same subject is A Survey of Old Testament Introduction, by G. L. Archer, Jr., Moody Press, 1964.

APPENDIX II

THE TRUTHFULNESS OF GOD AS RELATED TO SCIENTIFIC OBSERVATIONS

One of the basic principles of Christian theism is the truthfulness of God. This is in definite contrast to most heathen concepts of God's character. The truthfulness attribute of God is seen throughout the entire Bible, and is specifically declared in such passages as Psalm 138:2; John 3:33; 17:3; and Romans 3:4. Everything which God does, has done, or has revealed is in agreement with and consistent with his attribute of truth. In other words, there is perfect agreement between what God is and what He does.[1] In describing the revelations of God to man, A. H. Strong states, "All of (God's) revelations to creatures are consistent with his essential being."[2] This means that all that God reveals to man--whether in writing, in the observable phenomena of nature, or engraved in layers of fossil-bearing rock--is true, and in agreement with his eternal attribute of truth.

With the above principle in mind, we can be sure that what we see in the geologic record is true and reliable; for example, we will not find volcanic ash unless there was a volcano to produce it, nor sea shells unless there were sea-shell animals (such as mollusks) to produce them. We can be certain that since God is a God of truth, He never puts anything deceptive into his creations or revelations. A realization of this characteristic of God is especially necessary for the proper understanding of the physical world, which we recognize as having been created by God. It is true that the fiat creative acts of God in producing the earth, with whatever parts it originally contained, must have involved some appearance of age. For example, molecules of water surely did not "appear" to be new when they were first created. Then later, when living organisms were created, they must have appeared as though they had lived for an appreciable length of time. In no case, however, is there any necessity of postulating that parts or substances of the earth were originally formed with an appearance of great age. God's attribute of truthfulness definitely limited the types and extent of appearance of age which He could create. We will here cite a few examples of types which could not have been created by the God of truth:

1. Erosion--God did not create pre-formed marks of erosion. So wherever we find erosional topography there is no question but that it is a genuine example of erosional processes. A case in point is the existence of many deep river canyons on the continents, which show that they were formed primarily by the slow downcutting action of water. Such canyons, and the receding precipices over which the water often pours, have long inspired mankind with a sense of awe and wonder, but it has been only in the past 150 years that we have come to possess accurate means for study of such erosion. Because of these more precise means of identifying and measuring erosion we are now able to gain some idea of the immense periods of time which were required to wear away the hard rocks of such gorges as those of the Upper Nile River, and the Colorado River and its tributaries;

and of the gorges of many swift rivers which plunge off the Andes Mountains of Argentina, Chili, Bolivia, and Peru into the lowlands of these countries.

Thus we are frequently able to identify a literal "record-in-stone" provided by the work of erosion in cutting through thousands of feet of hard rock--types of rock such as granite, gneiss, and schist. Since these rock types are formed under the influence of great heat and pressure, they were fully hardened before the rivers began their courses over the rock masses. This means that their erosion has always been slow, and that a reliable time record has been provided for us where such rocks have been cut to great depths by a river. Since the amount and rate of the water flow in a given river have not always been the same, the total erosion time for a canyon is very difficult to determine. But where the rocks of the canyon have been of these or other types which were fully hardened before the river waters began to erode them, there can be no doubt but that we have a true and readable time record before us. For example, the Nile River, at the Semna rapids, between the second and third cataracts, is now downcutting through gneissic rock at the relatively fast rate of about one-twelfth of an inch per year.[3] The erosion rate may have been even several times this great at some time in the past, but there are very effective limits on the erosion, due to the fact that the rock has been hard and durable from the beginning, and due to the physical laws which limit the effect of water and its suspended sediments on a given amount of rock surface per unit of time. Therefore, we recognize that the natural records of erosion which God has left us are both true and reliable.

2. Fossils--These were a great mystery to man until it was discovered that the body structures of the fossils are equivalent to the body parts of related living organisms. Take the example of the muscle scars which are seen on the shells of both recent and fossil clams. If one dissects a freshly killed clam he will find two large muscles by which the clam closes the two halves of its shell for protection. Upon cutting these muscles away from the shell, one sees that there is a distinct depression in the material of the shell at the point where each of these muscles was attached. These depressions, and also a few other smaller ones to which other muscles attach, are called "muscle scars," and are seen in fossil clam shells as well as in shells of recent origin.[4] Now we must realize that any and all such muscle attachment scars which are seen on clam shells--even if they are very old fossils--represent the points at which real muscles of real, live clams were attached. To say, as some have, that God created these shells along with many other fossils in a ready-made state, and that these muscle scars thus never had any live muscles attached to them, is to accuse God of putting deception into his creation. (It is true that few, if any, creationist leaders currently hold that God created ready-made fossils and sedimentary strata, but at the "grass roots" level this view is still popular.)

The principle just stated can be illustrated thousands of times over as we observe the intricate fossilized structures of so many kinds of animals. For example, if the fossil corals found in the deepest strata were never living, why would they have calcareous septa as dividing partitions for their gastric cavities just as living ones do? If they were never more than pieces of rock, they would have no more need for calcareous septa than a piece of common sandstone would. And what about such structures as the elaborate chewing apparatus possessed by both fossil and modern sea urchins? This apparatus is composed of an intricate array of hard chewing plates which are arranged in essentially the same order in fossil sea urchins as in modern ones. Because of the hard, limy composition of these chewing plates they fossilized very well. Now the question arises, if the ancient fossil sea urchins were never alive, why did they need the same kind and shape of chewing apparatus that modern sea urchins have? So we see the absurdities at which one can arrive by indiscriminately using the idea of appearance of age. Now that modern paleontologic studies have discovered the detailed structure and the life habits of so many thousands of species of fossils, we must recognize these as a part of God's record of what has happened during the long periods of time since his original creation. This conclusion is based on the fact that God is a God of truth. Would God leave us with so much evidence that these were living, growing animals, when in reality they were not? We must further remember that these fossil species are also found in different stages of their growth, from small immature ones to adult, just as we observe development today. Surely the "One True God," as Christ spoke of Him, could never have left such a deceiving set of data as this in the fossil record!

There are some who cite the creation of wine by Christ at the wedding in Cana in support of the idea that God created sedimentary deposits in place, with an appearance of age. This is an entirely incongruous comparison: first, because this miracle was done openly so that the news of what had actually taken place soon got out, and has been carefully preserved in the Bible to the present day; and second, because the creating of wine was for the purpose of meeting a human need at a particular time--by bringing about a chemical change in some jars of a common chemical already in existence (H_2O). Thus the changing of water into wine is not really comparable to the forming of geologic deposits. A careful examination of all the cases where the Bible describes a miraculous production of appearance of age as a part of his dealings with man will reveal that none had to do with any long-lived substance or structure. Therefore, these have no bearing on geologic or paleontologic records. All of God's works, both in the past and during Bible times, are consistent with his attribute of truth.

FOOTNOTES

1. A. H. Strong, Systematic Theology, 1907, p. 260.

2. Ibid., p. 288.

233

3. W. L. Stokes, <u>An</u> <u>Introduction</u> <u>to</u> <u>Historical</u> <u>Geology</u>, 1960, p. 38.

4. R. R. Shrock, and W. H. Twenhofel, <u>Principles</u> <u>of</u> <u>Inverte-</u><u>brate</u> <u>Paleontology</u>, 1953, p. 386.

APPENDIX III

SOME OF THE MORE WELL-KNOWN THEOLOGICALLY CONSERVATIVE WORKS
FROM THE LATTER HALF OF THE NINETEENTH CENTURY

The following lists are given as an illustration of the progress which was made by evangelical Christianity in Great Britain after the subsiding of the long controversy over the age of the earth and the nature of the Biblical Flood. (See Chapter 10 for explanation.)

A. Authors

Most of these men were residents of the British Isles, but a few were American. The American ones, however, were in all cases largely dependent upon the work of British Bible scholars of the latter part of the 19th century.*

Henry Alford	George P. Fisher
Samuel J. Andrews	A. J. Gordon
Albert Barnes	William H. Green
Thomas D. Bernard	W. H. Griffith-Thomas
Andrew Bonar	Charles Hardwick
Horatius Bonar	Samuel Harris
A. B. Bruce	Charles Hodge
Robert S. Candlish	William Kelly
W. J. Conybeare	R. J. Knowling
A. B. Davidson	Henry P. Liddon
James Denney	J. B. Lightfoot
Alfred Edersheim	Joseph B. Mayor
Charles J. Ellicott	F. B. Meyer
Andrew M. Fairbairn	William Milligan
F. W. Farrar	Handley C. G. Moule
Andrew Murray	George Smeaton
G. F. Oehler	Charles Spurgeon
James Orr	James Stalker
Alexander Patterson	George B. Stevens
Alfred Plummer	H. B. Swete
E. B. Pusey	Milton S. Terry
Richard B. Rackham	Joseph H. Thayer
William M. Ramsay	Richard C. Trench
John C. Ryle	B. F. Westcott

Philip Schaff   Thomas Whitelaw

J. A. Seiss   Alexander Whyte

B. Some Outstanding British Bible Reference Works Published During
    the Latter Half of the Nineteenth Century

Cambridge Bible for Schools and Colleges

Cambridge Greek Testament for Schools and Colleges

Cooke's Explanatory and Critical Commentary

Dictionary of the Bible, by William Smith, Editor

Ellicott's Bible Commentary

Exposition of the Holy Scripture, by Alexander Maclaren

Expositor's Bible

Jamieson, Fausset, and Brown's Commentary

Young's Analytical Concordance

    *A few of these authors published their main work in the early
20th century, but their work was essentially a product of the 19th
century.

    Most of the authors listed are treated in the compilation of
Wilbur M. Smith, comprising the latter part of his book Profitable
Bible Study, 1951.

APPENDIX IV

THE PROBLEM OF DEATH BEFORE THE FALL OF MAN

It has been widely taught among theologically conservative Christians that all death originated at the time of the fall of man. This generalization apparently has occurred because the Bible, being primarily a book about God and man, does not specifically state what effects man's sin had upon the animal and plant kingdoms.

Some of the Scripture passages which are frequently cited in support of the claim that all death originated at the fall of man are: Genesis 3:17b, "Cursed is the ground because of you; in toil you shall eat of it all the days of your life." Romans 5:12, "Therefore, just as through one man sin entered into the world, and death through sin, and so death spread to all men, because all sinned." Romans 8:22, "...the whole creation groans and suffers the pains of child-birth together until now." If these passages really taught that no death of animals and plants had occurred up to the fall of man, then we would have to say that practically all fossils were formed after the fall of man. However, this is not at all the case. We of course agree that both spiritual and physical death in the human race originated with the tragic event of Adam's sin. But the beginning of death in the animal and plant kingdoms is simply not mentioned in any of the Scripture passages having to do with man's sin; nor is the time of the beginning of such death given in any other place in the Bible.

A consideration of the mutual relationships of the organisms, including man, which God placed in the Garden of Eden should be of great assistance in understanding this problem. According to the second chapter of Genesis, God "planted" the Garden of Eden with many kinds of growing plants and a great variety of animal life. Man was given the privilege of eating the fruits of the garden, and we certainly must assume that the "beasts of the field" and the "fowls" likewise supplied themselves with food from the garden. Thus we are led to the conclusion that the supply of the biological needs of animals and of man was basically the same in the Garden of Eden before the fall of man as it is today.

The fact of the eating of plant materials in the Garden of Eden is readily admitted by all. Since plants are living organisms, with living cells similar to those of animals, there is no question but that the terms "life" and "death" are appropriate in speaking of them. Thus when man, the beasts, and the birds ate and digested plant materials, they were bringing about the death of living organisms. This fact is intensified when we realize that seeds contain young, living embryos; so when Adam and Eve ate nuts and seeds they were killing the young embryos within those seeds. Also, the death of small animals must have been a regular occurrence in the Garden of Eden. It is difficult to conceive of the hoofed mammals roaming the fields day after day without crushing beetles and worms with their hoofs. And how could any sheep or cow pluck grass from the earth without eating the microscopic sized insects and mites which live on the blades and upper roots of the plants? Beyond this, how could such animals drink large quantities of water from streams and pools without ingesting many tiny aquatic arthropod animals? It should also be remembered that such tiny insects and mites are not insignificant specks, but that there is only one phylum of animals which is more complex than they, namely, the phylum which contains the vertebrates. Each such tiny insect is equipped with a complex nervous system, well-developed eyes, an elaborate respiratory system, a chemically efficient excretory system, etc.

Actually, we should not be surprised that the regular death of even complex organisms was included in the "way of life" before the fall of man. God created the whole animal kingdom, and much of the plant kingdom, with dependence upon the intake of food for the production of energy; and that food is always organic material produced by cells. In nearly all cases these cells which provide food for man and other organisms must die, either before being eaten or soon afterwards, as they are digested. Even most of the fungi and bacteria are dependent upon cellular organisms which have died, to provide their food for energy and growth. In fact, some kinds of fungi and bacteria are equipped with mechanisms to produce strong enzymes which digest the living cells of plants and animals which are their food. Thus if death were not a part of the original world of living organisms, then the entire basis of their lives would have had to be different from any principle known on the earth today. But, as we have seen, such a difference is not in keeping with the Genesis account of life in the Garden of Eden.

Death seems (and is) horrible to man, because man possesses an immortal spirit which is affected by death of the body. But from the viewpoint of the animals which are below man (if they had a viewpoint), there can be no such horror of death, because they possess no immortal spirit or personality. It is true that we sometimes attribute a fear of death to animals as we see them try to escape danger, but there is absolutely no justification for doing so. The Bible's teaching of the nature of man as distinct from the animals, and as being the only organism which possesses self consciousness, makes it absurd to attribute a conception of death to the animals. By divinely instilled, inherited instincts most kinds of animals try to avoid dangers and injuries; but they have no idea of death, nor fear of the same.

If one is still perplexed about the problem of death being inconsistent with God's perfect creation he should consider the following: (a) The passage in Rom. 5:12 is obviously emphasizing human death, and does not necessarily refer to animal death. (Note that the verse concludes, "so death passed upon all men.") (b) When God said to Adam, "cursed is the ground for your sake," this certainly tells us that the sin of man brought certain drastic disadvantages to the animal and plant world; but the statement does not necessarily imply that this was the beginning of death among non-human organisms.

(c) It is not possible for us as finite human beings to say that death in the <u>animal</u> world was not in the original, good plan of God, but that death in the <u>plant</u> world was in his plan. Who are we to say that plants are less "alive" than animals? Plants can carry out some activities which animals can not. Their cells are highly complex; and many plants produce motile reproductive cells--and even motile non-reproductive cells--which swim about by means of flagella just as actively as flagellated protozoans of the animal world.

(d) The same wisdom of God which led Him to ordain that plant life would serve as food for certain organisms could certainly have ordained that certain animals would also serve as food. For example, when God created the kinds of whales which live on microscopic organisms (as the blue whale), He surely foresaw that as they dashed through the water scooping up planktonic organisms their diet would include many kinds of tiny crustaceans which are very complex animals. Crustaceans belong to the same phylum as insects and have a degree of organization very similar to that of insects (see above on insects). Even if we might say that these whales may have originally eaten seaweed, we would have to remember that a vast number of these tiny crustaceans are found in among and clinging to the branches of the seaweed. (We do not mean to imply that we believe these whales ever lived on seaweed. The blue whale and its relatives have no teeth, but instead have a complex straining mechanism composed of many closely spaced, parallel plates of "whalebone" that hang down from the roof of the mouth, for straining out microscopic organisms from the water which they take in.)

A further evidence that many animals were originally designed by God for feeding on other animals is seen in the feeding reaction of lizards, salamanders, and adult frogs and toads. Each of these very rapidly snaps up its food (even if it is a piece of beefsteak presented to the animal on the end of a stick). Such a vigorous "all-out" attack on a "harmless" piece of beefsteak seems nonsense until one realizes that these animals live almost exclusively on rapidly moving insects, and that this "lightning speed" feeding mechanism has been necessary to their survival. Now the question comes, if these animals were vegetarians before the fall of man, how did they get this special feeding reaction? One might unwittingly say that these animals developed it on their own because of hunger, wrong feelings or such; but this is very unlikely. This feeding reaction requires special features of the nervous system which even man-- often under extreme conditions of hunger--has never been able to develop. Dr. T. H. Frazzetta, in his recent research on the feeding reaction of one species of lizard (an "alligator lizard," <u>Gerrhonotus multicarinatus</u>), has found that the length of time required for the lizard to capture an insect is approximately one-tenth of a second, at a temperature of 85° F.[1] Man is the most intelligent creature, with the most highly organized brain, and has often been hungry in the midst of many birds and other food animals, but he has been unable to develop an ability such as this.

It would not seem proper to say that Satan, at the time of the fall of man, gave the lizards and amphibians this ability; for the

Bible makes no hint that Satan has ever had the power to make a fundamental, permanent alteration in any segment of the animal kingdom. (It should be remembered that this rapid feeding mechanism requires not only a high degree of specialization of several parts of the nervous system, but also requires that there be precise and exact genetic programming present in the fertilized eggs of these animals to guide the formation of such specialized nervous parts and connections.) The only two alternatives we have left are either (a) that God originally created these animals as insect-eating creatures, with the necessary abilities and genetic programming, or (b) that He altered their nervous system and genetic make-up at the time of the fall of man. Of course God <u>could</u> have done the latter, but we surely have no grounds for saying that He did. He changed the life-habit and physiological make-up of the particular serpent which tempted Eve, but the Biblical account leaves us to assume that the remainder of the animals which suffered loss because of the fall were merely influenced by the degenerative forces which played upon them from then on (Romans 8:22). Therefore there is every reason to believe that God created the lizards and amphibians as they are now--or perhaps with even greater insect catching ability (since they may have undergone some degeneracy).

All these factors together, plus the fact that the Bible makes no specific reference to the origin of death in the animal, plant, or microscopic worlds, should explain at least most of the problem of the death of animals and plants before the fall of man. We are thus free to believe the testimony of the fossil-bearing strata: that many, many generations of animals and plants made their contributions to the earth, passed away, and were replaced by others, long before man was created. We can be satisfied that God's plan for living organisms, and for their provision of each other's needs, was a wise one. His organization of the living world and its biological principles may seem strange, or even sometimes repulsive, to us; but this is only because of our corrupted and imperfect understanding of the ways of God, together with our natural aversion to death which came upon us because of sin.

There is, however, one problem which seems to be particularly bothersome to us, concerning the existence of violence and death in the animal world. This is the pattern of behavior and way of life of the carnivorous mammals. The seemingly ruthless capturing of other mammals, and even of human beings by carnivores appears to be-- and perhaps is--contrary to what we believe concerning God's original creation. So we are quite willing to say that the carnivorous mammals may have begun their ruthless hunting of other animals only after the fall of man. (We have referred above to the likelihood that the curse mentioned in Genesis 3:17 did have detrimental and degenerating effects upon the natural world.) If the specialized flesh-tearing teeth of the carnivores make us wonder if they did not possess an instinct for ruthless hunting as soon as they were created, we should consider the possibility that in earlier times their diet was restricted to invertebrate animals (insects and sea-shore animals), and to fruits and other plant materials which their teeth could handle. After all, many carnivores even now eat large amounts of such foods. For example, cats eat grasshoppers; bears often eat fruit and honey; and raccoons eat corn, nuts, and other fruits, and even leaves and grasses.[2]

FOOTNOTES

1. T. H. Frazzetta, Department of Zoology, University of Illinois, Champaign, Illinois, personal communication, October, 1970.

2. T. I. Storer and R. L. Usinger, General Zoology, 1965, p. 652.

BIBLIOGRAPHY

Achauer, C. W., "Origin of Capitan Formation, Guadalupe Mountains, New Mexico and Texas," _American Association of Petroleum Geologists Bulletin_, v. 53 (1969), 2314-2323.

Anderson, R. Y., Walter E. Dean, Jr., et al., "Permian Castile Varved Evaporite Sequence, West Texas and New Mexico," _Geological Society of America Bulletin_, v. 83 (1972), p. 59-86.

Archer, G. L., Jr., _A Survey of Old Testament Introduction_, Moody Press, 1964.

Armerding, Hudson T., ed., _Christianity and the World of Thought_, Moody Press, 1968, 350 p.

Barrington, E. J. W., _Invertebrate Structure and Function_, Houghton Mifflin Co., 1967, 549 p.

Barss, D. L., et al., "Geology of Middle Devonian Reefs, Rainbow Area, Alberta, Canada," _in Geology of Giant Petroleum Fields_, M. T. Halbouty, ed., _American Association of Petroleum Geologists Memoir_ no. 14, 1970, p. 19-49.

Bathurst, R. G. C., _Developments in Sedimentology no. 12, Carbonate Sediments and their Diagenesis_, Elsevier Publishing Co., 1971, 620 p.

Bayne, Peter, _Life and Letters of Hugh Miller_, Boston: Gould and Lincoln, 1871, v. 1, 431 p.

Bebout, D. G., and W. R. Maiklem, "Ancient Anhydrite Facies and Environments, Middle Devonian Elk Point Basin, Alberta," _Bulletin of Canadian Petroleum Geology_, v. 21 (1973), p. 287-343.

Berry, W. B. N., _Growth of a Prehistoric Time Scale_, W. H. Freeman and Co., 1968, 158 p.

Birks, T. R., _The Bible and Modern Thought_, London: The Religious Tract Society, 1862, 520 p.

Blatt, H., et al., _Origin of Sedimentary Rocks_, Prentice-Hall, Inc., 1972, 634 p.

Buckland, William, _Geology and Mineralogy Considered with Reference to Natural Theology_, London: 1836, v. 1.

Buswell, J. O., _A Systematic Theology of the Christian Religion_, Zondervan Publishing House, 1962, v. 1.

Butler, G. P., "Modern Evaporite Deposition and Geochemistry of Coexisting Brines, The Sabkha, Trucial Coast, Arabian Gulf," _Journal of Sedimentary Petrology_, v. 39 (1969), p. 70-89.

242

Carson, R., The Edge of the Sea, Houghton Mifflin Co., 1955, 276 p.

Chilingar, G. V., et al., Developments in Sedimentology no. 9A, Carbonate Rocks: Origin, Occurrence and Classification, Elsevier
Publishing Co., 1967, 471 p.

Cohen, C. G., "Hermeneutical Principles and Creation Theories,"
Grace Journal, Grace Theological Seminary, Winona Lake, Indiana,
v. 5, no. 3, 1964, p. 17-29.

Cook, Harry E., "North American Stratigraphic Principles as Applied
to Deep-Sea Sediments," American Association of Petroleum Geologists Bulletin, v. 59 (1975), p. 817-837.

Custance, A. C., Without Form and Void, Doorway Papers, Box 291,
Brockville, Ontario, Can., 1970, 211 p.

Davies, T. A., "Oceanic Sediments and Their Diagenesis: Some Examples
From Deep-Sea Drilling," Journal of Sedimentary Petrology, v. 43
(1973), p. 381-390.

Davies, G. R., and S. D. Ludlam, "Origin of Laminated and Graded
Sediments, Middle Devonian of Western Canada," Geological Society
of America Bulletin, v. 84 (1973), p. 3527-3546.

Dean, Walter E., Jr., "Petrologic and Geochemical Variations in the
Permian Castile Varved Anhydrite, Delaware Basin, Texas and New
Mexico," The University of New Mexico, 1967 (Ph.D. Dissertation),
326 p.

Deep Sea Drilling Project, Initial Reports of the Deep Sea Drilling
Project, volumes 1-35, U. S. Govt. Printing Office, 1969-1976.

Deep Sea Drilling Project, (summary articles on drillings made),
Geotimes, v. 19 (1974), November, p. 16-18; v. 20 (1975), March,
p. 26-28, June, p. 22-24, July, p. 18-21, August, p. 16-19, December, p. 18-21; v. 21 (1976), January, p. 16, February, p. 23-26,
March, p. 21-22.

Elias, G. K., "Habitat of Pennsylvanian Algal Bioherms, Four Corners
Area," in Shelf Carbonates of the Paradox Basin, Four Corners
Geological Society Fourth Field Conference, 1963, p. 185-198.

Ellison, S. P., Jr., "Subsurface Woodford Black Shale, West Texas,
and Southeast New Mexico," in Bureau of Economic Geology, University of Texas Report of Investigations no. 7, 1950, p. 5-20.

Emery, K. O., et al., "Bikini and Nearby Atolls, Marshall Islands:
Part I, Geology," U. S. Geological Survey Professional Paper 260-A,
U. S. Government Printing Office, 1954, 263 p.

Feinberg, Charles L., ed., The Fundamentals for Today (revised),
Kregel Publications, 1958, 2 vols. 657 p.

Fisher, R. B., Science, Man, and Society, W. B. Saunders Co., 1971, 124 p.

Frair, Wayne and P. W. Davis, The Case for Creation, Moody Press, 1972, 93 p.

Friedman, G. M., ed., Depositional Environments in Carbonate Rocks, Society of Economic Paleontologists and Mineralogists, Special Publication no. 14, 1969, 209 p.

Friedman, G. M., "Generation of Laminated Gypsum in Sea-Marginal Pool, Red Sea" (abstract), American Association of Petroleum Geologists Bulletin, v. 57 (1973), p. 780.

Friedman, G. M., "International Congress of Sedimentology," Geotimes, v. 21, February 1976, p. 18.

Fuller, J. G. C. M., and J. W. Porter, "Evaporite Formations with Petroleum Reservoirs in Devonian and Mississippian of Alberta, Saskatchewan, and North Dakota," American Association of Petroleum Geologists Bulletin, v. 53 (1969), p. 909-926.

Gebelein, C. D., "Distribution, Morphology, and Accretion Rate of Recent Subtidal Algal Stromatolites, Bermuda," Journal of Sedimentary Petrology, v. 39 (1969), p. 49-69.

Gillispie, C. C., Genesis and Geology, Harvard University Press, 1951, 315 p.

Goodell, H. G. and R. K. Garman, "Carbonate Geochemistry of Superior Deep Test Well, Andros Island, Bahamas," American Association of Petroleum Geologists Bulletin, v. 53 (1969), p. 513-536.

Gross, M. G., Oceanography: A View of the Earth, Prentice-Hall, Inc., 1972, 581 p.

Haber, F. C., The Age of the World: Moses to Darwin, The Johns Hopkins Press, 1959, 303 p.

Hancock, J. M., and P. A. Scholle, "Chalk of the North Sea," in Petroleum and the Continental Shelf of Europe, A. W. Woodland, ed., 1975, v. 1, p. 413-425.

Hanshaw, B. B., "Inorganic Geochemistry of Carbonate Shelf Rocks," American Association of Petroleum Geologists Bulletin (abstract), v. 53 (1969), p. 720.

Harper, H. E., Jr., and A. H. Knoll, "Silica, Diatoms, and Cenozoic Radiolarian Evolution," Geology, v. 3 (1975), p. 175-177.

Hays, J. D. et al., Initial Reports of the Deep Sea Drilling Project, v. 9, U. S. Government Printing Office, 1972, 1205 p.

Heckel, P. H., and J. M. Cocke, "Phylloid Algal-Mound Complexes in Outcropping Upper Pennsylvanian Rocks of Mid-Continent," American Association of Petroleum Geologists Bulletin, v. 53 (1969), p. 1058-1074.

Heezen, B. C., and I. D. MacGregor, "The Evolution of the Pacific," Scientific American, v. 229, November 1973, p. 102-112.

Hitchcock, Edward, The Religion of Geology and its Connected Sciences, Boston: Phillips, Sampson, & Co., 1851, 510 p.

Hoffmeister, J. E., "Growth Rate Estimates of a Pleistocene Coral Reef of Florida," Geological Society of America Bulletin, v. 75 (1964), p. 353-358.

Hriskevich, M. E., "Middle Devonian Reef Production, Rainbow Area, Alberta, Canada," American Association of Petroleum Geologists Bulletin, v. 54 (1970), p. 2260-2281.

Hsü, K. J., et al., "Glomar Challenger Returns to the Mediterranean Sea," Geotimes, v. 20 (1975), August, p. 16-19.

Hsü, K. J., "When the Mediterranean Dried Up," Scientific American, v. 227, no. 6 (Dec. 1972), p. 26-36.

Hughes, P. W., "New Mexico's Deepest Oil Test," in Fifth Field Conference Guidebook, New Mexico Geological Society, 1954, p. 124-130.

Ilich, M., "Hydrothermal-Sedimentary Dolomite," American Association of Petroleum Geologists Bulletin, v. 58 (1974), p. 1331-1347.

Illing, L. V., "Bahaman Calcareous Sands," American Association of Petroleum Geologists Bulletin, v. 38 (1954), p. 1-95.

Jamieson, R., A. R. Fausset, and David Brown, A Commentary on the Old and New Testaments, Wm. B. Eerdmans Publishing Co., 1948, 6 volumes. (The original edition was published in 1871, in England.)

Johnson, J. H., Limestone-Building Algae and Algal Limestones, Colorado School of Mines, 1961, 297 p.

Kaneps, A., "Deep Sea Drilling Project," Geotimes, v. 21, January, 1976, p. 16.

Kendall, C. G. St. C., "An Environmental Re-interpretation of the Permian Evaporite-Carbonate Shelf Sediments of the Guadalupe Mountains," Geological Society of America Bulletin, v. 80 (1969), p. 2503-2521.

Kendall, C. G. St. C., and Sir Patrick A. D'E. Skipwith, "Holocene Shallow-Water Carbonate and Evaporite Sediments of Khor al Bazam, Abu Dhabi, Southwest Persian Gulf," American Association of Petroleum Geologists Bulletin, v. 53 (1969), p. 841-869.

Kinsman, D. J., "Modes of Formation, Sedimentary Associations, and Diagnostic Features of Shallow-Water and Supratidal Evaporites," American Association of Petroleum Geologists Bulletin, v. 53 (1969), p. 830-840.

Klingspor, A. M., "Middle Devonian Muskeg Evaporites of Western Canada," American Association of Petroleum Geologists Bulletin, v. 53 (1969), p. 927-948.

Kraft, John C., "Carbonate Analogs--Modern and Ancient," in Field Guide to Some Carbonate Rock Environments, Florida Keys and Western Bahamas, H. G. Multer, ed., Fairleigh Dickenson University, 1971, p. 134-136.

Ladd, H. S., and Schlanger, S. O., "Bikini and Nearby Atolls, Marshall Islands, Drilling Operations on Eniwetok Atoll," U. S. Geological Survey Professional Paper 260-Y, U. S. Government Printing Office, 1960, 43 p.

Ladd, H. S., "Reef-building," Science, v. 134 (1961), p. 703-715.

Landes, K. K., Petroleum Geology, Jn Wiley and Sons, 1951, 660 p.

Lang, W. B., "Basal Beds of Salado Formation in Fletcher Potash Core Test, Near Carlsbad, New Mexico," American Association of Petroleum Geologists Bulletin, v. 26 (1942), p. 63-79.

Lang, W. B., "Cycle of Deposition in the Salado Formation of the Permian of New Mexico and Texas" (abstract), American Association of Petroleum Geologists Bulletin, v. 60 (1949), p. 1903.

Langton, J. R., and G. E. Chin, "Rainbow Member Facies and Related Reservoir Properties, Rainbow Lake, Alberta," American Association of Petroleum Geologists Bulletin, v. 52 (1968), p. 1925-1955.

Larsen, G., and G. V. Chilingar, Developments in Sedimentology No. 8, Diagenesis of Sediments, Elsevier Publishing Co., 1967, 551 p.

Larson, R. L., et al., Initial Reports of the Deep Sea Drilling Project, v. 32, U. S. Govt. Printing Office, 1975, 980 p.

Leopold, E. B., "Bikini and Nearby Atolls, Marshall Islands, Miocene Pollen and Spore Flora of Eniwetok Atoll, Marshall Islands," U. S. Geological Survey Professional Paper 260-II, U. S. Government Printing Office, 1969, 53 p.

Maatman, R. W., The Bible, Natural Science, and Evolution, Reformed Fellowship, Inc., 1970, 165 p.

Machielse, S., "Devonian Algae and Their Contribution to the Western Canadian Sedimentary Basin," Bulletin of Canadian Petroleum Geology, v. 20 (1972), p. 187-237.

Mao, Han-Lee, "Bikini and Nearby Atolls, Marshall Islands, Physical
Oceanography in the Marshall Islands Area," U. S. Geological Survey
Professional Paper 260-R, U. S. Government Printing Office, 1955.

Matthews, S. W., "This Changing Earth," National Geographic, v. 143,
January 1973, p. 1-36.

Mayor, A. G., Papers from the Department of Marine Biology of the
Carnegie Institute of Washington, Publication No. 340, v. 19 (1924).

Mayor, A. G., "Growth Rate of Samoan Corals," in Papers from the
Department of Marine Biology of the Carnegie Institute of Washington, Publication no. 340, v. 19 (1924), p. 51-72.

McCamis, J. G., and L. S. Griffith, "Middle Devonian Facies Relations,
Zama Area, Alberta," American Association of Petroleum Geologists
Bulletin, v. 52 (1968), p. 1899-1924.

McKee, E. D., and R. C. Gutschick, History of the Redwall Limestone
of Northern Arizona, Geological Society of America Memoir 114,
1969, 726 p.

Menard, H. W., Marine Geology of the Pacific, McGraw-Hill, 1964,
271 p.

Meyer, R. F., Geology of Pennsylvanian and Wolfcampian Rocks in Southeast New Mexico, New Mexico Bureau of Mines and Mineral Resources
Memoir 17, 1966, 123 p.

Miller, Hugh, The Testimony of the Rocks, Boston: Gould and Lincoln,
1858, 502 p.

Moore, J. R., "Charles Lyell and the Noachian Deluge," Journal of
the American Scientific Affiliation, v. 22 (1970), p. 107-115.

Morris, H. M., Biblical Cosmology and Modern Science, Craig Press,
1970, 146 p.

Newell, N. D., and J. K. Rigby, "Geological Studies on the Great
Bahama Bank," in Regional Aspects of Carbonate Deposition, A Sym-
posium, Society of Economic Paleontologists and Mineralogists,
Special Publication no. 5, 1957, p. 15-72.

Newell, N. D., et al., The Permian Reef Complex of the Guadalupe
Mountains Region, Texas and New Mexico, W. H. Freeman and Co.,
1953, 236 p.

O'Brien, Charles F., Sir William Dawson, A Life in Science and Religion, American Philosophical Society, 1971, 207 p.

Packer, J. I., Fundamentalism and the Word of God, Wm. B. Eerdmans
Publishing Co., 1958, 191 p.

Pember, G. H., Earth's Earliest Ages, New York: Fleming H. Revell,
c.1876, 469 p.; and London: Hodder and Stoughton, 9th ed., 1901.

Peters, W. G., "Field Evidence of Rapid Sedimentation," Creation Research Society Quarterly, v. 10 (1973), p. 92-94.

Pettijohn, F. J., Sedimentary Rocks, Harper and Row, 1957, 718 p.

Prescott, G. W., The Algae: A Review, Houghton Mifflin Co., 1968, 436 p.

Price, G. M., The New Geology, Pacific Press, 1923, 706 p.

Ramm, B., The Christian View of Science and Scripture, Eerdmans Publishing Co., Grand Rapids, 1954, 256 p.

Reno, Cora A., Evolution on Trial, Moody Press, 1970, 192 p.

Riley, W. B., The Bible of the Expositor and the Evangelist Vol. 1, Genesis, Union Gospel Press, 1926.

Ryan, W. B. F., Hsü, K. J., et al., Initial Reports of the Deep Sea Drilling Project, vol. 13, pt. 1 and pt. 2, U. S. Govt. Printing Office, 1973, 1447 p. (NS 1.2: D36/2/v. 13/pt. 1, pt. 2.)

Sandeen, E. R., The Roots of Fundamentalism, British and American Millenarianism 1800-1930, University of Chicago Press, 1970, 328 p.

Sanders, J. E., and G. M. Friedman, "Origin and Occurrence of Limestones," in Developments in Sedimentology no. 9A, Carbonate Rocks, Elsevier Publishing Co., 1967, 471 p.

Schaeffer, Francis A., Escape From Reason, Inter-Varsity Press, 1968, 96 p.

Schaeffer, Francis A., The God Who Is There, Inter-Varsity Press, 1968, 191 p.

Scholle, P. A., "Diagenesis of Upper Cretaceous Chalks from England, Northern Ireland, and the North Sea," in Pelagic Sediments on Land and Under the Sea, International Association of Sedimentologists, Special Publication no. 1, 1974, p. 177-210.

Scoffin, T. P., "Fossilization of Bermuda Patch Reefs," Science, v. 178, Dec. 22, 1972, p. 1280-1282.

Scofield, C. I., et al., The Scofield Reference Bible, Oxford University Press, 1917.

Shelton, J. S., Geology Illustrated, W. H. Freeman and Co., 1966, 434 p.

Shepard, F. P., The Earth Beneath the Sea, The Johns Hopkins Press, 1967, 242 p.

Shinn, E. A., "Coral Growth Rate, An Environmental Indicator," Journal of Paleontology, v. 40 (1966), p. 240.

248

Shrock, R. R., and W. H. Twenhofel, Principles of Invertebrate Paleontology, McGraw-Hill Book Co., 1953, 816 p.

Sloss, L. L., "Evaporite Deposition from Layered Solutions," American Association of Petroleum Geologists Bulletin, v. 53 (1969), p. 776-789.

Smith, L. A., "Messinian Event," Geotimes, v. 22 (1977), March, p. 20-23.

Smith, Wilbur M., Profitable Bible Study, W. A. Wilde Co., 1951, p. 227.

Sonnenfeld, P., "The Significance of Upper Miocene (Messinian) Evaporites in the Mediterranean Sea," Journal of Geology, v. 83 (1975), p. 287-311.

Stokes, W. L., An Introduction to Historical Geology, Prentice Hall, 1960.

Storer, T. I., and R. L. Usinger, General Zoology, McGraw-Hill Book Co., 1965, 741 p.

Strong, A. H., Systematic Theology, The Judson Press, 1949, 1166 p. (First edition published in 1907)

Taylor, S. E., "The Mystery Tracks in Dinosaur Valley," Bible-Science Newsletter, v. 9, April 1971, p. 1-7.

Tazieff, Haroun, "The Afar Triangle," Scientific American, v. 222, Feb. 1970, p. 32-40.

Thomson, William, editor, Aids to Faith, A Series of Theological Essays, London: John Murray, 1861, 469 p.

Toulmin, S., and J. Goodfield, The Discovery of Time, Harper Torchbooks, 1965.

Tracey, J. I., Jr., et al., Initial Reports of the Deep Sea Drilling Project, v. 8, U. S. Govt. Printing Office, 1971, 1037 p.

Von der Borch, C. C., J. G. Sclater, et al., Initial Reports of the Deep Sea Drilling Project, v. 22, U. S. Govt. Printing Office, 1974, 890 p.

Walter, M. R., et al., Developments in Sedimentology no. 20, Stromatolites, Elsevier, 1976, 790 p.

Wells, J. W., "Bikini and Nearby Atolls, Marshall Islands, Fossil Corals From Bikini Atoll," U. S. Geological Survey Professional Paper 260-P, U. S. Govt. Printing Office, 1954.

Wertenbaker, Wm., The Floor of the Sea, Little, Brown, & Co., 1974, 275 p.

Weyl, P. K., Oceanography, Jn. Wiley and Sons, 1970, 535 p.

Whitcomb, J. C., Jr., The Early Earth, Baker Book House Co., 1972, 144 p.

Whitcomb, J. C., Jr., The World That Perished, Baker Book House Co., 1973, 155 p.

White, A. D., A History of the Warfare of Science with Theology in Christendom, New York, George Braziller, 1955, v. 1, 415 p.

Wiersbe, Warren, "Truth: A Responsibility," Brethren Missionary Herald, v. 34, Dec. 23, 1972, p. 36.

Williams, Emmett, and G. Mulfinger, Physical Science, Bob Jones University Press, 1974.

Wimpenny, R. S., The Plankton of the Sea, London: Faber & Faber Ltd., 1966, 426 p.

Winterer, E. L., et al., Initial Reports of the Deep Sea Drilling Project, v. 7, U. S. Govt. Printing Office, 1971, 1757 p.

Winterer, E. L., J. I. Ewing, et al., Initial Reports of the Deep Sea Drilling Project, v. 17, U. S. Govt. Printing Office, 1973, 930 p.

Wray, J. L., "Archaeolithophyllum, an Abundant Calcareous Alga in Limestones of the Lansing Group (Pennsylvanian), Southeastern Kansas," Kansas Geological Survey Bulletin no. 170, Part 1, 1964, p. 1-10.

Young, E. J., Studies in Genesis One, Presbyterian and Reformed Publishing Co., Philadelphia, 1964, 105 p.

Zenger, D. H., "Dolomitization and Uniformitarianism," Journal of Geological Education, v. 20 (1972), p. 104-124.

Zenger, D. H., "Significance of Supratidal Dolomitization in the Geologic Record," Geological Society of America Bulletin, v. 83 (1972), p. 1-12.

Zimmerman, Paul A., editor, Rock Strata and the Bible Record, Concordia Publishing House, 1970, 209 p.

INDEX*

age, absolute, 53

algae, as producers of sediments and rock, 23, 31, 36, 53-54, 56, 87,
  95, 110(#7), 111(#13), 117, 131-138, 151-154, 159ff, 215

ancient and modern deposits compared, 69, 74, 75, 85-90, 118, 120,
  124, 134-138, 140, 143-145, 175

anhydrite, defined, 99, 177, (also see "evaporites")

antithesis, principle of, 20-21

appearance of age, doctrine of, 49-51, 61-62, 189-190, 210, 230-232

aragonite, defined, etc., 115-117

atolls, 23ff, 75-76

Augustine, Saint, 224-225

Bacon, Francis, 8, 20

Bahama banks, 113ff

basalt, 25, 158

beachrock, 120

Bible and science (see "science and truth")

biologically produced rock formations, 23ff, 48, 95-96, 113ff, 128-142,
  148ff

Birks, T. R., 198-199

boring and encrusting of rock layers, 129-131

brachiopods, defined, etc., 52, 109

bryozoan, defined, 95-96

Buckland, Wm, 187-188

* Note--This index does not list all of the men referred to in this
manual. Only those from Chapters 1, 2, 10, and 11, and the appendices,
who were of considerable importance or prominence in the history of
Bible-science thought are listed. The reader will of course find
other names listed in the footnotes at the end of each chapter, and
in the bibliography.

Mediterranean Sea floor, 170-178

metabolic processes of growth, 16-17, 28, 33-34, 59, 151-154, 237

micron, defined, 154

Miller, Hugh, 195-196, 202

Miocene Epoch, 171ff

miracles, 60, 191, 207, 232

Mississippian Period, 112, 140

mollusks, 52, 65

nannofossils, 151-154, 159ff, 180(#31)

natural laws, stability of, 16-17, 33-34, 57-59, 105, 125, 154, 164, 186, 231

nature, defined, 5

nature (see "natural laws")

"numerical adjective argument," 215, 227-228

ocean sediments, 64, 117, 148ff

oöid, defined, etc., 115-117, 123

"ordinal number argument," 215, 227-228

Ordovician Period, 51, 52

organic banks, 95ff, 113ff, 132-134

organic layers in evaporite deposits, 79-80, 100-104, 177

ostracods, defined, 109

pelagic organisms, defined, etc., 178(#2), 148-155, 158, 162, 165, 172

pellets, fecal, 44, 95, 115, 125

Pember, G. H., 206

plants, creation of, 215, 236, 238

plants, flowering, 53-54, 215, 236, 238

Pleistocene Epoch, 35, 160, 172

Pliocene Epoch, 172